DID YOU KNOW . . .

AVERAGE AMOUNT OF TIME THE AVERAGE AMERICAN SPENDS GOING THROUGH JUNK MAIL IN A LIFETIME: 8 MONTHS.

PROPORTION OF AMERICAN TEENAGE GIRLS WHO SAY THAT STORE-HOPPING IS THEIR FAVORITE ACTIVITY: 93%.

NUMBER OF GUNS BROUGHT TO SCHOOL EACH DAY IN THE UNITED STATES: 135,000.

AMERICANS WHO CLAIM TO HAVE BEEN ABDUCTED BY ALIENS: 3.7 MILLION.

AVERAGE AMOUNT OF TIME PATIENTS ARE ALLOWED TO SPEAK BEFORE BEING INTERRUPTED BY THEIR DOCTORS: 18 SECONDS.

NUMBER OF TIMES EVERY YEAR THAT HACKERS INFILTRATE THE PENTAGON'S COMPUTER SYSTEM: 160,000.

PROPORTION OF CORPORATE DOWN-SIZINGS THAT HAPPEN ON A TUESDAY: 55 PERCENT.

THE GAP BETWEEN THE TOTAL VALUE OF WORLD IMPORTS AND WORLD EXPORTS IF YOU ADD UP THE OFFICIAL STATISTICS OF EVERY COUNTRY: $245 BILLION (THEY SHOULD ADD UP TO THE SAME AMOUNT, OF COURSE).

PROPORTION OF CARS ON ALBANIAN ROADS BELIEVED TO HAVE BEEN STOLEN FROM ELSEWHERE IN EUROPE (1997): 80%.

PROPORTION OF MEDICAL COLUMNS IN CANADIAN NEWSPAPERS JUDGED TO BE GIVING "POTENTIALLY LIFE-THREATENING" ADVICE: 28%.

TIME YOU HAVE TO YELL TO PRODUCE ENOUGH SOUND ENERGY TO HEAT A CUP OF COFFEE: 8 YEARS, 7 MONTHS AND 6 DAYS.

THE SUM OF OUR

DISCONTENT

THE SUM OF OUR

DISCONTENT

1 2 3 4 5

HOW NUMBERS MAKE

US IRRATIONAL

DAVID BOYLE

TEXERE

New York • London

Published by

TEXERE
55 East 52nd Street
New York, NY 10055

Tel: 212.317.5106
Fax: 212.317.5178
www.etexere.com

In the UK:

TEXERE Publishing Limited
71–77 Leadenhall Street
London EC3A 3DE

Tel: 20 7204 3644
Fax: 20 7208 6701
www.etexere.co.uk

This publication is designed to provide accurate and authoritative information in regard to the subject matter covered. It is sold with the understanding that the publisher is not engaged in rendering legal, accounting, or other professional services. If legal advice or other expert assistance is required, the services or a competent professional person should be sought.

Designed by Victoria Kuskowski

Library of Congress Cataloging in Publication Data has been applied for.

ISBN 1-58799-060-1

Printed in the United States of America

This book is printed on acid-free paper.

10 9 8 7 6 5 4 3 2 1

FOR JOANNA, BEN, AGATHA, AND FRANCES

WHILE YOU AND I HAVE LIPS AND VOICES WHICH

ARE FOR KISSING AND TO SING WITH

WHO CARES IF SOME ONEEYED SON OF A BITCH

INVENTS AN INSTRUMENT TO MEASURE SPRING WITH?

e.e. cummings

CONTENTS

INTRODUCTION

THE TYRANNY OF NUMBERS

We recognize that in the past testing has helped reduce unfairness in allocating opportunities and directing resources to the economically disadvantaged, and has been useful for making decisions. However, the growing over-reliance on testing over the past several decades deprives the nation of all the talent it needs and sometimes conflicts with the nation's ideals of fairness and equal opportunity.

National Commission on Testing and Public Policy, 1998

There are no such things as still lifes.

Erica Jong

I

I am writing just as the courtroom battle over numbers, votes, and machines in the 2000 presidential election is coming to a head. Despite a political season where competing statistics were flung over the networks with ever more abandon, it has probably never been so clear just how muddling, subjective, and confused by human error the business of counting and measurement is. Far from being an objective measure of the will of the people, you can clearly count Florida's votes in any one of scores of different ways.

Like other kinds of statistics in modern life, votes are supposed to be a pretty exact way of finding a new democratic leader. But if you want them to be absolutely *precise*, the whole edifice starts to unravel. It isn't just a question of whether it's the popular vote or the electoral college votes that should be counted—that's just the equivalent of sporting rules about which teams stand where in the league—it's the business of finding an absolutely exact score. And when the winner hangs on 327, or 300, or 900 votes out of six million or so from Florida, then every vote counts. But, as the pundits and politicians soon discovered, whether or not a vote was really a vote might depend on how much the ballot has been punched through. It was the constant recounting in some of Florida's counties that put the little word chad—the little bits of cardboard normally knocked out of a ballot—firmly into the English language lexicon.

Although the modern world obsessively tries to measure everything, the hard fact is that only when laboratory conditions are precise—if they ever can be—can you ever get anything like precision. And when really important issues involving people are at stake, like education or economics or voting, then you never get anything like laboratory conditions. Try as they might to recreate them at the recounts, it just couldn't work. There were rules in Palm Beach that nobody could talk and anyone whose cell phone rang would be kicked out, and—in Volusia—exactly what color pens the counters were allowed (red) and where they could put their purses (next to the guard). It was no good: Any count—even one carried out by machines—is going to be subject to interpretation. At one stage, sheriffs' deputies in Broward County took custody of 78 tiny chads as evidence of potential ballot tampering. The police put them into an envelope marked: CRIME. FOUND PROPERTY. Another official was even accused of eating chad.

The irony was that, thanks to what George W. Bush calls "fuzzy math"—from both sides—the election had been more of a clash between meaningless measurements than ever before. There were statistics about crime, schools, health care, and of course tax cuts. There were bizarre comparisons, and—although most of the statistics used may have been correct—they were so selective and hard to compare, that they might have been using another language. And even when Bush got in his "fuzzy math" jibe, he followed it up quickly with an accusation that 50 million people wouldn't receive Gore's tax cut.

Statistics in politics are a way to "condemn and indict in a hurry," according to the anthropologist David Murray of the Statistical Assessment Service. "You get both authoritativeness and no accountability." The trouble is, brandishing numbers doesn't work anymore. They mean little and they have plunged us into a world packed full of figures, where almost every aspect of our lives is measured—from our purchases to our insurance risk—and transformed into numerical half-truths. This obsessive calculation of things that can't be measured is one of the most extraordinary features of the modern world, yet it comes in for remarkably little debate. We simply accept it.

II

Numbers now dominate our lives. There are personal calculations to be made each day, about investments, journey times, bank machines, and credit cards. There are professional figures at work, in the form of targets, statistics, workforce percentages, and profit forecasts. As consumers, we are counted and aggregated according to every purchase we make. Every time we are exposed to the media, there is a positive flood of statistics controlling and interpreting the world, developing each truth, simplifying each problem. "Being a man is unhealthy," said the front page of one newspaper recently, adding—like every similar newspaper article about statistics—the word "Official." As if we had been wondering about the truth all these years and, thanks to the counters, we now know; as if the figures are so detached that there is no arguing with them. But of course we keep arguing. We take our collective pulses 24 hours a day with the use of statistics. We understand life that way, though somehow the more figures we use, the more great truths still seem to slip through our fingers. Despite all that calculating, and all that numerical control, we feel as ignorant as ever.

If you are said to be "calculating," people could mean one of two things about you—both related and equally repellent. It could mean that you are constantly comparing what is best for you in any given situation. This is not a compliment. It implies something cold, fishlike, and completely self-interested. But it could also mean you are someone who counts too much, someone who measures things but can't see the reality behind them.

There is something equally cold about that, but disinterested rather than self-interested. A calculating person, in this sense, is someone for whom the world past the end of their nose is a foreign country. And although we have become exactly that with all our counting, and increasingly so, it can send a shiver down the spine when you come across extreme examples.

Like the eighteenth-century prodigy Jedediah Buxton in his first trip to the theater to see a performance of Shakespeare's *Richard III* in London. Asked later whether he'd enjoyed it, all he could say was the number of steps during the dances was 5,202 and the number of words spoken by the actors was 12,445. Nothing about what the words said; about the winter of our discontent made glorious summer; nothing about the evil hunchback king.

Today, Buxton would probably be described as autistic. It is particularly horrifying to hear that his numbers turned out to be exactly right.

The story is funny now as then, but it is also faintly disturbing—and I have been wondering why this is. It could be that we see Jedediah Buxton as a fearsome symbol of the modern age, counting everything but seeing the significance of nothing. But I think it is deeper than that. There is something inhuman about it—not so much the ability to count, but the failure to be moved. We shiver, I think, at anybody with no emotions—as if they were completely amoral, like Dr. Strangelove. We shrink from white-coated doctors, too, like cold calculating machines. Even doctors should be slightly fallible.

Even so, we encounter these "calculating" machines almost every day. It's hard not to turn on the news without audibly tripping over one of them. Like the academic who refuses to pass judgment on any problem, however urgent, because there hasn't been enough research. Or the politician who is so obsessed with the polling figures that he can no longer trust his gut instincts. Or the social scientist who has laboriously proved with the use of statistics something that anybody else with an ounce of common sense knew already—that the death of a parent can scar a child for life, or that alcoholics have an unusually high depression rate. It's "official," they say. Like the University of Michigan study that revealed that children who don't exercise and eat junk food tend to be overweight. Or the recent research that showed that areas of high unemployment tend to have fewer jobs.

Then there are the familiar people who muddle up the numbers with the truth. Or, even worse, those who think you can change the truth just by changing the statistics. Don't forget those British agriculture ministers who urged the public to listen to the scientists over the safety of BSE beef—and really believed it—even though they were also quietly suppressing the research of anybody arguing it might not be safe to eat.

These are modern monsters, but none of us can completely escape the accusation. We're all tied up with figures, even if they are just batting statistics and lottery numbers.

Romantics and leftists traditionally say this is a bad thing. Romantics think that it reduces the individual to mere figures. Leftists think it's a kind of tyranny. They are both wrong in the sense that we do need to be able to count—but they are right too. The strange thing is that ratcheting up the calculations has often been done for excellent humanitarian reasons, driven by impeccably radical reformers. Of course, in the history of the tyranny of numbers over life there are crazed scientists and Nazis with branding irons that stalk through the pages. This is no scientific history of counting, and there is no account of the great statistical pioneers like Herbert Spencer or Karl Pearson. Nor have I covered the byways of scientific research or IQ—or the people who really believed you could control individuals by counting them.

But counting could also be a way of improving the world. Maybe they wanted to find ways of cutting population growth, like Robert Malthus. Maybe they wanted to find a way of aggregating the national accounts to defeat Hitler, like John Maynard Keynes. Or maybe they wanted to force politicians to worry about people's happiness, like Jeremy Bentham. Or make industry more efficient and merit-based, like Frederick Taylor. All the historic interludes I've chosen in this book fall into that category. They are people who—for the best of motives—brought forth the flood of numbers and calculations into the nonscientific parts of our lives.

It still is a way of improving the world. Are your schools not performing as well as they should? Then measure their results. Are you worried about the performance of a city, a company, a great institution, a hospital? Send in the auditors, set some standards as benchmarks. You don't trust the professionals? Summarize their decisions in number form, send in the cost-benefit experts, and keep your beady eye on them. It is the modern way. Numbers—like money—drive out the mysterious power of the elite, the clubbable atmosphere of the professions, the we-know-best patronizing attitudes of those thick-set people with glasses and firm handshakes who used to lord it over our lives. We can control them if we can reduce their complex professionalism to numbers.

The trouble is that the numbers have proliferated, and it's sometimes hard to breathe—still less tell the difference between one statistic and another, which ones are good and which ones are bad. It's almost enough to make you coldly calculating.

III

If presidential candidates can't agree which statistics to use, or how to measure intangibles like wealth, success, rehabilitation, or wisdom—they absolutely agree about the vital importance of measuring. And nowhere more so than in the increasingly controversial area of education. Despite campaigns to persuade them otherwise, both Bush and Gore believed in expanding the standardized tests in reading and math and introducing wide-scale testing of teachers too.

The tests already decide a student's class ranking and whether they can graduate or not. They can also affect how much money the school gets from the state, how many of its own decisions it can make, and whether or not it stays open. "Testing makes standards meaningful, promotes competition, and empowers parents and teachers to seek change," said Bush. "Investment without accountability is a waste of money," said Gore. But in practice, say opponents, schools cram for the tests, education gets narrower, children get increasing pressure—as well as private tutoring on weekends and in the evenings, homework until after 10:00 P.M. Teachers in North Carolina get three chances to pass a basic skills test before they are thrown out: But if the test doesn't really measure whether they're good or not, then it's a blunt instrument that could lose a large number of teachers.

High school students in Massachusetts and Denver refused to take their tests recently. Louisiana parents even went to court. And in Massachusetts in 1998, so many trainee teachers failed (56 percent) that the state education board had to reduce the passing grade. The tests show that "standards" are rising as a result—but they are such narrow standards. And compulsory testing, according to the National Commission on Testing and Public Policy, probably takes up 20 million school days and costs anything up to $900 million.

Despite the proliferation of measurements, somehow the numbers are still not providing an effective lever. Why? Because so often you can't measure what's really important. But it's all very well to say it is impossible: Decisions still have to be made—and if you don't count what's really important, it gets ignored. It doesn't count. There are only so many resources, so doctors must compare the quality of life of a 70-year-old with heart failure against that of a suicidal teenager with a long history of depression. Elected officials have to compare the pleasure and disruption brought by a new 18-screen cinema with the contentment given by keeping it as a park. Investors have to compare a notoriously polluting oil company with a dodgy record in human rights with a tremendously successful Internet company with three employees and no profits.

It's impossible, of course, but they have to try, because otherwise the wrong decision will be made or their rivals will steal an advantage. So they find themselves isolating something that *can* be counted. Then they measure, measure, measure, knowing that what they measure is alive and will not keep still, and suspecting also maybe that—however much they count—they will not capture the essence of the question they are asking. Things have to keep static if you're going to count them: that's probably why the first statisticians were known as "statists."

But real life isn't still.

How, for example, can businesses measure what they are worth when value is increasingly ephemeral—encompassing things that go way beyond traditional balance sheets? How can we measure our national or local success when our measuring rods are so inadequate, and yet so important to our politicians? Yet, without measuring rods, it is hard to know whether we are making any progress.

But if politicians had a difficult time, it was nothing compared to what was happening in the business world, as managers struggled to find ways of measuring customer loyalty, brand reputation, or staff morale. And as they did so, Internet companies that had never made a profit and were selling intangible products rushed past them up the Wall Street indices. When the balance sheet of a company like Microsoft shows assets worth only 6 percent of its stock market value, they needed to find an answer.

It's all a bit like a computer game. What really matters can't be counted, but it's a much worse situation than that. If you make the attempt but measure the wrong thing, it isn't just wasted effort. It can destroy everything you've worked for. Like the school league tables that make teachers concentrate on getting borderline pupils through at the expense of their weaker classmates. Or the hospital waiting lists that fell because only quick simple problems were treated. It's a familiar story, just as unemployment statistics bear no relation to the number of people who actually want to work. It all comes down to definitions: Governments prefer to count people on welfare rather than unemployed people. To count things, you first have to define them in measurable ways, and magically the system can manipulate the figures by narrowing the definition.

This amounts to a kind of crisis. We need answers, but we also know that what is most important to our lives simply can't be pinned down like still life. The crisis has led business to realize that success depends also on intangibles like know-how or ethics. It has led schools to realize they also need to embrace feelgood or self-esteem, and politicians to embrace quality of life. But then they try to put those intangibles into numerical measurements—and that's where it all goes horribly wrong.

IV

The trouble is that numbers can't capture the sheer complexity of human life. They simplify, and they pile up unused in data banks as if they were the repository of all truth. In 1999, nearly three-quarters of top United States companies weren't even using those vast screeds of numbers they get from laboriously measuring customer buying data. We desperately try and measure all those things that worry us or entrance us, failing to capture in figures our happiness or our frustration with progress. Trying, in other words, somehow to capture the sum of our discontent—when we can't.

All of which would be fine, if that were the end of the story—but it isn't. We can't leave things as they are because all those numbers are making us misunderstand things. They give us the illusion of authority and knowledge—a dangerous thing in the hands of politicians and bureaucrats—but they actually make us more ignorant, because measuring things means defining them and reducing them. We lose some of the magic in it. In fact, every time a new set of statistics comes out, I can't help feeling that some of the richness and mystery of life gets extinguished. Just like the individual stories of passion and betrayal get hidden by the marriage statistics, or the whole meaning of the Holocaust gets lost in the number 6 million. There is a sort of deadening effect, a distancing from human emotion and reality. Not much, but just enough for it to matter—like Jedediah Buxton trying to understand Shakespeare's masterpieces by counting the words.

Magic is about breaking out of categories, words, and definitions, and I should declare an interest—I want a bit more of it. Measuring things takes away the childish sense of wonder where things are really possible. This is, no doubt, extremely naive of me. A serious-looking man with a white coat and clipboard—one of those disinterested people who counts a lot but feels little—will have to put me right and tell me off for filling people's minds with airy-fairy nonsense.

Luckily I'm not the first writer to point out the problem. The last time the world plunged into measuring itself with such single-mindedness, the novelist Charles Dickens was there to show what a world governed by dry facts and even dryer numbers might mean. He did so in his novel *Hard Times*, which remains a testament to the case against counting, and in the monstrous character of Thomas Gradgrind—hardware merchant and utilitarian—the man who believes that only demonstrable countable facts are important. Yet you can define something precisely, count every attribute, and measure it in every way, Dickens implied, and still not know much about it.

He describes how the warmhearted circus girl Sissy Jupe is adopted into Gradgrind's dry-as-dust household. Sissy knows all about horses because she was brought up with them, but asked to define one in class and she finds herself tongue-tied and overshadowed by one of her more experienced fellow pupils. "Quadruped," he says. "Graminivorous. Forty teeth, namely twenty-four grinders, four eye-teeth, and twelve incisive. Sheds coat in spring; in marshy countries, sheds hoofs, too. Hoofs hard, but requiring to be shod with iron. Age known by marks in mouth". . . And so on.

"Now girl number twenty," says Gradgrind, turning back to Sissy. "You know what a horse is."

A SHORT HISTORY

OF COUNTING

Know then thyself, presume not God to scan,
The proper study of mankind is man.

Alexander Pope, *An Essay on Man*

I have often admired the mystical way of Pythagoras,
and the secret magic of numbers.

Sir Thomas Browne, *Religio Medici*

I

IT WAS SEPTEMBER 12, 1904. The Kaiser was on the throne, the *Dreadnought* was less than a few rivets on the ground, and Freud was in his Vienna consulting rooms, thinking the unthinkable. In Berlin, the unthinkable appeared to be becoming a reality. Numbers, once the domain of high priests—accessible to only the holiest of the holy—suddenly seemed to be within the grasp of a horse called Hans. Rumor had it that Hans could count.

As many as 13 of the city's greatest scientific minds were convinced of it. The leading psychologists, veterinary surgeons, physiologists—even the director of the Berlin zoo—had come away from the demonstration shaking their heads, worrying slightly for their professional reputations. Yet they had just signed a paper: the horse they had spent the day watching was not responding to signals from its owner when it demonstrated its considerable mathematical powers. Clever Hans, in other words, was not a circus act. He really was clever.

Clever Hans sounds more like the title of a Grimm fairy tale or one of Freud's more spectacular patients. Actually he was just a horse belonging to retired math teacher Wilhelm von Ostein, who exhibited Hans in a northern suburb of the city every day at noon, wearing a hard black hat over his streaming white hair and beard. Von Ostein believed passionately in Hans's ability to do complicated multiplication and division—even fractions—tapping out the answer with his hoof and manipulating sets of numbers up to six decimal places. What's more, by converting his answers into numbers, Hans could also read, spell, and identify musical tones. He communicated zeros with a shake of the head.

Leading German biologist Carl Stumpf had become fascinated with the Hans phenomenon and had invited 13 eminent scientists—the so-called Hans Commission—to defend him and Von Ostein from ridicule in the press. To defend their own reputations, the commission recommended further study by a rising young psychologist, Oskar Pfungst. In the six weeks that followed, Pfungst had been severely bitten by Hans, Von Ostein had withdrawn his horse in a rage, and—with a sigh of relief—modern science had cracked the mystery of the counting horse.

First of all, Pfungst noticed that Hans got excited if he couldn't see the questioner and made strenuous efforts to see around his blindfold so that he could. They also found that the horse lost the arithmetical plot if he was asked questions that the questioners didn't know the answers to themselves. Clearly he must be responding to some kind of unconscious signal from the person asking the questions.

Pfungst argued, completely convincingly, that Hans was able to pick up the slight incline of the questioners' heads when they had finished asking the question and expected the answer to be tapped out. When Hans had reached the right number of taps, he was able to notice the tiny relaxation, the minute straightening up or raised eyebrow with which the questioners betrayed themselves, and he stopped tapping. Hans also tapped faster when he knew it was a long answer—a practice that added to his intellectual reputation—and this, too, said Pfungst, he was able to derive from tiny changes of facial expression.

Pfungst's own reputation was made, modern science had been vindicated—animals could not count. Von Ostein died a few months later. History does not relate what happened to Hans, but I'm not hopeful.

II

So we can all breathe a sigh of relief—animals can't count. For centuries, counting was accepted as one of the key differences between human beings and animals. "Brutes cannot number, weigh, and measure," said the great pioneer of quantification, the fifteenth-century cardinal Nicholas of Cusa. The arrival of a mathematical horse was a serious challenge to the numerical worldview: Numbers are supposed to be the exclusive domain of humans and, before that, the exclusive domain of the gods.

Numbers have been in constant use for the past 6,000 years, but we have never quite resolved what they are. Are they intellectual tools for humans, invented by us for our own use—or are they fantastical concepts, preexisting in the universe before Adam, which we had to discover, like everything else, along with the North Pole and the laws of thermodynamics? Which came first: man or numbers? Are they available for any species to use or just an aspect of mankind? Are they real or human?

In prehistory, they were exclusively the province of the gods. The ancient world believed that numbers were holy things, which meant something in their own right, and that the proper people to deal with them were a fearsome bunch of accountant-priests—an unpleasant combination. There is a fresco in Syria that shows this early form of mystical bureaucrat counting and writing down, part of the business of managing the Assyrian Empire—numbers and empire have gone hand in hand since the earliest times. But without written calculations, which everybody could see and check, the early accountants made the most of the mystery and ritual in counting, wrapping their professional expertise in a cloak of fearsome religion.

This tradition came to a head in the 6th century B.C. with the ancient Greek philosopher Pythagoras, who was the great believer in the natural God-given beauty of numbers. For Pythagoras, numbers corresponded to a natural harmony in the universe, as bound up with the music of the spheres as they are with calculations. Numbers were the underpinning of music and beauty. The story goes that Pythagoras was hearing a blacksmith hammering away, heard the musical notes made by the anvil, and realized that different lengths of hammer generated them—and that there were perfect ratios of halves, thirds, and quarters that generated perfect chords. They were the secret harmonies generated by the real numbers in nature. Another legend says that he learned about such things from the wisest people among the Egyptians and Phoenicians, and spent 12 years studying with the Magi after being taken captive and imprisoned in Babylon.

Numbers existed even before the universe itself, according to Pythagoras. But even that was too mild for St. Augustine of Hippo, who declared that six was such a perfect number that it would be so even if the world didn't exist at all. "We cannot escape the feeling," said the mathematician Heinrich Hertz, "that these mathematical formulae have an independent existence and an intelligence of their own, that they are wiser than we are, wiser even than their discoverers, that we get more out of them than was originally put into them."

Numbers rule the universe, said Pythagoras and his followers. Anything less than the perfect harmonious numbers that Pythagoras based his system on—oddities like negatives or fractions—was "unutterable" and initiates were sworn to secrecy about them. According to his follower Proclus, the first people who mentioned such possibilities all died in a shipwreck. "The unutterable and the formless must be concealed," he said. "And those who uncovered and touched this image of life were instantly destroyed and shall remain forever exposed to the play of the eternal waves."

Counting was always about power. Imperial managers needed to count their wealth and empire to control it: The bigger the empire, the more it needed to be counted. But if numbers were mystical God-given tools, it meant that those who guarded them were also mysterious and powerful people. Although we have long since decided that numbers are a tool of mankind rather than magic spells, we still share just a hint of this sense of the mystique of numbers. As if the accountants or technicians are a little apart from the world, in their white coats or carrying their computer programs that the rest of us can never hope to understand.

But even the ancients recognized that numbers were related to mere humans. We count in base 10 probably because people had 10 fingers to use. Palaeolithic people used not just their hands, but knuckles, ears, toes, finger joints. By the 16th century, the Chinese had organized a hand-counting system using two hands to count to over a billion. Societies that used fingers to count with would often punish thieves by cutting off their hands, without which they could no longer use numbers at all. They became what Nicholas of Cusa called "brutes."

Body counting remains in the language. In New Guinea, the word for six is *wrist*. The word for nine is *left breast*. The Venerable Bede listed these things: The number 50,000, for example, was indicated by pointing the thumb of your extended hand to your navel. The Holy Roman Emperor Frederick II—famous for his scientific experiments that involved drowning criminals in barrels—also wrote a famous book on falconry where he explains one hand movement "as if indicating the number 75." Counting meant moving your body, and that meant ritual—ritual that evolved into the mysterious movements the accountants made with the abacus.

III

We now live in an age that's pragmatic about numbers and counting. Numbers are simple, everyday human tools for us, but we use them to control things and describe things—for research or sometimes just for shock value—but at the same time, we have lost something too. Numbers are no longer divine. They are now, in a sense, more human. Or perhaps humans have become more godlike. But what have we lost in the exchange? We have lost the ancient art of understanding numbers as beautiful and meaning something beyond themselves, and numbers without souls can have a deadening effect on us.

The first nail in the coffin was irrational numbers. When the intellectual descendants of Pythagoras opened up the new world of paradoxes, irrationality, bizarre computations, negative numbers, square roots, then nothing ever seemed the same again. What did minus 2 mean, after all? What does 0.333333 recurring mean? What about π? When the mathematicians got started, as they did even in the lifetime of Pythagoras, the idea of harmony in numbers seemed to disappear. They didn't seem in the least perfect.

There were philosophical problems too. Counting means definition and control. To count something, you have to name it and define it. You have to categorize. You have to be able to see the similarity in things and their differences, and decide which are important, before you can count them. "It must have required many ages to discover that a brace of pheasants and a couple of days were other instances of the number two," said the philosopher Bertrand Russell. But it wasn't ever as simple as that, because actually no two things are exactly the same.

But once you have grasped the concept of two, there are so many other categories you have to create before you can count how many people there are in your tribe. Do you count children? Do you count foreigners who happen to live with you? Do you count people who look completely different from everybody else?

Numbers ceased to be divine when they had to be put to practical work. This was another nail in the coffin, the second way that numbers lost their souls. Empires and bureaucracies needed to stop admiring them and put them to work, helping them control the world around them. They needed them to be precise. It is no coincidence that it was the ancient Sumerian civilization, the first real empire, that developed the idea of writing down numbers for the first time. They had to if they were going to manage an imperial culture of herds, crops, and people. Yet any definition you make simply has to be a compromise with the truth. And the easier it is to count, the more the words give way to figures, the more counting simplifies things that are not simple. Because although you can count sheep until you are blue in the face, actually no two sheep are exactly alike.

The old world didn't need precision. Numbers merely supported natural or supernatural events. If Christ's resurrection was important, it wasn't terribly vital to know what the actual date was. Instead, Europeans used numbers for effect—King Arthur was described as killing tens of thousands in battles all by himself. Modern politics is the last remaining profession that does this, claiming unwieldy figures that they have achieved personally and pretending a spurious accuracy by borrowing the language of statistics, when actually they are using the numbers for effect like a medieval chronicler. It was the English king Henry I who defined a yard as the distance from his own nose to the tip of his middle finger on his outstretched arm. Accuracy wasn't so important that he bothered to measure anybody else's nose-to-finger reach. An acre was originally the area that a team of eight oxen could plow in a morning, which is probably the most vague possible definition. Nor were the numbers medieval people used—bulky Roman symbols— much good for calculation.

And when it came to measuring time, accuracy was completely irrelevant. There were 12 hours in the medieval day and 12 hours of the night too, but without proper tools for measuring time, these were expanded and compressed to make sure the 12 hours into the light and the dark. An hour in the summer was much longer than an hour in the winter, and actually referred to the "hours" when prayers should be said.

Clocks were the manifestation of how numbers were put to practical use. Nobody knows who invented clocks, though legend has it that it was the mysterious Gerbert of Aurillac—a medieval monk who spent time in Spain learning from the wisdom of the Arabs—and who, as Sylvester II, was the Pope who saw in the last millennium. He was said to be so good at math that contemporaries believed he was in league with the Devil. It was not for 250 years that clocks arrived in the mass market, but once they had, you couldn't argue with their accuracy. From the 1270s, they dominated the European townscapes, insisting that hours were all the same length and that trading times and working times should be strictly regulated. Counting in public is, after all, a controlling force—as the people of Amiens discovered in 1335 when the mayor regulated their working and eating time with a bell, attached to a clock.

Clocks had bells before they had faces and were machines of neat precision, as you can see by the fourteenth-century one still working in the nave of Salisbury Cathedral, with its careful black cogs swinging backward and forward—the very model of the new medieval exactitude. Soon every big city was imposing heavy taxes on themselves to afford the clock machinery, adding mechanical hymns, Magi bouncing in and out, and—like the one in Strasbourg in 1352—a mechanical cockerel that crowed and waggled its wings.

Where would they stop, these medieval calculators? Scholars at Merton College, Oxford, in the 14th century thought about how you can measure not just size, taste, motion, heat, and color, but also qualities like virtue and grace. But then these were the days when even temperature had to be quantified without the use of a thermometer, which had yet to be invented. They must have been heady days, when the whole of quality—the whole of arts and perception—seemed to be collapsing neatly into science.

Anyone still dragging their feet really was holding back history. Some dyed-in-the-wool conservatives insisted that people know pretty well when it was day and night, and when the seasons change, without the aid of the new counting devices. But anyone who thinks that, said the early Protestant reformer Philip Melanchthon, deserves to have someone "shit a turd" in his hat. The new world of number crunchers had arrived.

The third nail in the coffin was commerce. The new merchants needed simple Arabic figures, and they needed to be accurate. The Church at Florence briefly banned the new numbers—brought back from the Middle East by Crusaders—in 1229 because they seemed dangerously Muslim. But the new literate, numerate mercantile classes needed them, as they dispatched fleets for kings and managed the processing of wool with their new counting boards.

There were other nails in the coffin to come—the powerful new concepts of zero and negatives. The Arabic zero was one of the main reasons why the 13th century Church banned non-Roman numbers: Zero seemed to mean infinity and infinity meant God, yet there it was bandied around the least important trade calculations for fish or sheep for everyone to see. Despite that, it was probably a monk who brought zero to Europe. Raoul de Laon was a particularly skillful exponent of the art of the abacus—who used a character he called *siphos* to show an empty column. The word came from the Arabic *sifr*, meaning "empty"—the origin of the word *cypher*. It was immediately controversial.

It wasn't just the Church that objected. Even more potent were the fears of the Italian bankers, who were afraid this little symbol would lead to fraud. It can, after all, multiply other figures by 10 at one slip of the pen. But despite the ban, the enormous increase in trade because of the Crusades and the activities of the Hanseatic League meant that something of the kind was needed. Italian merchants increasingly used zero as an underground sign for "free trade." Bootleggers and smugglers embraced the idea with enthusiasm. Like the V sign across the continent under Nazi tyranny, zero became a symbol of numerical freedom, a kind of medieval counterculture.

What normally happens with countercultures is that everyone adopts them, and that's exactly what happened. Soon everyone was using zero quite openly and adding and subtracting happily using a pen and ink. Written computations had no mystery. There was something open and almost democratic about them, and they needed no priests to interpret them. Calculation was no longer a mysterious art carried out by skilled initiates.

Soon the abacus had died out so much that it became a source of fascination. One of Napoleon's generals was given one in Russia when he was a prisoner of war, and he was so astonished that he brought it back with him to Paris to show the emperor. Though don't dismiss the abacus completely. In occupied Japan in 1945, the United States army organized a competition between their automatic calculator and skilled Japanese abacus users. The abacus turned out to be both quicker and more accurate for every computation except multiplication.

The final nail in the coffin of divine numbers was the arrival of accountancy, bookkeeping, and—with the books—negative numbers in the form of debt. Double-entry bookkeeping may not have actually been the brainchild of a friend of Leonardo da Vinci, the Milan math teacher Fra Luca Pacioli, but it was Pacioli's destiny to popularize it. The writer James Buchan described his method as a "machine for calculating the world." It was one of the "loveliest inventions of the human spirit," according to Goethe. It could work out, at any moment, when your complex deals were profitable, allowing you to compare one deal with another.

Pacioli was a Franciscan monk who knew all about profit. He had special dispensation from the pope—a friend of his—to own property. "The end and object of every businessman is to make a lawful and satisfactory profit so that he may sustain himself," he wrote. "Therefore he should begin with the name of God." Pacioli and his followers duly wrote the name of God at the beginning of every ledger. Before Pacioli, traders tended to give any fractions to the bank. After Pacioli they could record them. They could grasp at a glance where they stood while their cargoes were on high seas, or while they waited two years or more for them to be fabricated into something else. They could make them stand still to be counted.

A neo-Platonist, fascinated by Pythagoras and his ideas of divine proportion, Pacioli filled his book with other stuff like military tactics, architecture, and theology. He chose a potent moment to publish it: the year after Columbus arrived back from discovering America. But despite his Pythagorean roots, Pacioli provided the foundations for a more complex idea of profit and loss, of assets and liabilities, making all of them clearly measurable. His critics feared he had abolished quality altogether. All that you could put down in the double entries was quantities—numbers of sheep, amounts of wool: There was no column for qualities like good or bad. The numbers had taken over, simplifying and calculating the world in their own way.

Within three centuries, accountants had developed into the professional you called in after bankruptcy—a kind of undertakers for the business world—which is why the British Companies Act 1862, which regulated such matters, became known as "the accountant's friend." "The whole affairs in bankruptcy have been handed over to an ignorant set of men called accountants, which was one of the greatest abuses ever introduced into law," said Mr. Justice Quinn during a British bankruptcy case in 1875.

In 1790, the post office directory for London lists just one accountant. By 1840 there were 107 of them and by 1845—right in the middle of the railway boom—there were 210, ready to assist cleaning up the mess in the financial collapse the following year. They might have been responsible for the rash of suicides in London in 1846; maybe they helped prevent more. We shall never know. Either way, it was just the beginning for the accountants. By the turn of the century there were more than 6,000 in England and Wales and a similar number in the United States. Now there are 330,000 members of the American Institute of Certified Public Accountants alone, and that doesn't count the fraud examiners, chartered accountants, government accountants, management accountants, and all the other branches of the profession, but—as far as I know—no counting horses left at all.

IV

Pacioli and his spiritual descendants have helped create the modern world with its obsession with counting—and the strange idea that once you have counted the money, you have counted everything. There is a hardheaded myth that numbers are serious and words are not—that counting things is a rigorous business for a serious man's world. "When you can measure what you are speaking of and express it in terms of numbers, you know something about it," said the scientist Lord Kelvin a little over a century ago. "When you cannot express it in terms of numbers your knowledge of it is of a meager kind."

Armed with this attitude, Lord Kelvin dismissed radio as pointless, airplanes as impossible, and X rays as a hoax, so we might reasonably doubt his opinion here. But is my knowledge really of such a meager kind? Can I express something about myself in numbers? If Lord Kelvin's successors managed to express my entire genetic code in numbers, would they know me better than I do myself when I can do no such thing? Well, in some ways, maybe they can—but I doubt it. Any more than the Nazis could know anything about the victims in concentration camps by branding a unique number on their arms.

We are more than branded now. We are in a world obsessed with numbers, from National Insurance and interest rates to buses, from bank balances and bar codes to the cacophony of statistics forced on us by journalists, politicians, and marketers. We seem to agree with Lord Kelvin that numbers provide us with a kind of exactitude. Actually they are exact about some of the least interesting things, but silent on wider and increasingly important truths.

We have to count. Numbers can surprise us and show something is wrong: They have shock value. And in case anyone thinks I'm a total hypocrite for using them myself in this book, it is in that sense that they are used. Not counting is like saying that numbers are evil, which is even more pointless than saying that money is evil. We need to be able to count, even if the results aren't very accurate. "Without numbers, we can understand nothing and know nothing," said the philosopher Philolaus in the fifth century B.C.—and he was right. But twenty-five centuries after Philolaus, the French philosopher Alain Badiou put the other point of view—and he was right too: "What arises from an event in perfect truth can never be counted." The world is just too complex to be expressed in figures.

Both Philolaus and Badiou are right. The more we rely on numbers to understand problems or measure aspects of human life, the more it slips through our fingers and we find ourselves clinging to something less than we wanted. Because every person, every thing, every event is actually unique and immeasurable.

This is the paradox this book is all about. If we don't count something, it gets ignored. If we do count it, it gets perverted. We need to count, yet the counters are taking over our lives. "The measurable has conquered almost the entire field of the sciences and has discredited every branch in which it is not valid," said the French poet Paul Valéry. "The applied sciences are almost completely dominated by measurement. Life, itself, which is already half enslaved, circumscribed, streamlined, or reduced to a state of subjection, has great difficulty in defending itself against the tyranny of timetables, statistics, quantitative measurements, and precision instruments, a whole development that goes on reducing life's diversity, diminishing its uncertainty, improving the functioning of the whole, making its course surer, longer, and more mechanical."

The problem happens when we use numbers to count things that can never be counted, and when we confuse the two. That's when the old world and the new world collide. It's happening all around us as the technocrats try to count the universe.

This book is intended as a reminder of the time when numbers stood for something in themselves, just at a time when things, people, and institutions seem so complex that counting them no longer seems an

adequate way of controlling them. It is an old way of looking at numbers—the discredited and forgotten wisdom of Augustine, Pythagoras,
and Plato—but it may also carry within it the seeds of a new way.

We snigger patronizingly when we read how, in 1245, Gossoin of
Metz worked out that—if Adam had set off the moment he was created,
walking at the rate of 25 miles a day—he would still have to walk for
another 713 years if he was going to reach the stars. We laugh at the
great alchemist Roger Bacon, striving to measure the exact arc of a rain-
bow from his laboratory above Oxford's Folly Bridge, when he calculated that someone walking 20 miles a day would take 14 years, seven
months, and just over 29 days to get to the moon.

We stare back uncomprehendingly when we read St. Thomas
Aquinas's solemn injunction that 144,000 would be saved at the end
of time. Though the last thing he meant was that literally 144,000
people would make it to heaven. To Aquinas, a thousand meant per-
fection, and the 144 is the number of the apostles multiplied by itself.
"I speak in parables of eternal wisdom, my honored sir," he might have
said, like a character in Andrew Sinclair's novel *Gog*. "I leave statistics to
plumbers."

The old way of looking at numbers, what the medieval historian
Alfred Crosby calls the "Venerable Model," means nothing to us now.
"We sniff and cluck at its mistakes—that the earth is the center of the
universe, for instance—but our real problem with the Venerable Model
is that it is dramatic, even melodramatic, and teleological: God and Purpose loom over all," he wrote. "We want (or think we want) explana-
tions of reality leeched of emotion, as bloodless as distilled water."

But do we want that? Like those medieval scientists, modern number crunchers are attempting to measure the unmeasurable as a way of
controlling a complicated world. It's a dangerous era for anyone who
believes there's more to life than that.

Truth is complex, after all. Yet when we reject the idea that a horse
is extraordinary, intelligent, and prodigiously sensitive just because it
can't count after all, we are in the grip of a modern simplifying disease.

2

BENTHAM AND THE
MEASURE OF HAPPINESS

*Nature has placed Mankind under the governance of two sovereign
masters, pain and pleasure. It is in them alone to point out what we
ought to do, as much as what we shall do.*

Jeremy Bentham

*There is nothing which has yet been contrived by man, by which so
much happiness is produced as by a good tavern or inn.*

Samuel Johnson, March 21, 1776

LONDON, 1832

I

IT WAS ONE of the strangest funerals ever held. Three days after his death on June 6, 1832, the body of the great utilitarian philosopher Jeremy Bentham—dressed in a nightshirt—was unveiled to his friends and admirers, gathered together at the Webb Street School of Anatomy in London. It was a stormy early evening, and the grisly occasion was lit by flashes of lightning from the skylight above, as Bentham's young doctor, Thomas Southwood Smith, began his oration—a speech that included a demonstration of the dissection on his old friend.

Among the faithful were some of the great figures of reform from the immediate past and future, the radical tailor Francis Place and the future sanitation reformer Edwin Chadwick in the shadows. In their minds, we might imagine, was a sense of enormous achievement—two days before, the Great Reform Act, which had been the focus of all their hopes, had been given Royal Assent. There might also have been the occasional less welcome echo from Mary Shelley's gothic novel *Frankenstein*, published 14 years before, as Southwood Smith's scalpel glinted in the gaslight—with all its warning for the Godless who meddle with the untouchable moments of birth and death.

They might also have been wondering whether this was the right way of remembering their hero. Dissection was then regarded as such an appalling end that it was handed out as an extra punishment for the murderers who normally found themselves cut open in this room. Southwood Smith the former preacher managed to keep his voice steady, but his face was as white as the corpse's. Bentham's funeral guests would have reassured themselves that they were carrying out the details of his will, and that they were men of the new age of science, and could put aside those old-fashioned notions of superstition, emotion, and shame.

Could those things even be measured in Bentham's new political morality of "utility"? The facts—yes, the rigorously logical fact—was that it was more "useful" to dissect the philosopher's body than it was to bury it. And as Bentham had written himself, if you were going to have statues or portraits of him, it was more "useful" to use the real thing rather than let it go to waste in a coffin in the earth.

When Smith finished his work of cleaning and embalming, Bentham's body was to be an "Auto-Icon," a modern monument and a more exact replica of the man than any artist could possibly achieve. It would be dressed in Bentham's own clothes, with his walking stick—which he used to call Dapple, after Sancho Panza's mule—firmly in his hands. It would remain in a glass case in University College, London, which he had done so much to turn into the reality of bricks and mortar.

The plan didn't go quite as expected. Despite Bentham's best endeavors to study the head-shrinking methods of the Maoris, his own head shriveled ghoulishly and extremely fast. A few years later, the college decided to replace it with a waxwork. The original was placed between his legs, from where it has occasionally been stolen. And there Bentham's Auto-Icon remains, wheeled gravely into important college meetings and still on display to the professors and students of London University and anybody else who wanders in, together with some very un-Benthamite rumors about ghosts.

It was a fittingly scientific end to the life of the man who gave us the philosophical school of utilitarianism. Because it was Bentham who told us that what is good and right is what most promotes human happiness—not necessarily what it says in law or the Bible. And it was Bentham who launched the world's politicians on an increasingly determined set of calculations, so they can know what this "good" is in any given situation.

The daily outpouring of figures and statistics that now so dominate our conversations began partly with Bentham, but he was also a symptom of his time. At the beginning of his life, London was dirty, foul smelling, and dangerously brutal, with one congested bridge over the river. By the end there were eight bridges over the Thames, the streets were lit by gaslight, and steam trains—"self-moving receptacles," as he described them—were beginning to change the shape of cities. What's more, his native land had experienced no fewer than 30 years of census returns and was about to start the compulsory registration of births, marriages, and deaths.

The number crunchers had arrived. Some people even predicted it at the time. "The age of chivalry is gone," moaned Edmund Burke in the House of Commons. "That of sophisters, economists, and calculators has succeeded, and the glory of Europe is extinguished for ever." And if one person could be blamed for that, you would probably waggle the finger at Jeremy Bentham.

Now that almost two centuries have gone by since his death, you would think it might be possible to get more perspective on the man who did so much to start the numbering of the modern world. But that still seems impossible. Because for all his mild manners and gentle unemotional ways, Bentham has inspired passionate feelings of distaste ever since. Carlyle described his contribution as a "pig philosophy." Karl Marx went even further, describing Bentham as "the insipid, pedantic leather-tongued waste of the commonplace bourgeois intelligence of the 19th century." Trotsky was immediately converted by reading his works at the age of 17, but later condemned them as "a philosophy of social cookbook recipes." For anyone with a hint of ideology, anyone with the least utopian dream, Bentham and his social measuring tape were anathema.

The humorless Nietzsche was even moved to verse to describe him:

Soul of washrag, face of poker,
Overwhelmingly mediocre.

Looking at Jeremy Bentham's face now, in the glass case, it does have a little of the poker about it. Even his clothes seem ludicrous, as if they have been borrowed from a Disney cartoon, and don't seem nearly dangerous enough to inspire such hatred. Nor do the stories of the old boy jogging from his home in Westminster to Fleet Street well into his 70s, about his ancient cat—which he called the Reverend Dr. John Langhorn—and his determined early-morning walks around the garden. Why insult the poor fellow just because he wanted to squeeze the passion out of politics by counting?

Reading his books doesn't supply the answer. His works are impenetrable and his autobiography was bowdlerized and put into an unreadable third person by his incompetent assistant John Bowrigg, so it is hard to get a sense of the man. The overwhelming impression to us now is that here was a mild, vain, fastidious, pedantic, irritating obsessive who never really lived a full life—hardly loved and barely lost—but who brought about a revolution that is still such an important part of our lives that it remains as ambiguous as ever.

But let's go back to the beginning.

II

Jeremy Bentham was born on February 15, 1748, the son of a successful City of London lawyer who provided him with such a miserable, monotonous, and gloomy childhood that he put the attainment of happiness at the center of his philosophy. His mother died when he was 10, and life with Jeremy's overbearing and demanding father meant no games and little fun. No other children were ever asked to the house.

Instead of embracing the law as his father was insisting, Bentham spent his small allowance on the works of the philosophers David Hume and Claude-Adrien Helvétius. In them, he found the basis for his philosophy—that you could estimate happiness from a number of different pleasures and that public "utility" was the basis of all human virtues. Reading Helvétius and walking a little way behind his family—you can picture their exasperation at this gauche and bookish adolescent trailing along after them—he asked himself: "Have I a genius for anything?"

Adolescents tend to ask themselves this question. But to Bentham, the answer came like an appearance by the angel Gabriel. He took the clue from the book he was reading, in which Helvétius gave his opinion that legislation was the most important of earthly pursuits, an opinion widely approved by legislators the world over. "And have I indeed a genius for legislation?" said the young Jeremy to himself. "I gave myself the answer, fearfully and tremblingly—Yes."

Enthusiastically, and already packing his mind with this sense of historic mission, he devoured as much as he could from the works of moral and political philosophy he could get his hands on. Tom Paine was starting to think up *Rights of Man*, there was simmering discontent in the American colonies, and ideas were dangerous world-shifting things. Bentham flung himself in. But it was when he traveled back to Oxford to vote as a university graduate in the 1768 parliamentary election—the great British universities had their own members of Parliament until well into the 20th century—that he had his real breakthrough. He was rummaging through the small library in Harper's Coffee House when he came across the pamphlet by the chemist Joseph Priestley that included the phrase "the greatest happiness of the greatest number." Bentham let out a sharp "Eureka!" and dashed out to make the phrase his own.

It remains the phrase for which Bentham is best known. Priestley never used it again—he didn't need it, said Bentham—so he adapted it as the center of his philosophy. And there it is, in the first page of the first work he ever published, the *Fragment on Government*: "It is the greatest happiness of the greatest number that is the measure of right and wrong."

Before Bentham—or so he believed—the laws of England and the morality on which they were based were a hopeless jumble of superstition, tradition, contradiction, and privilege. After Bentham—or so he believed—there would be a clear logical reason for laws, and governments would know automatically what to do. It would no longer be a matter of balancing distrust of the people with fear, as Gladstone said later, but a simple piece of arithmetic. Government action—all action in fact—should be based on what would make most people happiest.

For the rest of his life, Bentham devoted most of his intellectual effort to working out how his Greatest Happiness Principle might become clear in practice. Borrowing the popular thinking at the time that classified diseases or the Linnean classification for plants and animals into families, he set about classifying pleasures to meet the strict demands of his legislative theory. By the end of his life, Bentham had defined 14 broad kinds of pleasure—from the pleasures of skill and wealth to the pleasures of what he called "malevolence" and "relief"—and sent a generation of followers and enthusiasts away to measure them.

I wish I could return in six or seven centuries time, he was fond of remarking, so that I can see the effects of my work. "Alas! His name will hardly live so long," wrote the essayist William Hazlitt—putting his finger on the whole problem with utilitarianism in one neat sentence: "There are some tastes that are sweet in the mouth and bitter in the belly, and there is a similar contradiction and anomaly in the mind and heart of man."

Despite this put-down, Bentham has managed to remain famous for more than a century and a half—and, for a long time, it didn't seem as if he would ever achieve it. He was much better known abroad. Hazlitt was also right when he said that Bentham's fame was in inverse proportion to the distance from his house in Westminster. When the traveler and writer George Borrow found himself arrested in Spain, he was released from prison on the grounds that he shared a nationality with the man his captor called "The Grand Bentham." And when he visited Paris toward the end of his life—an honorary French citizen after the Revolution—the lawyers at the courts of justice rose to receive him.

"The case is, though I have neither time nor room to give you particulars," he wrote in 1810, "that now at length, when I am just ready to drop into the grave, my fame has spread itself all over the civilized world."

III

What kind of man was the legislator for the world; the philosopher who thought you could calculate human happiness? The answer is: not a very worldly one. You know instinctively that anyone who calls his morning walks something as pompous as "antejentacular circumgyrations" is likely to be pretty cut off from life. This, after all, was someone with sufficient mental space to have a pet name, not just his walking stick, but for his teapot (Dick)—and who probably never talked to women at all, except for his cook and housemaid. Who was never once drunk, and who fell in love briefly twice—but without obvious effect.

Bentham surrounded himself with luxuries of bread, fruit, and tea, but he never read literature. He covered his walls with Hogarth prints, and happily wandered round and round his garden in Queens Square Place, Westminster, scrupulously dressed and with his straw hat on his head.

He loved animals more than people. It somehow makes him a little more human and endearing to think of him encouraging mice to play in his office while he struggled to classify human experience, though it was difficult to manage their relationship with his beloved cats. Nevertheless, it hardly seems like the description of a man so fired with life that he could settle down and measure the immeasurable passions. His interpreter John Stuart Mill certainly thought so, and he knew him. "He had neither internal experience, nor external," Mill said of Bentham. "He never knew prosperity and adversity, passion nor satiety; he never had even the experiences which sickness gives. . . . He knew no dejection, no heaviness of heart. He never felt life a sore and a weary burthen. He was a boy to the last."

It was a description that was later applied to Bentham's successors, who believed that anything could be measured. Believing that pleasure or pain, or anything important can be measured precisely is a mistake made by people who haven't really experienced the complexity of the world. It's a boyish mistake.

Bentham's writing has only clouded the issue. He would start gigantic projects of classification with enthusiasm, the first chapter of which would turn out to be so voluminous that he would have to concentrate on that and abandon the rest. It was a pattern that continued for the rest of his life. He began by writing a long critique of the distinguished jurist William Blackstone, part of which came out as *A Fragment on Government* in 1776. The rest was expanded and expanded, and abandoned because it was out of control. Next, there was the *Treatise on Punishments*. Only the introduction was ever anything near finished. The rest had once again expanded beyond control and had to be turned into a study on laws in general. And so on and so on, collating, noting in margins, packed with expletive and rage, then putting the papers aside never to be looked at again.

Luckily, according to the historian Leslie Stephen, he "formed disciples ardent enough to put together these scattered documents as the disciples of Mahomet put together the Koran." Even so, it was hardly enough to make him a best-seller. One reviewer in his lifetime described his style as "the Sanskrit of modern legislation"—and those were the days when nobody could understand Sanskrit. "He has parenthesis within parenthesis, like a set of pillboxes," wrote his erstwhile secretary Walter Coulson. "And out of this habit have grown redundancies which become tiresome to the modern reader."

What really changed Bentham's life was his idea for an entirely different type of prison, where—like modern auditors and their all-seeing figures—one prison guard could watch all the inmates simultaneously all the time. The Panopticon was his own invention, built in the shape of a flower, with the prison keeper at the center. The governors would run the new institutions as profit-making concerns, which would use the prisoners as motive power for a range of inventions that would make a profit—and at the same time "grind the rogues honest."

The idea was a masterpiece of enlightenment, Bentham thought. Because the new prison governors relied for their profit on the prisoners' health, it was in their interest to keep them healthy and well fed. It never happened, so we shall never know whether the prisoners would actually have thanked him—as Bentham believed they would have done. But, since he was intending to work them 14 hours a day with another hour on the treadmill for exercise, it's hard to believe their gratitude would have been overwhelming.

Even so, for the next 20 years, Bentham barraged the government with his plans, and with some effect. They even bought a site for it on London's Millbank where the Tate Gallery stands today, but the final signature was frustratingly difficult to obtain. Bentham was so certain the money would come through that he sank at least £10,000 of his own money into the project as early as 1796, and he soon found himself on the verge of imprisonment for debt. Day after day he wandered the Treasury corridors, writing letters, his hopes rising when William Pitt was replaced as prime minister by Henry Addington, only to be dashed again. "Mr. Addington's hope is what Mr. Pitt's hope was," he wrote in despair, "to see me die broken-hearted, like a rat in a hole."

He asked everyone he could for help. "Never was any one worse used than Bentham," wrote the antislavery campaigner William Wilberforce. "I have seen the tears run down the cheeks of that strong-minded man, through the vexation at the pressing importunity of creditors and the insolence of official underlings."

In the meantime, he turned himself into a bizarre generator of crazy ideas. He tried to interest the Treasury in currency schemes—always a sign of mild instability—and speaking tubes. He suggested the idea of a train of carts drawn at speed between London and Edinburgh. He told the Americans they should build a canal across Panama, and suggested to the city authorities that they should freeze large quantities of vegetables so that there could be fresh peas available at Christmastime. Not content with that, he linked up with Peter Mark Roget, later to write the first Thesaurus—a Benthamite project of classification if ever there was one—to invent what he called a fridgidarium to keep food cold. He told the Bank of England how they could create an unforgeable banknote. He wrote widely in favor of votes for women and proposed, in unpublished writings, that homosexuality should be legal, at a time when you could be hanged for sodomy. "How a voluntary act of this sort by two individuals can be said to have any thing to do with the safety of them or any other individual whatever, is somewhat difficult to be conceived," he wrote.

Absolutely none of these ideas was taken up during his lifetime. He had more luck with inventing new words. *International* is one of his. So are *codify* and *maximize*. He had less success renaming astronomy as "uranoscopic physiurgics." Still less renaming biology as "epigeoscopic physiurgics." And his letters urging the British government to rename the country "Brithibernia" remained in the minister's in-trays. His attempts to reshape the cabinet also had to wait more than a century. There should be 12 ministers, he said—including one for education, one for "the preservation of the national health," one for "indigence relief," one for "preventive service"—to stop accidents—and an "interior communication minister" (transport). In fact, he died the year before the government first voted any money to education at all.

The hopelessly old-fashioned shape of the government was probably why the Panopticon stayed stubbornly incomplete. That is certainly what Bentham thought, even when a parliamentary committee took pity on him in 1813 and voted him £23,000 in damages, with which he paid off his debts. The Panopticon story is important here because it made him realize that the whole of government needed reform. If Lord Spencer could hold up the project for a generation simply because it was near his London landholdings, then the whole system was corrupt. He needed a method of government to calculate right from wrong, rather than letting it fall to whomever happened to have the ear of the prime minister of the day. If the system of government could not see that it was in the general interest to adopt his plan, then how could you construct a system of government that would automatically want to improve human happiness?

"All government is in itself one vast evil," said the frustrated philosopher, who set about doing something about it. So, with a sigh of relief, he went back to writing his impenetrable prose. And in 1802, it all came right. Despite his inability to finish writing anything, the Swiss publisher Pierre Dumont at last managed to get Bentham to agree to publishing some of his work. By the time Dumont had finished with it, it was even easy to read and was attracting attention in Paris, Moscow, and Madrid. This was the *Traites de Législation Civile et Pénale*. It included crucial parts of Bentham's *Introduction to the Principles of Morals and Legislation*, and it was the first of many.

He soon found he had a good deal more influence abroad than he did in London, though still not much power. By the time he had sent out his constitutional code to the revolutionary governments of Spain and Portugal, both had succumbed to counterrevolution. He sent it in nine installments to the provisional government in Greece, with much the same effect. His ideas were welcomed at first by Rivadavia in Argentina and Bolívar in Columbia, though it wasn't long before Bolívar was busily banning his works from the universities. His letter bombardment of Sir Robert Peel seemed to leave him cold. And the Duke of Wellington did not respond to his promise that his name would be as great as Alexander's if he took Bentham's advice on law reform. He had more success in Italy because Cavour remained a fan. Tsar Alexander even sent him a ring, which he returned with the seal unbroken because he thought it looked too much like a bribe. And thanks to Lord Macaulay, he did have an influence in shaping the new laws of India.

So, he was increasingly optimistic. In a calculation reminiscent of those by his medieval forbears, he predicted that his code would finally be adopted in every country in the world in the year 2825—presumably exactly a thousand years since he made the prediction. It was a letter from Guatemala that same year that gave him the title, which stuck, *legislador del mundo*—the Legislator for the World.

The idea of measuring happiness was central to almost everything he wrote. He began to consider exactly how the formula would work—something his followers had to tackle after his death—and he fell back on the moderate thought that any kind of calculation was better than none. "In every rational and candid eye, unspeakable will be the advantage it will have over every form of precision being ever attained because none is ever so much as aimed at," he wrote. All you needed was the formula, and that meant calculating the pleasures and pains against their intensity, duration, certainty, rapidity, fecundity, purity, and extensiveness. Simple!

And from the start he realized that this principle, whatever it was called, depended on being able to measure the way people felt. "Value of a lot of pleasure or Pain, How to be Measured," was the title of chapter 4 of *Introduction to the Principles of Morals and Legislation*. He imagined that this was a simple proposition—"Who is there that does not calculate?" he asked airily—but the complete absence of any official figures made him think again. Where was the raw data? He asked the Bank of England how much paper money was in circulation. They didn't know. Neither had the Foundling Hospital any idea about the cost of living for paupers.

In a sudden burst of enthusiasm for figures, he persuaded the great agricultural reformer Arthur Young to use his *Annals of Agriculture* to send out a questionnaire about rural poverty. Young even wrote an encouraging introduction to it. Unfortunately, Bentham's enthusiasm got the better of him, and the questionnaire included no fewer than 3,000 questions. Not surprisingly, only a handful of answers ever arrived back at Queens Square Place.

And even if they had poured in, how could you compare these different pleasures and pains. You couldn't count the number of people affected by them and you certainly couldn't compare how much they were feeling them. What if slaves were happy—did that make slavery right? This was a difficult question for Bentham, who was a lifelong critic of slavery. And how do you compare the one person who gets a great deal of pleasure from building a multiscreen cinema on a well-known beauty spot with the thousands of people who are mildly inconvenienced? It's still an absolutely impossible question to answer satisfactorily.

Luckily for the utilitarians, there was an answer to some of these practical problems in the new "science" of economics. You might not be able to tackle the big questions like slavery or natural rights—Bentham famously regarded the phrase "we hold these truths to be self-evident" as "nonsense on stilts"—but for the sheer complexity of balancing most people's pain and pleasure, you could use money. He called it the "only common measure in the nature of things." Using money means you can find the zero point between pleasure and pain, he said. So Bentham plunged himself into all things economic, getting to know the pioneer economist David Ricardo and seeing the new economists as the intellectual force that would put his movement into practice.

It wasn't really an answer. Counting it with money meant that the rich could buy more happiness than the poor. He worried that people would think only money had any value—a "vulgar error" he said. And toward the end of his life he worried that people would think only the majority mattered if he used the phrase the "greatest number." By 1831, just a few months before his death, he had carefully reformulated what he meant: The optimal goal is "provision of an equal quantity of happiness for everyone." But that makes the calculations even more difficult to manage. Especially these days, when the happiest people in the world are thought to be the Mexicans (the poorest) and the most miserable are thought to be the Americans (the richest). As always, it depends how you work it out.

And what about beauty? If you convert morality into a pseudo-science, how do you recognize the great benefits of creativity? What about spirituality? Bentham had three pianos and loved music, but it was Cardinal Newman who pointed out that he had "not a spark of poetry in him." This was confirmed in a letter the philosopher wrote to Lord Holland. The difference between poetry and prose, he explained, is that poetry has lines that don't reach the margin.

This was the stick with which his critics have beaten him ever since. And he seems to have agreed with them, in his great defense of the game of shove-halfpenny: "Prejudice apart, the game of push-pin is of equal value with the arts and sciences of music and poetry." Fripperies, fripperies.

IV

When Bentham died on June 6, 1832, he was surrounded by 70,000 pieces of unindexed paper. It was left to his adoring disciples to do something with it, the first task of the political utilitarians before they got down to measuring the world. And foremost among them was James Mill, one of those frighteningly dour and driven Scots pioneers who had built the reputation of the country in the 18th century. Mill needed someone to hero-worship, and he found it in Bentham. Bentham needed followers and a driven mind to organize them. It was a perfect match. Rigid and stern though he was, Mill signed his letters to Bentham as your "most faithful and fervent disciple."

In turn, Mill was conducting a major educational experiment of his own—his eldest son. When he wasn't writing his gigantic history of India, he was using every spare moment he had to concentrate on young John Stuart Mill's education.

And so began a strange intensive indoctrination, which involved starting to learn ancient Greek at the age of three, with grueling studies from 6:00 to 9:00 A.M. and from 10:00 A.M. to 1:00 P.M. every day. There were no holidays. There was no birching, but his father's sarcasm was almost as unpleasant. There was to be no mixing with other children—the young John wasn't even allowed to go to church. What he learned in the morning, he was expected to pass on to his eight brothers and sisters in the afternoon.

John could not exactly love his father tenderly, he said later in his *Autobiography*. He described him as "the most impatient of men," and we can imagine what that simple sentence conceals. For the rest of his life, he confessed that his conscience spoke with his father's voice. But his father certainly gave him a 25-year head start over his contemporaries, which must have helped him slip into the role of the great Liberal philosopher of the Victorian age.

The only area of human knowledge that he was kept in ignorance of was utilitarianism: This he had to choose for himself, his father decided. Mill senior needn't have worried. When he introduced the idea to his 16-year-old son in a series of "lectures" as they walked along, demanding an essay on the subject the next morning, which would be rewritten and rewritten again, John Stuart was so enthusiastic that he formed his own Utilitarian Society. James Mill's friend's looked on in astonishment at this youthful force-feeding of knowledge. There was no doubt that John was a prodigy, said Francis Place, but he would probably end up "morose and selfish." Unfortunately, Place was right.

It is hard to warm to Mill, or any of the unemotional utilitarians. Bentham said that his sympathy for the many sprang out of his hatred for the few. He despised passionate emotions, describing them as a kind of madness. He showed almost no feelings at all—except for one: He was unable to hide how much he disliked his wife. James Mill "had scarcely any belief in pleasure," according to his son. "He would sometimes say that if life was made what it might be, by good government and good education, it would be worth having: but he never spoke with anything like enthusiasm even for that possibility."

James Mill lived only a few years longer than Bentham. The dust he inhaled in his regular journeys to his country cottage in Mickleham gave him a serious lung hemorrhage in 1835, and he died on June 23 the following year—leaving it to his son John as the third generation to carry the baton for utilitarianism. It was John who gave the movement its name: He found it in a novel called the *Annals of the Parish* about a Scottish clergymen who warns his parishioners not to abandon God.

At 20, John Stuart Mill—regarded by both his father and Bentham as their spiritual heir—set to with a will to finish Bentham's *Rationale of Evidence* for publication. "Mr. Bentham had begun his treatise three times at considerable intervals, each time in a different manner, and each time without reference to the preceding," he wrote. He spent months unpicking Bentham's crabbed handwriting, chopping his sentences up into manageable parts, and finally sending five volumes off to the printers. The following year he had a nervous breakdown. The Victorians called it a "mental convulsion." The breakdown took the form of a series of doubts about the whole Bentham legacy.

> "Suppose that all your objects in life were realized; that all the changes in institutions and opinions which you are looking forward to, could be completely effected at this very instant: Would this be a great joy and happiness to you?" And an irrepressible self-consciousness distinctly answered, "No!" At this my heart sank within me: "The whole foundation on which my life was constructed fell down. All my happiness was to have been found in the continual pursuit of this end. The end had ceased to charm, and how could there ever be any interest in the means? I seemed to have nothing left to live for."

It was an important question and it seemed to fly in the face of everything that Bentham stood for, just as the harsh unemotional education that he had received at the hands of his father seemed completely inadequate to deal with it. If the question couldn't be answered, how could any calculation of pleasure come to that conclusion? Life seemed complex beyond anything Bentham could have imagined. For much of the year, Mill could hardly work at all. Music was a relief, and so were the poems of William Wordsworth—who he was convinced, had experienced something similar himself. But—still in the grip of Bentham—Mill worried about music. If there were only a limited number of notes, wouldn't the music run out? Can you calculate the number of pieces of music in the world? Experience shows that it is too complicated to count, just as you can't count the combination of possible poems by the 26 letters of the alphabet. But these are the fears of a utilitarian who has looked into the abyss.

He never fully recovered. A decade later, he had another collapse, and for the rest of his life he suffered from a nervous twitching over one eye.

With antecedents like Bentham and Mill, it is touching to think of John Stuart struggling to find some kind of emotional meaning. He found it by coming out of his reclusion to dine twice a week with Harriet Taylor, the intelligent wife of a wholesale druggist. Mr. Taylor seems to have been generous enough to overlook whatever was going on between them. His family roundly condemned him for the relationship and he retired from the world completely, finding that any reference to her by anybody else made him overexcited.

Instead, he wrote a book about logic, then his magnum opus, *Political Economy*. And when Taylor died in 1849, he married Harriet. She probably enabled him to humanize the utilitarian gospel. She certainly inspired him to write *The Subjugation of Women* in 1869, and his lifelong support for votes for women. When she died in Avignon of congestion of the lungs, he was absolutely devastated and bought a house there so he could spend half his time near his wife's grave. "The highest poetry, philosophy, oratory, and art seemed trivial by the side of her," he said. At last, love had come to the utilitarians.

John Stuart Mill understood very well the impossibility of measuring people's happiness. He was only able to make sense of life at all only by breaking with the style of Bentham and his monstrous father. He could see the uncountable complexity of human hopes, but he never abandoned the creed. On May 5, 1873, he walked 15 miles in a botanical expedition near Avignon, and he died unexpectedly three days later. In a sense, he was the last of the line; in another sense, he was just the beginning. After Mill came a long tradition of counting pioneers who unleashed the flood of statistics on the modern world, and then had serious doubts.

V

"All emotions were abhorrent to his cold, precise but admirably balanced mind," wrote Sir Arthur Conan Doyle, introducing the great detective Sherlock Holmes to the public just over half a century after Bentham's death. You can point to other figures, from Victor Frankenstein to the Duke of Wellington, who provided role models for human beings as calculating machines—Wellington's dispatch from the battle of Waterloo was so modestly written that the American ambassador reported back home that he had lost. But it was Bentham the "reasoning machine"—who tried to strip morality and government of its emotional and traditional baggage—who made Sherlock Holmes possible, with all his logic and detailed knowledge of inks and papers.

"He was, I take it, the most perfect reasoning and observing machine that the world has seen," went on Conan Doyle on the opening page of his first Sherlock Holmes story, "A Scandal in Bohemia." "He never spoke of the softer passions, save with a gibe or a sneer. . . . For the trained reasoner to admit such intrusions into his delicate and finely adjusted temperament was to introduce a distracting factor which might throw a doubt upon all his mental results."

Holmes could use his delicate and unemotional brain to see through the complex fogs of London to the truth, just as Bentham wanted to be able to do with the confusing mists of government. Whether you can actually get to any truth coldly and calculatingly—certainly any truth worth having—is an issue for which we still don't know the answer. The 20th century has rehearsed the arguments backward and forward, balancing the respective claims of the so-called Two Cultures, and probably the 21st century will as well. Can science find meaning? Can scientists make any kind of progress without leaps of imagination? We still don't agree, but we do now live in Bentham's world. He didn't have the necessary figures to make his calculations; we are drowning in them. He couldn't see some of the moral consequences of his ideas; we have some of the more unpleasant utilitarian creeds of the century etched on our hearts. But he made the rules.

Bentham's creed was softened enough by John Stuart Mill to make it the Western world's dominant moral creed, among government ministers just as it is among everyone else. Mill also recognized that Bentham may have been a "mere reasoning machine" and said the same could have been said of himself before he learned to appreciate the value of emotions, though there are still precious few of those in his *Autobiography*. Life is not clear-cut, Mill said. His repeated depressions showed him that happiness must not be the conscious purpose of life, or—paradoxically—it would slip through our fingers.

DAMAGE BY NUMBERS

I said to my soul, be still, and wait without hope,
For hope would be hope for the wrong thing; wait without love
For love would be love of the wrong thing.

T. S. Eliot, "East Coker"

In the years ahead, we must get beyond numbers and the language
of mathematics to understand, evaluate and account for such
intangibles as learning, intellectual capital, community, beliefs
and principles, or the stories we tell of our tribe's values
and prosperity will be increasingly false.

Dee Hock, founder of the Visa network

I

SUPPOSE YOU GET everything you want, wondered John Stuart Mill at the start of his first nervous breakdown and his rejection of Bentham's puritanical legacy. "Would this be a great joy and happiness to you? And the irrepressible self-consciousness distinctly answered, 'No.'"

Mill's self-consciousness definitely got it right. The human psyche is too complex and far too fleeting to be pinned down in quite that way. You can carry out Bentham's calculations of happiness with incredible accuracy, you can measure what you want precisely, but somehow the psyche slips away and sets up shop somewhere else. Or, as Gershwin put it, "Just when you get what you want, you don't want it." While Mill was locking himself into his bedroom, the poet Samuel Taylor Coleridge was coming to similar conclusions: "But *what* happiness?" he said to the Benthamites with a rhetorical flourish. "Your mode of happiness would make *me* miserable."

Modernity has not yet learned that numbers can be elusive and their slipperiness can be dangerous. As a society, we have not yet undergone Mill's self-doubts and solid renunciations. We admit that numbers can't reveal everything, but we try to force them to anyway. We tend to solve the problem by measuring ever more ephemeral aspects of life, constantly bumping up against the central paradox of the whole problem, which is that the most important things are just not measurable. The difficulty comes because they can *almost* be counted. And often we believe we have to try just so that we can get a handle on the problem. And so it is that politicians can't measure poverty, so they measure the number of people on welfare. Or they can't measure intelligence, so they measure exam results or IQ. Doctors measure blood cells rather than health, and people all over the world measure money rather than success. They might sometimes imply almost the same thing, but often they have little more than a habitual connection with one another. They tend to go together, that's all.

Anything can be counted, goes the watchword of management consultants McKinseys, and anything you can count you can manage. It's an approach that's shared by their competitors too. That's the modern way, as we desperately attempt to bring scientific precision to human problems. But the truth is, even scientific measurement has its difficulties. Chaos theory, for example, shows that very tiny fluctuations in complex systems have very big consequences. Or as the gurus of chaos put it: The flapping of a butterfly's wings over China can affect the weather patterns in Texas. The same turned out to be true for other complex systems, from the behavior of human populations to the behavior of share prices, from epidemics to cotton prices.

II

The man who dramatically undermined the idea that numbers are complete truths was a Lithuanian Jew born in Warsaw before World War II, the son of a clothing wholesaler who found himself working for IBM's research wing in the United States. Benoit Mandelbrot is probably the best known of all the chaos pioneers because of the extraordinary patterns, known as fractals, that he discovered by running the rules of chaos through IBM's computers. And he got there with a simple question that makes the kind of statistical facts the Victorians so enjoyed seem quite ridiculous. The question was: "How long is the coastline of Britain?"

On the face of it, this seems easy enough. You can find the answer in encyclopedias. But then you think about it some more and you wonder whether to include the bays, or just to take a line from rock to rock. And, having included the bays, what about the sub-bays inside each bay? And do you go all the way around each peninsula however small? And having decided all that, and realizing that no answer is going to be definitive, what about going around each pebble on the beach? In fact, the smaller you go, to the atomic level and beyond, the more detail you could measure. The coastline of Britain is different each time you count it and different for everyone who tries. Numbers don't—can't—count.

There was a time when accountants were able to deal with this kind of uncountable world better than they are now. In the early days of the American accountancy profession, they were urged to avoid numbers if they possibly could. "Use figures as little as you can," said the grand old man of American accounting, James Anyon. "Remember your client doesn't like or want them, he wants brains. Think and act upon facts, truths, and principles, and regard figures only as things to express these, and so proceeding you are likely to become a great accountant and a credit to one of the truest and finest professions in the land."

Anyon had arrived in the United States from England in 1886 to look after the firm of Barrow, Wade, Guthrie, and Co.—set up three years before by an English accountant who realized that there was a completely vacant gap in the accountancy market in New York City. Thirty years later, he was giving advice to young people starting out in what was still a new profession. "The well trained and experienced accountant of today . . . is not a man of figures," he explained again. "He is rather a man of facts and truths, and figures become subordinate and are used only as a means of expressing such facts and truths."

But Anyon's successors ignored his advice, and for a very familiar reason. The public, the politicians, and their business clients wanted control. They wanted pseudo-scientific precision and were deeply disturbed to discover that accountancy was not the exact science they thought it was. Every few years, there was the traditional revelation of a major fraud or gigantic crash, and a shocked public opinion could not accept that accounts might ever be drawn up in different ways. How could two accountants come to different conclusions? How could some companies keep a very different secret set of accounts? For the same reason that the length of Britain's coastline is different for everyone who measures it.

Often it's only the figures that matter, even when everybody knows they are a bit fudged. One paper on this phenomenon by the economist Gerry Gill—called "Okay, the Data's Lousy but It's All We've Got"—was a quote by an unnamed American economics professor explaining his findings at an academic conference. Which is fine, of course, unless the data is wrong—because people's lives may depend on it.

"Yet professionals, especially economists and consultants tight for time, have a strong felt need for statistics," says the development economist Robert Chambers in his angry book *Whose Reality Counts?*:

> Status, promotion and power come less from direct contact with the confusing complexity of people, families, communities, livelihoods and farming systems, and more from isolation which permits safe and sophisticated analysis of statistics. . . . The methods of modern science then serve to simplify and reframe reality in standard categories, applied from a distance. . . . Those who manipulate these units are empowered and the subjects of analysis disempowered: counting promotes the counter and demotes the counted.

Since the foundation of the General Accounting Office in 1921—America's preeminent government auditing office—and the gradual rise to prominence of its equivalents around the world, counting, measuring, and auditing have become an increasing part of modern life. We now have an array of national and international measuring standards designed to assess environmental performance, training standards, or management efficiency in companies large and small. We have GAAP (Generally Accepted Accounting Principles) and a range of other systems for measuring financial achievements. We have another range of educational measurements, standards, and qualifications, and then more qualifications to qualify the accountants, examiners, and consultants to use the standards to measure anybody's performance—and auditors behind each one, measuring, measuring, measuring.

By 1992, environmental consultancy alone was worth $200 billion around the world. Counting things is a lucrative business. Which is one of the reasons the private-sector auditing firms, like Arthur Andersen, PriceWaterhouseCoopers, and KPMG, entered such a boom period in the 1980s. Since the 1980s private sector auditing companies have been attracting as many as one in 10 university graduates. "We are in the middle of a huge and unavoidable social experiment," says professor of accounting at the London School of Economics Michael Power—calling this very modern phenomenon an "audit explosion."

Whole armies of number crunchers have descended on every institution, or set up their empires of internal audit inside them, and focused everyone's attention on what can be counted. The tragedy has been that this has often not been the most important aspect of life. Their activities have given a pseudo-scientific glamour to their numbers, which has made their rule hard to challenge. Yet in every area of life, we have had to live with the consequences, which means the people satisfy the target not the real objective. How do you measure the success of a military unit in the Vietnam War? Answer: Body count. Result: terrible loss of life among the Vietnamese, civilian, and military, but no American victory. How do you make sure schools are living up to parents' expectations? Answer: Test the children as much as possible. Result: exhausted kids who can see no further than exams. How do you make sure the new generation of call centers are providing value for money? Answer: Measure the delay before answering the phone and the time spent on each call. Result: frustrated, alienated customers and frustrated, miserable staff. Modern management is by quantifiable targets, which will always—almost by definition—miss the point.

Auditors deal in universal norms, methods of counting, targets, standards—especially in disciplines like psychology and economics that try to improve their standing by measuring. This is how economics transformed itself into econometrics, psychology transformed itself into behavioral science, and both gained status—but all too often lost their grip on reality. Sociologists tackled their perceived lack of "scientific" respectability by organizing bigger and bigger questionnaires to confirm what people knew in their heart of hearts anyway. Even anthropologists, who need a strong dose of interpretation provided by the wisdom, understanding, and imagination of a researcher on the ground, began to lose themselves in matrices and figures. Scientists have to simplify in order to separate out the aspect of truth they want to study—and it's the same with any other discipline that uses figures.

The trouble with auditors of any kind—accountants or academics— is that they are applying numerical rules to very complex situations. They wear suits and ties and have been examined to within an inch of their lives about their understanding of the professional rules. But their knowledge of life outside the mental laboratory may not be very complete. Sometimes it's extremely sketchy. And when Western consultants arrive in developing countries with their clipboards, like so many Accidental Tourists, it can do a great deal of damage.

Robert Chambers has revealed just how much damage can be done by faulty figures in developing countries. The number crunchers he describes are like innocents abroad, deluded by local elders in distant villages. Sometimes deliberately. As a result of what may have been an insect-damaged cob, consultants convinced themselves during the 1970s that African farmers were losing up to 40 percent of their harvest every year. The real figure was around 10 percent, yet by the early 1980s American aid planners were diverting up to $19 million a year into building vast grain silos across Africa to tackle a problem that didn't exist, while ignoring those that did.

Then there was the UN Food and Agriculture Organization's notorious questionnaires in the early 1980s, which completely ignored mixed farms in developing countries. They asked only about the main crop— anything else was too complicated. As a result, production rates in developing countries seemed so low that multinationals came to believe they needed genetically manipulated seeds to help relieve famine. But then, as Emerson said, people see only what they want to see. That's the trouble with questionnaires.

Chambers found that there were 22 different erosion studies in one catchment area in Sri Lanka, but the figures on how much erosion was going on varied as much as 8,000-fold. The lowest had been collected by a research institute wanting to show how safe their land management was. The highest came from a third-world development agency showing how much soil erosion was damaging the environment. The frightening part is that all the figures were probably correct, but the one thing they failed to provide was objective information. For that you need interpretation, quality, imagination.

"In power and influence, counting counts," Chambers wrote. "Quantification brings credibility. But figures and tables can deceive, and numbers construct their own realities. What can be measured and manipulated statistically is then not only seen as real; it comes to be seen as the only or the whole reality." Then he ended up with a neat little verse that summed it all up:

Economists have come to feel
What can't be measured, isn't real.
The truth is always an amount
Count numbers, only numbers count.

III

The great Belgian pioneer of statistics, Adolphe Quetelet, summed it up: "We can say in advance how many individuals will sully their hands with the blood of their neighbors, how many of them will commit forgeries, and how many will turn poisoners with almost the same precision as we can predict the number of births and deaths. Society contains within it the germ of all the crimes that will be committed." Numbers can seem pretty eerie sometimes.

It's a frightening thought, just as it was frightening for Quetelet's contemporaries to hear him say it in the 1830s. But he and his contemporaries had been astonished by how regular the suicide statistics were. There were the occasional bumper years, like 1846, 1929, and other economic crash periods, but generally speaking it was there. People didn't seem to be able to help themselves. Amidst a constant number of individuals, the same number would take it into their heads to murder as much as get married. Statistics were powerful.

Quetelet was among the most influential of the statisticians trying to solve the confusion of politics by ushering in a nice clean, unambiguous world, urging that we count things like the weather, the flowering of plants, and suicide rates in exactly the same way. The collapse of politics and ideology into numbers is probably more responsible than anything for the intense dullness of politics these days, as fewer people are prepared to take part in the political process. "Statistics should be the dryest of all reading," said Quetelet, and goodness, wasn't he right?

To help the process along, Quetelet invented the dryest of all people— the monstrous intellectual creation with Frankensteinian connotations, *l'homme moyen*, or Average Man. Mr. A. Man is seriously boring: He has exactly average physical attributes, an average life, an average propensity to commit crime, and an average rather unwieldy number of children—which used to be expressed as the cliché 2.4. But Average Man exists only in the statistical laboratory, measured at constant room temperature by professional men with clipboards and white coats. The whole business of relying on numbers too much goes horribly wrong simply because Mr. Average is the Man Who Never Was—counted by people who know a very great deal about their profession or science but precious little about what they are counting. The Man Who Never Was measured by the Men Who Don't Exist. Quetelet's *l'homme moyen* is the first and most important paradox of the whole dangerous business of counting.

PARADOX #1: YOU CAN COUNT PEOPLE, BUT YOU CAN'T COUNT INDIVIDUALS

Average Man belongs to the Industrial Revolution and the Age of the Masses, but we just don't believe most of that Marxist stuff anymore. It belongs in the 20th century world of mass production, where people were transformed into cogs in giant machines, as pioneered by the great industrialist Henry Ford—the man, you may remember, who offered his customers "any color you like as long as it's black." Mass production and Average Man had no space for individuality. Figures reduce their complexity, but the truth *is* complicated.

Now, of course, you can almost have your car tailor-made. You can mass-produce jeans using robots to create designs that perfectly match the peculiarities of individual bodies on the other side of the world. The days have gone when your clothes issued by the military didn't fit, when you struggled to keep up with the speed of the production line, with your tasks individually timed for Average Person by the time-and-motion experts. And we can see more clearly how difficult it is to categorize these widely different individuals who make up the human race. But in the hands of a bureaucratic state, people who don't conform to the norm get hounded and imprisoned. Or, these days, social workers visit them and remove their children.

And after all that, when you get to know Mr. Average, you find he has a bizarre taste in underwear, extraordinary dreams about flying through galaxies, and a hidden collection of ABBA records. He isn't average at all. Counting him as *l'homme moyen* means stripping him of his individuality, which in, turn, makes sure he *doesn't* actually count.

Policies that are measured so that they fit Mr. Average precisely won't actually suit anybody very much. He is a symptom of reducing human beings to numbers and forgetting there are any other dimensions to human beings that make a difference. And so we have the modern belief that a single gene will make someone intelligent, or homosexual, or a drug addict—when common sense tells us that it is the complex interaction between a whole range of genes and environments, and goodness knows what else, that makes people what they are. And we have British Telecom's revolutionary "Soul Catcher" project, an attempt to capture every human sensory experience digitally—

and claiming that the average 80-year life would fill the equivalent of precisely 7,142,857,142,860,000 floppy disks.

PARADOX #2: YOU CHANGE WHAT YOU'RE COUNTING BY COUNTING IT

It sounds like quantum mechanics, and maybe it is—but the Uncertainty Principle also holds sway for corporations and governments too. Simply because it is so hard to measure what's really important, governments and institutions pin down something else. They have to. But the consequences of pinning down the wrong thing are severe: All your resources will be focused on achieving something you didn't mean to.

Governments and pressure groups latch onto the wrong solutions and then busily measure progress toward them. They thought that shifting to diesel fuel for cars would clean up polluted air in European cities and measured progress toward achieving it. Result: air full of carcinogenic particulate matter, because diesel creates its own pollution. They thought more homework for primary-school children was the solution to underachievement and measured progress toward it. Result: miserable, dysfunctional kids. They thought setting targets for train punctuality would make them run on time. Result: Train companies simply lengthen the official journey times.

The business psychologist John Seddon tells the story of one company where managers couldn't understand why customers were still complaining, costs were still going up, but all the sales, production, and delivery targets were being met. It turned out that salespeople were meeting monthly targets by holding orders back or moving them forward. Sometimes they were even booking dummy orders, only to cancel them later. Delivery targets were being met sometimes by delivering orders before they were actually finished. Numerical targets change people's behavior—that's what they're for—but only to meet the targets, not to tackle the complex problem that lies behind them.

It has all the makings of a fairy tale. If you choose the wrong measure, you sometimes get the opposite of what you wanted. And any measure has to be a generalization that can't do justice to the individuals who are included.

PARADOX #3: NUMBERS REPLACE TRUST BUT MAKE
MEASURING EVEN MORE UNTRUSTWORTHY

When farmers and merchants didn't trust each other to provide the
right amount of wheat, they could use the standard local barrel stuck to
the wall of the town hall, which would measure the agreed local
bushel. When we don't trust our corporations, politicians, or professionals now, we send in the auditors—and we break down people's jobs
into measurable units so that we can see what they are doing and check
it. If doctors hide behind their professional masks, then we measure
their deaths per patient, their treatment record, and their success rate,
and we hold them accountable. When politicians look out of control,
we measure their voting records and their popularity ratings—just as
the TV commentators break down a sporting performance into opportunities, misses, aces, broken services, and much else besides.

It wasn't always like that. Previous generations realized that we lose
some information every time we do this—information the numbers
can't provide. They realized, like James Anyon, that we could never
fully measure what a doctor does. They still have intuition born of
experience, they still have know-how that slips through the measurement. But we need some standard. The aristocratic establishment used
to be quite happy to accept the word of the professionals if they were
"trustworthy gentlemen of good character." But from the outside, that
trust looked like a cozy nepotistic conspiracy. And probably it was. Even
now, auditors will tell you that they can only ever hope to count a representative sample: You can never measure everything.

It was this kind of political problem that led to the growth of cost-
benefit analysis: a fair and "objective" means of making trustworthy
decisions. This was originally used by French officials to work out what
tolls to charge for new bridges or railways, but it was taken up with a
vengeance in 20th-century America as a way of deciding which flood-
control measures to build. After the Flood Control Act of 1936, there
would be no more federal money for expensive flood-control measures
unless the benefits outweighed the costs. Only then would the public
be able to see clearly that there was no favoritism for some farmers over
others. It was all going to be clear, objective, nonpolitical, and based on
the numbers.

The U.S. Army Corps of Engineers—in charge of the flood-control
analysis—tried to make the process sound as if it were a mandate from
God. "It is calculated according to rather a complex formula," a corps

official told a Senate committee in 1954. "I won't worry you with the details of that formula." It couldn't last. The more they were faced with angry questioning, the more their calculations had to be public.

But how far do you go? What do the numbers really mean? Do you, as they did for some flood-control schemes, work out how many seagulls would live in the new reservoir, and how many grasshoppers they would eat, and what the grain was worth that the grasshoppers would have eaten? Do they work out what these values might be in future years? Do they value property when no two real estate agents can name the same price? "I would not say it was a guess," one of their officials told the U.S. Senate about property values. "It is an estimate." And after all that, it is economists who persuaded the U.S. secretary of the interior Bruce Babbitt to start demolishing the dams their predecessors laboriously calculated.

So here's the paradox. Numbers are democratic. We use them to peer into the mysterious worlds of professionals, to take back some kind of control. They are the tools of opposition to arrogant rulers. Yet in another sense they are not democratic at all. Politicians simply like to pretend that numbers take the decisions out of their hands.

PARADOX #4: WHEN NUMBERS FAIL, WE GET MORE NUMBERS

Because counting and measuring are seen as the antidote to distrust, any auditing failure must need more auditing. That's what society demanded the moment financier Robert Maxwell had fallen off his yacht into the Bay of Biscay. Nobody ever blames the system—they just blame the auditors. Had they been too friendly with the fraudsters? Had they taken their eyes off the ball? Send in the auditors to audit the auditors.

If the targets fail, you get more targets. Take the example of a large manufacturer that centralizes its customer care to one central call center. After a while, they find that the customers are not getting the kind of care they were used to before. What does the company do, given that it can't measure what it really needs to—the humanity and helpfulness of its service to customers? They set more targets—speed answering the telephone, number of calls per operator per day. They measure their achievements against these targets and wonder why customers don't get any happier.

The same issue has repeated through corporations many times over. As internal audits multiply, corporations find they have been measuring the wrong thing. Scandinavian Airlines SAS once revealed how they insisted on measuring the success of their cargo division by the amount of weight it carried every month, until they discovered that their customers wanted something far more complex. A closer examination of their performance showed that, although the weight carried was rising steadily, the deliveries were on average four days late.

Management gurus a decade ago were urging colleagues to shift the emphasis from financial measures to more intangible ones, like customer satisfaction or quality. But that hasn't worked either. Even for SAS, the exact mixture of prompt, accurate, and friendly service was different for each customer. Any measure misses the point because it assumes that every member of staff, every customer, every aggregated group is exactly the same. No matter how the customers are divided, that simply isn't true. "People do what you count, not necessarily what counts," said business psychologist John Seddon, and he's right.

PARADOX #5: THE MORE ACCURATELY WE COUNT, THE MORE UNRELIABLE THE FIGURES

Number crunchers can't leave anything out if they're going to be absolutely precise. So you get a peculiar phenomenon when the cost-benefit experts spend enormous efforts getting a figure absolutely correct—only to throw something else in that is simply plucked from the air.

This has a long tradition, back to the French statistician Adolphe Jullien in 1844, who worked out precisely the cost of moving one unit of traffic on France's new rail system. He finally came up with a wonderfully exact figure of 0.01254 francs per kilometer. But what about administration and the interest on capital? Ah yes, he says—but these were more difficult to assess, so he arbitrarily doubled the figure. Or the U.S. Corps of Engineers, who would spend months on the exact cost-benefit of new waterways they liked, then shoved in a notional $600,000 for national defense and $100,000 for recreation.

Many figures are an unusual amalgam of the precise and the arbitrary. It's like Lewis Carroll's story about the little boy who comes up with a figure of 1,004 pigs in a field. "You can't be sure about the four," he is told. "And you're as wrong as ever," says the boy. "It's just the four I can be sure about, 'cause they're here, grubbling under the window. It's the thousand I isn't pruffickly sure about."

PARADOX #6: THE MORE WE COUNT, THE LESS
WE UNDERSTAND

Numbers are the international tools of scientists. They allow experts to "speak one and the same language, even if they use different mother tongues," said the philosopher Karl Popper—whose libertarian beliefs made him enthusiastic about anything like this with the potential to break down totalitarian regimes. The auditors look for measurements with no human content—like the meter, one 10-millionth of the distance from the pole to the equator—in their search for pure objectivity. It is a scientific dream of the kind you often get after revolutions, in this case the French. Could taking decisions like this usher in an era of facts after all that political confusion? Answer: no.

Because to do this, everyone has to count in exactly the same way, in laboratory conditions, taking no account of local variation or tradition, so the figures are not as informative as they might be. That may just be possible in a laboratory, but the whole point about schools, offices, and cities is that they are not. Decisions by numbers are a bit like painting by numbers. They don't make for great art. When you reduce something to figures or the bottom line, you lose information—and the Tower of Babel comes tumbling down again.

This is an international language based on centrally imposed definitions and understanding. It's a kind of modern imperialism, with all the respect for local understanding of the glass towers of the international architectural style. Can we really believe the European Union was getting accurate comparisons in their recent mega-survey asking 60,000 people if they "could make ends meet"? As if a German, a Greek, and a Brit would all understand the same by that. When Pepsi had their slogan "Come alive with the Pepsi generation" translated into Chinese, it was understood as "Pepsi brings your ancestors back from the grave." Microscopic differences in definition have big effects. It's chaos theory all over again.

PARADOX #7: THE MORE WE COUNT, THE LESS WE CAN
COMPARE THE FIGURES

Just as it is difficult to compare accurate figures from one culture to another, it's even harder to compare them from one era to another—and for the same reason. Hard objective measures take no account of how people at the time understood the categories you're counting.

"The past is a foreign country," wrote the novelist L. P. Hartley. "They do things differently there."

Take crime figures, for example. If you stare too long at the figures, you'd be forgiven for thinking the world is descending into a moral morass. It may be, but the figures won't prove it. The way people understand crime is different for different generations, and it changes surprisingly quickly. The crimes they feared the most were different. Others simply weren't reported.

Take New York City, for example. The successful bid to cut soaring crime in the 1990s involved shifting resources from tackling major to minor offences—leading to a height of 101,000 drug arrests in 1997 alone, more than at the height of the crack epidemic. It led to a tripling of the number of prisoners in New York State: so many that, in the early 1990s, the violent offenders were let out early to make way for all the low-level drug offenders and the people caught urinating in the street. A look at the statistics during that time would have told you much more about what the police chief was concentrating on—often offences that would never have been recorded in the statistics before—than how much crime there was.

A century ago, for example, crime was recorded much more informally, and different crimes horrified people. What would have been seriously violent now might then just have been charged as a simple assault or drunkenness. Crimes against property really upset people a century ago, but violence was often regarded as something the lower classes did to each other, and it concerned them less. A century ago, as many as one in four London policemen were assaulted every year. Two centuries ago, in the days of Bentham's middle age, the chaplain of London's Newgate Gaol was complaining that all the boys in prison kept a mistress. That included those aged nine and ten.

The truth is that every generation believes that crime is getting worse. "The morals of children are tenfold worse than previously," the social reformer Lord Ashley told the House of Commons in 1843, using a bogus statistical style that would be much copied. At the same time, the communist pioneer Friedrich Engels calculated that crime had risen seven times over since the Battle of Trafalgar in 1805. A generation later, in 1862, British society was horrified by the outbreak of "garrotings"—a kind of mugging by throttling the victim. By the 1890s, it was "hooligans," hitting old ladies in the street and brandishing pistols—which were then available by mail order from the department store Gamages. Then there was the sudden 90 percent rise in bag-snatching in England between the wars, mainly because police statistics stopped reporting thefts as "lost property." Simple figures can't possibly compare such different worlds.

PARADOX #8: MEASUREMENTS HAVE A MONSTROUS LIFE OF THEIR OWN

Stalin announced his first Soviet Five Year Plan in 1928, an enormous undertaking planned to increase gross industrial output by 235.9 percent and labor productivity by 110 percent. But don't be fooled by these figures, which were completely spurious. The fake precision was to lend a scientific air to the whole enterprise. The actual effect of the plan was to reduce real per capita income by half and starve millions on what Stalin referred to as the "agricultural front." Even so, he declared the first five-year plan a success 12 months early in 1932, and the second one started right away. The numbers were meant to give an air of legitimacy to an otherwise untenable plan.

Stalin's figures were widely believed, even in the West. But not only were nearly all the figures falsified—something you can do during a reign of terror—but they carried within them a terrible authoritarianism to try to force them to be true. Which is why strikes had to be redefined as "sabotage," and why after 1939, employees had to be fired if they were once more than 20 minutes late for work. It was also why one in eight of the Soviet population were either shot or sent to a labor camp. Figures are frightening sometimes.

Stalin was an extreme case, but all numbers relate to empire. We use them now to enforce outlying businesses or offices to conform to the bureaucrat's view of "quality"—and in a way, this is one of the most dangerous aspects of all. "Best practice" simply locks them into a dull and uninspired version of what was once the best, the hopelessly second rate, as we measure progress toward hideous concepts like BAT-NEEC (Best Available Techniques Not Entailing Excessive Cost). You don't have to be Stalin to destroy innovation by counting.

PARADOX #9: WHEN YOU COUNT THINGS, THEY GET WORSE

In quantum physics, the mere presence of the observer in subatomic particle experiments can change the results. In anthropology, researchers have to report on their own cultural reactions as a way of offsetting the same effect. And once you start looking at numbers you keep falling over a strange phenomenon, which is that the official statistics tend to get worse when society is worried about something. For the sake of argument, I'll call it the "Quantum Effect."

We all recognize the phenomenon of medical scares that publicize a problem—often it's something like Lyme disease—only to find that the number of cases has shot up as people suddenly start reporting the same symptoms. It's the same whenever society is gripped by moral panic. Take the case of child sex abuse. The UK statistics toddled along at the 1,500-a-year mark until 1984, when an unprecedented wave of publicity on both sides of the Atlantic catapulted the issue to the top of the public agenda. Between 1984 and 1985, child sex abuse shot up with a 90 percent increase in reported cases. And in the following year a similar rise was reported.

Child-abuse campaigners would say that the actual rate of child abuse is never reflected properly in the statistics. They may well be right—the same would be true of the figures for racist attacks. All I am saying is that the actual statistics wouldn't have told you anything, except how strongly the public felt about child abuse at the time. So often, the statistics start rising *after* the panic rather than the other way round, as an eagle-eyed society tries to stamp out the unforgivable. That's the Quantum Effect.

It's difficult to know quite why the figures go up. Sometimes the definitions change to reflect greater public concern. Sometimes people just report more instances of it because it is in the forefront of their minds. Sometimes they borrow the category as a useful place to hang phenomena they hadn't defined before. Sometimes, maybe, what we fear the most comes to pass.

PARADOX #10: THE MORE SOPHISTICATED YOU ASPIRE TO BE, THE LESS YOU CAN MEASURE

This is true for politicians who try to measure the elusive source of "feelgood" in their populations and long for the days when they knew they could just measure wages. And it is true for the doctors who used to measure disease but know there is some other kind of psychic health that allows people to recover from operations—but that they cannot count under the microscope. But it's most urgent for business.

Business leaders increasingly recognize that the key to success is realizing that their assets are intangible qualities, which are extremely hard to measure directly—like knowledge, information, or reputation.

Count up the value of their fixed assets and you come up with a figure wildly different from the actual value of their company on the world markets. Microsoft is an extreme example. Its balance sheet at one time listed assets amounting to only about 6 percent of what the company was worth. "In other words," said the futurist Charles Leadbeater, "94 percent of the value of this most dynamic and powerful company in the new digital economy is in intangible assets that accountants cannot measure."

What's really important can't be measured—perhaps we should call that the "McKinsey Fallacy." It may also be why the best things in life are still free. Yet if your competitors are going to try, then you have to try too. That's why, for politicians or business strategists, measurement is a growing headache.

IV

So why do we count at all? The answer is that numbers are an absolutely vital tool for human progress. They mean we can test hypotheses, seek out the fraudulent and inefficient. They give us some control over our unpredictable world. They allow us to take problems by surprise, so to speak—to force ourselves to look at them in new ways. They can prove us wrong. It's just that they are not objective, nor the final answer, and they dull our good sense and intuition—and, by no means least, they're dangerous. Especially when we have reached the point when numbers don't work anymore.

If you're in politics or business and you need to measure the unmeasurable in order to make things happen—and your career and our lives may depend on you being able to do so—then you have a crisis. It is a counting crisis.

The word *crisis* is overused—especially by people who then launch into a stream of statistics—so I should use the word carefully. It certainly isn't the kind of crisis that commentators usually trumpet about, and isn't the kind campaigners can put on a graph—the crisis hasn't grown by 6 percent since last February or dropped by 3.5 miles—but it is a crisis nonetheless. It's that number crunchers don't have the necessary tools for the new world.

The whole of Western culture is geared to measuring. All around us, we can hear the noise of the modern world applying sports-style league tables to complex political or business problems. Or searching for the single, measurable gene that causes complex human attributes like love or learning or intelligence. You can hear it submitting these delicate problems to the men in white coats who will apply general rules about complex individual peculiarities. You can hear us all shifting the power from one kind of professional to another, in the name of democracy— from teachers and doctors to accountants, auditors, and academics. And they have their own secretive rituals that exclude outsiders like a computer instruction manual.

Yet if you don't try putting figures to what's really important, then you also know your competitors will do it for you, the regulators and politicians will impose some fancy numerical code on you, and the pressure groups will demand what they call "accountability." Without putting numbers to your business case, your report, or your argument, you risk sounding woolly, or not completely serious. Serious academics, funders, bankers, and brokers will shun you.

It's hard to resist the pressure.

4

ROBERT MALTHUS AND THE
DEATH OF MORAL STATISTICS

*This unlucky attempt to give numerical precision to things which do
not admit of it . . . is wholly superfluous to his argument.*

John Stuart Mill on Malthus

*When will they learn that a virtuous and happy population is
worth more than mere numbers, that a wise and free people are
infinitely more to be desired than a nominally rich nation of
Tyrants, Slaves and fools.*

Francis Place to James Mill

LONDON, 1780

I

IT WAS A unique moment in history. Suddenly those old gentleman
politicians with their powdered wigs, pink coats, and fox-hunting weekends—those who had run the country for so long with their own brand
of bluff pomposity—felt out of their depth. "Throughout the whole
progress of this important measure, I have daily attended and listened
to every conversation respecting it, but I have hitherto not voted once,"
complained one English MP in the House of Commons during a trade

debate. "And the reason is—I am not ashamed to make the avowal—it has not been in my power to understand the resolutions. . . . I by no means stand alone in this predicament."

Those sturdy farmers and squires, who made the exhausting journey to Westminster or Washington regularly to represent their local taxpayers, would soon be echoing that admission privately to themselves. They were capable of passing laws, even declaring national independence and creating a nation. They sat in judgment on their fellow men as magistrates on the bench. But the language of government suddenly seemed too much for them. And the reason was the disturbing and overwhelming onslaught of figures. Good sense, good morals, and balanced disposition were no longer enough—there were trade figures, bills of mortality, marriage figures, and population extrapolations. Suddenly you had to be an "expert."

Counting the nation had always appealed to the most imperial rulers because it allowed them to collect tax better. That was why William the Conqueror drew up the Domesday Book, with its intricate listing of people and sheep. That was why Henry VIII's unpleasant sidekick Thomas Cromwell made the clergy responsible for collecting local statistics about baptisms and deaths. But, generally speaking, life before the 18th century was comparatively number-free. What figures there were certainly couldn't be compared to anything today. In fact, a quick glance at one so-called Bill of Mortality for London during the Great Plague of 1665 would make anyone realize just how little you can compare figures from one generation to another. Categories of deaths meant different things then:

Ague and Feaver	5,257
Executed	21
Teeth and Worms	2,614
Frighted	23
Gout and Sciatica	27
Grief	46
Plague	68,596
Lethargy	14
Griping in the Guts	1,288

I defy any modern statisticians to compare categories like Grief and Lethargy to anything today (ME perhaps), or even a century later, when Bentham was first calling for a national population register. Still less "griping in the guts" (diarrhea or appendicitis perhaps). The Bills of Mortality were "gothic ruins, which is wasting time to prop and plaster," said a medical contemporary of Bentham's, but there wasn't anything else. It wasn't until 1770 that the word *statistics* was first coined in English, in a translation of the German word *Staatenkunde*.

Once the word was out there, the utilitarians seemed to feel the urgent need to find something for it to refer to. As Bentham had discovered to his horror, there were almost no official statistics at all, and the statistic that most muddled his contemporaries was how many people there were. Nobody in England had much idea what the population of the country was, and the prevailing opinion was—with a typical kind of English pessimism—that it was dropping like a stone. Counting people seemed like a good modern idea. It would help the tax authorities or provide information on the number of paupers. It might even help plan a local police force.

The man behind the idea was the former secretary of the Prince of Wales and son of the archbishop of Canterbury, Thomas Potter—"a man of more than middling abilities," according to *Gentleman's Magazine*, "and somewhat conceited of his own parts." It might perhaps have helped the counting cause if Potter hadn't been a member of the orgiastic Hellfire Club—motto: "Do as thou shalt wish"—but that became a scandal some months in the future, and probably nobody knew at the time. No, his proposal was widely admired and showed every sign of being passed into law.

The fact that Britain did not become the first country in the world to hold a census was down to the efforts of one man. Almost single-handedly, York MP William Thornton mustered enough votes to defeat the idea in a series of bravura performances that amounted to a contemporary critique of statistical thinking. In the first vote, he was the only MP against. By the time it reached the House of Lords, he had so stoked up the opposition that they threw it out.

His main arguments were that this was a backdoor attempt to bring in nasty French institutions like the police, and that official counting was a pointless activity that changed nothing and undermined the privacy of true Englishmen. It would also make parish officials much too powerful—just to molest every family in the kingdom for the sake of what he called "political arithmetic."

"Can it be pretended, that by the knowledge of our number, or our wealth, either can be increased?" he asked fellow MPs. "And what purpose will it answer to know where the kingdom is crowded, and where it is thin, except we are to be driven from place to place as graziers do their cattle? If this be intended, let them brand us at once; but while they treat us like oxen and sheep, let them not insult us with the name of men."

It is easy to laugh from two and a half centuries later, in these days when we count almost everything. Yet there was something rather noble about Thornton's defense—bone-headedly English for all that. After all, how can counting the population stop people leaving for America, as contemporaries were afraid they were doing? Why should press gangs create armies when volunteers surely fight better? It was true when he said it, just as it is now.

Consequently, Britain didn't get its first census for nearly half a century more, by which time Sweden had carried out the first modern census, followed closely in 1790 by the United States—which wasn't even a nation when Thornton and Potter slugged it out across the House of Commons. By the time Britain got around to counting its population, it was under blockade at the height of the Napoleonic War, and they badly needed to know the food requirements of the nation.

By the end of the 18th century, the population debate had turned itself on its head and become the central issue of the age. Under the influence of the Benthamite clergyman Robert Malthus, people were suddenly afraid the working population was increasing very much faster than the available food. Now the fear was that there were too *many* people, and on both sides of the Atlantic, the two tribes of radicals—the Romantics and the Benthamites—battled it out with increasing vitriol. They were soon awash with population figures, and we have been ever since.

Malthus's theories have been immensely influential. His work made him the father of population study, of eugenics, of contraception—though he refused to accept the "abominable" idea himself. Together with Bentham, he almost invented political statistics and was, as such, one of the coauthors of the modern world. It also brought him the most appalling abuse in his own lifetime and ever since. Malthus claimed that he never minded—but he kept on bringing out new editions of his influential book, complete with brand-new prefaces, just to refute the hurtful allegations.

After the first fortnight, the abuse never kept me awake for a minute, said Malthus—one of the least excitable propagandists in history. But it wasn't entirely true: He did mind, and he did want to make a difference. Malthus was writing at a time when hardly any of the statistics he needed for his theories were available. Together with Bentham, he campaigned for more figures, and helped set up the organization that was eventually to become the Royal Statistical Society. He wanted the figures to be tough, scientific, and objective—but he had another agenda too. He wanted them to shock people into taking action, to delay their marriages and *do* something—though he was always a bit hazy what they should do—to limit the size of their families. He didn't just want facts; he wanted what would shortly be called "moral statistics." He wanted numbers that could change the world.

We've had them ever since, but—like an antibiotic that doesn't work anymore—we've grown immune to them. In two centuries, the power behind moral statistics seems to have worn itself out.

II

"A tall, thin, pale, grave looking personage peeped from the aperture," said the opening of a chapter of a popular novel published in 1817:

> "This is Mr. Fox," said Mr. Forester, "the champion of calm reason, the indefatigable explorer of the cold clear springs of knowledge, the bearer of a torch of dispassionate truth, that gives more light than warmth. He looks on the human world, the world of mind, the conflict of interests, the collision of feelings . . . as a mathematician looks on his diagrams, or a mechanist on his wheels and pulleys, as if they were foreign to his own nature, and were nothing more than subjects of curious speculation."

Any reader of the novels of Thomas Love Peacock—like Malthus, a lifelong employee of the East India Company—would have found this at the start of a chapter in *Melincourt* titled "The Principle of Population."

Nobody would have been in any doubt that this was intended as a portrait of "Population Malthus," the puritanical butt of public jokes, the misunderstood "Parson Malthus," the much-reviled pioneer number cruncher. This was a portrait of a man who fitted the mould of Bentham and Sherlock Holmes, preparing—in one almighty leap—to count the world. Actually Malthus was probably just as dispassionate as Peacock painted him, but not nearly as cold.

Thomas Robert Malthus—he called himself by his second name—was born on February 13, 14, or 17, 1766, depending on the source, near Dorking in Surrey, the polite rural hinterland south of London. It's a strange thought that the future prophet of "moral restraint" may actually have been born on St. Valentine's Day.

His father was a Romantic and prolific correspondent with the French philosopher Jean-Jacques Rousseau, who famously coined the phrase "the noble savage" and who looked forward with great anticipation to the perfectibility of mankind. Like Bentham, Frederick Winslow Taylor, and the other great pioneers of numbers, Malthus became what he was by reacting against his dad.

But only very mildly. As a second son, his path was mapped out before him. He would go into the church, and he arrived at Jesus College, Cambridge, at the late age of 22 to study for the ministry. Malthus did what he was told. At Cambridge, he was a contemporary of the future prime minister William Pitt the Younger and the future scourge of the slave trade, William Wilberforce. And as a fellow of the college, he was probably one of those who voted to throw out the poet Samuel Taylor Coleridge unless he paid his tutor's bill.

From there Malthus went to be curate of the small village of Okewood in Surrey, famous throughout the century for the enormous number of baptisms and the tiny number of deaths. It was a symbolic place to start work.

All the contemporary accounts say that Malthus was charming company, with his red side whiskers and deep blue eyes, and that he would have been extremely good-looking were it not for one major fault. He had a harelip. It was a relatively common problem, and easily remedied these days—but not then. The one portrait of him still in existence fudges the issue by having his mouth in an uncomfortable twist.

Quite apart from what he looked like, it would have made it hard for him to speak clearly and distinctly. People would have found it hard to hear him, and somehow you feel that it was this, not the disfigurement, that he minded most. There is in his writing a sort of exhausted frustration that he wasn't being understood, even when he wrote things down. And he *wasn't* understood. But Malthus, being Malthus, accepted this patiently, without excitement or surprise. He was, after all, one of the most placid men who ever lived.

Even so, it's a strange thought that the father of eugenics would probably have been disposed of as imperfect by some of his most extreme followers. Marie Stopes—the pioneer 20th-century birth-control campaigner—refused to speak to her daughter because she married a man she considered a less than perfect human specimen just because he wore glasses. Poor old Malthus wouldn't have had a second look.

As a young man, he spent his time gently arguing with his father about justice, perfectibility, and the remains of Rousseau's idealism. It just won't work, Malthus told him, because population will always grow faster than food. "Why not put your ideas down on paper," replied his father, and Malthus obediently did. He did what he was told, after all.

SURREY, ENGLAND, 1798

III

Napoleon had just occupied Rome and taken the pope prisoner, Wordsworth and Coleridge had changed the world of Romantic poetry forever with their book *Lyrical Ballads*, and Malthus was busy preparing the text of his anonymous pamphlet, intended to do little more than refute his father's idealistic romanticism. He called it, *An Essay on the Principles of Population, as It Affects the Future Improvement of Society; with Remarks on the Speculations of Mr. Godwin, Mr. Condorcet, and Other Writers.* As a title it was a bit of a mouthful, but it was also one of the most influential essays ever written—and a virtual manifesto for the number crunchers.

The basic point was very simple, and it was the first census in the United States that particularly spurred him on to write it. What the census seemed to show was that, in one generation of 25 years—though probably helped by immigration—the American population had doubled. That was Malthus's big idea: that if it isn't checked, human population carries on doubling every quarter century, while the ability to grow food to support it increases only arithmetically. "The human species would increase as the numbers 1, 2, 4, 8, 16, 32, 64, 128, 256; and the subsistence as 1, 2, 3, 4, 5, 6, 7, 8, 9," he wrote. "In two centuries the population would be to the means of subsistence as 256 to 9; in three centuries as 4,096 to 13, and in two thousand years the difference would be almost incalculable."

Failure to lower the birth rate would lead to unemployment, crime, and poverty, he said—and to what Malthus called "vicious practices." It wasn't a very hopeful book, but it wasn't a new idea either. The French revolutionary Count de Mirabeau had already said, "men will multiply up to the limits of subsistence like rats in a barn." But Malthus had caught the public mood of crisis, with the new war in Europe and a looming blockade by Napoleon, and the pamphlet was a sensation.

This was also partly because the writings of the great anarchist William Godwin—the man named in the title—were the talking point of the moment. "All education is despotism," said Godwin, who condemned marriage as "a system of fraud" and ended his life on a government pension. The other writer named in the title had already ended his life. Marie-Jean-Antoine-Nicholas de Caritat, Marquis de Condorcet, had written his great idealistic history of human progress while he was hiding in Paris from the revolutionaries, and had escaped to wander in the forests outside the city like a pauper, with a long beard and no identity card. He was caught by a Jacobin spy, imprisoned, and poisoned himself before he could be recognized.

The controversy crashed around the still anonymous author of the *Essay*. Most writers had traditionally thought that a bigger population was a good thing. Hadn't God told them to go forth and multiply, after all? Malthus had appeared to turn the accepted order on its head.

God had also urged people to be relatively kind to the poor, and here again Malthus seemed to be urging people not to—on the grounds that it encouraged people to have too many babies. The *Essay* took another ten years to appear in the United States, but the reaction was the same there. Malthus was wrong, said his critics. For one thing, there was lots of food—it just wasn't distributed very well. "Human institutions are the real cause of all the misery with which we are surrounded," said one mysterious and anonymous author, calling himself Piercy Ravenstone. "And he who in the arrogance of his folly would trace them to any other source, as he renders hopeless all improvement to our condition, is equally an enemy to man whom he oppresses, and to God, whom he maligns."

Nor were his figures right, said Ravenstone. If Adam and Eve had food enough for two in 4004 B.C.—the traditional date of the Creation—Malthus's principles would mean the earth couldn't support more than 1,328 people, and rather more had in fact popped up. But it was Godwin who came up with the classic and unanswerable killer blow: "If Mr. Malthus's doctrine is true, why is the globe not peopled?"

A good question and it worried Malthus too. To find out the answer, he set out on the first of a series of investigative journeys to Norway, Sweden, and Russia. From there, he came back with trunkfulls of population statistics and strange stories collected from Captain Cook of the fierce methods other cultures use to avoid overpopulation in other parts of the world—anything from prostitution and infanticide to leaving baby girls outside to die.

In Norway, he discovered that working men weren't allowed to marry until the local minister had signed a certificate agreeing that they were able to support a wife and children. He was horrified by the Russian state hospitals, where the children of poor mothers were handed in to nurses—no questions asked—and then handed back again when they could prove they could support them. This condemned the children to live in such unsavory conditions that on average 100 of them would die every month. Malthus blamed charity: "It seems to me that the greatest part of this morality is clearly to be attributed to these institutions miscalled 'philanthropical.'"

IV

Perhaps Mathus's most important encounter was with his Swiss driver during a second visit in the middle of the brief peace between Britain and France in 1802. The country's going to the dogs, the driver kept telling him, because people were getting married younger and younger. Why, in his day . . .

Malthus was inspired by this salt-of-the-earth type. So the 1802 edition of the *Essay* was five times as long as the first, and it was packed with statistics—including some of the results of the first British census when it appeared in 1801, showing that the population was growing very fast. But this time, the message wasn't nearly so bleak. This was Malthus, and he was optimistic that humanity could change after all.

Malthus reengineered solution was what he called "moral restraint." He was a bit hazy about exactly what he meant by this, but it seemed to mean not having sex—which he claimed would make the passion between the sexes burn "with a brighter, purer, and steadier flame." The world wasn't convinced—and who can blame them—and assumed that he meant contraception. No matter how many times he condemned the whole idea, nobody listened. It was his usual problem back again.

To make absolutely clear that he really *did* mean moral restraint—and to avoid the prevailing opinion that he was being sacrilegious—he signed all the following editions of his books "Reverend." It only gave fuel to his critics. From then on, he was christened with the patronizing "Parson Malthus."

The solution favored by Parson Malthus was pure "caring conservatism." Having children outside marriage should be regarded with disapproval. Society should be tough on people who break the rules of chastity—especially women, he said. Mothers should be told that, after a certain date, no new children would be given welfare. Clergymen should explain to couples what a bad idea it was to marry recklessly. And there should be a national system of education set up, along with a national system of savings banks. There are 20,000 Londoners, said Malthus—plucking another unsupported statistic from the air—who get up every morning without knowing how they would pay for their meals.

"Hard as it may appear, dependent poverty ought to be held disgraceful," wrote Malthus, sounding just like Bentham, who sat up and took notice in his cold study in Westminster. "Such a stimulus seems to be absolutely necessary to promote the happiness of the general mass of mankind."

His attitude chimed in with the prevailing public mood. The cost of welfare in England had quadrupled in the 30 years or so between Malthus's birth and the publication of his *Essay*, and there was a growing sense that something should be done about it. This wasn't welfare as we understand it today—measured and controlled by gigantic federal agencies—it was the old Elizabethan Poor Law from the 16th century, which said that every parish was responsible for providing for paupers. It was managed by an unreliable mixture of local landlords, magistrates, and publicans—sometimes cruelly, sometimes with enlightenment. It was a hit-or-miss affair, but probably no more unpleasant than its measured and counted equivalent today.

Something was going to have to give, but it seemed strange to people that a minister should be calling for a more brutal world. Here was a clergyman warning the rich against charity and warning the poor against marriage—it was nothing short of scandalous, said Malthus's great critic William Hazlitt: "Is marriage a worse sin than fornication?"

Malthus didn't reply to questions like that, but he stuck to his own principles. Plato said that the correct age for a man to marry was 37. Malthus, who did what he was told, married at 38, having been given the living of rector of Walesby in Lincolnshire. And despite Karl Marx's theory that he had taken a solemn vow of chastity, he actually fathered three children. And in 1815, the year of the Battle of Waterloo, he was appointed the first ever professor of political economy anywhere in the world—at Haileybury College.

Haileybury was an unusual school owned and run by the East India Company—which was also at the time employing both James and John Stuart Mill and Thomas Love Peacock. The school had a very unusual curriculum, suited to the education of the company's future representatives in the ports of the world. It included classes in Sanskrit, Persian, and Hindi. Malthus spent the rest of his life there in quiet seclusion.

He is normally dismissed as a bit of a monster, and there is always something monstrous in trying to impose numbers on people—forcing the little numbers to fit the big ones. But he was also motivated by the horror of rural poverty that he saw as a country curate; the starving elderly; the laborers who couldn't feed their burgeoning families; and the respectable couples ruined by the rising price of bread. They were the people for whom his other great enemy, William Cobbett, wrote *Cottage Economy*, with its furious diatribe against tea drinking. He wanted to do good, and all the contemporary descriptions are of a man who was polite and pleasant company, if only you could hear what he was saying.

But then again, there was something colorless about Malthus, something emotionless—like old Bentham. He never got angry, never got excited, never got miserable, and was never rude. He never said anything nasty about anyone, even behind their backs. He read the appalling things people wrote about him and sighed at people's ignorance in a way that just infuriated them even more. He was the quintessential Benthamite gentleman—not quite a machine, but calculating nonetheless.

But his figures certainly made things happen, as he brought out more and more editions of his *Essay* with even more population statistics and projections than before. They seemed to have an effect, despite his trenchant opposition to the idea of contraception. It wasn't that men didn't use the early 19th century version of condoms—it was just that they were actually designed to protect them from disease when they visited prostitutes. The idea of using them with your wife was scandalous. Certainly Malthus wanted nothing to do with the idea.

So it was left to the "radical tailor" Francis Place—who we last met in the shadows at Bentham's funeral-autopsy—to tell the world how to prevent too many children. He had cause to know: He married at the age of 19 and had 15 of them. Place thoroughly agreed with Malthus, but as a sensible man of the world, he didn't believe "moral restraint" was very practical. So he issued a series of handbills for the poor, explaining exactly what to do.

The pamphlet caused moral outrage around the country, and continued to do so for the next century whenever an enlightened reformer did anything similar. The irony is that by the time Malthus was an old man, contraceptives had become known as "Malthusian devices." Poor old Malthus: People never heard him very clearly.

V

Sometime in the 16th century, a new word started appearing in English dictionaries. *Pantometry* meant counting everything. You needed a word for it when the idea was so unusual. But by the end of the 18th century it had slipped out of use, probably because there wasn't anything remarkable about pantometrists by then. Yet it would have been a useful way of describing the prevailing mood of the new generation—the one that had caused such confusion to the old-style politicians—who believed, as no other generation before them, that the world could be changed by counting it.

By the 1830s, the pantometrists were suddenly in the majority. There was the reforming British prime minister Sir Robert Peel, who set up the new Statistical Department of the Board of Trade in 1832 to provide him with the figures he needed. There was the brilliantly numerate British president of the Board of Trade, William Huskisson, whose life ended abruptly at the opening of the Liverpool-Manchester Railway, when he tried to get out of the way of the new steam engine *Rocket* by running along the tracks.

Behind them was a whole new class of government statisticians, like George Richardson Porter, a leading member of the Society for the Diffusion of Useful Knowledge and appointed to run Peel's new department. He leapt into action, sending letters to towns across England and

Ireland asking for figures for everything back to 1820 and sat back waiting to process the results. All he got was a few notes from Waterford
and one from Limerick. Manchester followed a few months later, and
then the answers dried up completely. Next he wrote to customs officials, and absolutely none volunteered any help. Most didn't even
bother to reply. It was hard being a pantometrist in those days.

There were the medical campaigners like William Farr, who took
over the new General Register Office in London with great enthusiasm—
measuring literacy rates, proving that copycat suicides and murders
tended to follow gory newspaper reports, and working out a neat statistical law of annual mortality. The number of people who die in the year
is twice the number in the spring plus the autumn, or twice the number
dying in the summer plus the winter. "Neat but useless," said one historian later.

Everything could suddenly be quantified. From the 1830s, the new
statistical societies were sending out their amateur counters in house-to-
house surveys of school books, bible ownership, religiosity, illness, house
design, sleeping arrangements, crime, and anything that appealed
to them, publishing table after table in closely argued pamphlets and
reports.

They were ridiculed by their contemporaries, just as Malthus was,
but on both sides of the Atlantic, nobody was hated as much as the census officials and registrars. As late as 1839, the press was still supporting
the wife of a laborer in the English county of Leicestershire who was
tried for refusing to give information about her new baby to the regis-
trar. The London *Times* bellowed its support for her, quoting the leader
of the medieval Peasants' Revolt, Wat Tyler, about what English people
should do "under a tyranny leading to the violation of the decencies of
domestic life." She was found guilty but not punished.

It was the same in the United States, where Alexander Hamilton's
former assistant, Tenche Coxe—the pantometrist's pantometrist—was
described by one contemporary as having "more than a hint of fact-
benumbed pedantry." Just like Porter in London, the Connecticut Acad-
emy of Arts and Science sent a letter to every town in the state asking 32
questions about the population, number of suicides, carriages, coaches,
and clergymen. Ten years later, only 30 of them had replied.

Yet time was on their side. The truth was that a profound change
had come over America in its attitude to numbers. In 1701, a pompous
visiting English mathematician condemned America as "barbarous"
because most people could "hardly reckon above 20." But when the

English traveler Thomas Hamilton arrived in Philadelphia a century later—objecting to the city's carefully measured grid pattern as "an infringement on the rights of individual eccentricity"—he saw something quite different. Americans were so obsessed with numbers and able to compute, he said, that it set them apart from Europeans.

What had happened? Maybe it was the constant requests from the various settling companies in London for population figures. Maybe it was the fascination all revolutionaries have with such things—Jefferson opted for a decimal currency, but sensibly didn't take the next French step of a 10-day week. Maybe it was Benjamin Franklin's passion for frugality and early rising. If you stayed up until 11:00 P.M. and got up two hours after dawn, calculated one American guidebook to life, your bill for candles would be $182.50 over half a century.

Maybe it was also a feeling that the new nation could avoid political parties if it could only calculate the answer to every political question objectively. Measurement was a way of being scientific about politics. It was a brave idea, but it unraveled when it came to managing a census.

The legislation for the first British census was finally drawn up by Bentham's stepbrother Charles Abbott, and was rushed through Parliament on New Year's Eve 1800. Three months later, the census counted 9.2 million people living in England and Wales. The trouble was that those responsible for actually counting—the "overseers of the poor"—muddled up the number of people with the number of households. The population still wasn't clear.

Similar confusions were getting into the U.S. census returns, and the more ambitious the pantometrists, the more confusing it became. Future president James Madison campaigned successfully to make sure the 1810 census counted people in five categories—free white females, free black people, slaves, free white males over 16, and free white males under 16. Ten years later, they categorized people according to their occupations as well. This was a critical mistake, repeated over and over again by development economists ever since. By counting people with three or more jobs according to just one category, the figures painted a simplistic picture of communities struggling to make ends meet strictly divided into upper, middle, and peasant classes. The truth was that complex social networks allowed people to use their skills and resources far more efficiently than the simple figures suggested.

It was one of the most important sins of pantometry—oversimplification, and the peculiar way that official figures seem to mold the world into their image. These days, most of us have the simple single jobs that they can count easily, however hard we try to rebuild those complex local links that used to blur work and leisure and provide people with subsistence. But worse, generations of simplistic economic "answers" have been imposed on poor communities around the world, based on exports, imports, and economic specialization—and ignoring the wealth that comes from lots of jobs, mixed farms, and complex social interaction. When development economists measured African or Indian communities in the 20th century, they often categorized farms according to their main crop—entirely ignoring all their other resources—just as the 1820 census ignored everybody's other jobs. The world was never as simple as that, and numbers couldn't convey it. It isn't surprising that those rich interconnected local economies of rural America or rural India are almost gone for good. That's what happens when you count in the wrong way.

Still, it was the 1840 census that caused the most immediate trouble. That one also counted prisons, disabled people, people in mental hospitals, and much else besides. Two decades before the American Civil War, with the slavery issue heating the debate, it was political dynamite. The figures seemed to show epidemic rates of insanity among the black population in the North. Not just that, but from Louisiana to Maine, there was a line of rising figures for deaf-dumb black people, black people in prison, and much else besides. The defenders of slavery seized on the census to show that freedom wasn't very good for slaves.

There was even a government inquiry. It turned out that tens of thousands of people had refused to fill in the forms because they didn't trust the government. The assistant marshals complained that they weren't being paid enough to collect the information, so many didn't. Many had also just put all old people considered senile in the column marked simply, in the politically incorrect language of the time, "idiot blacks." There were far more older people in the North than the South—hence the result.

The 1840 census taught Americans that statistics could sometimes mislead. Let's face it, they could sometimes lie. But if the word "pantometry" slipped out of the language, the idea carried on.

VI

Statistics weren't enough for Malthus and his followers. Back in England, another man we last met at Bentham's funeral was using them—

just as Malthus intended—to change the world. By the age of 36, Edwin Chadwick had been the mainstay of two vital royal commissions, and their hefty reports—each one packed with tables of figures—were largely his work. It was Chadwick's assistants who were being sent out across the country to count and collect not just numbers, but numbers that would create change. Not just statistics but what Chadwick called "moral statistics." Chadwick wasn't just the first modern civil servant, he was also a pioneer of modern campaigning.

"Here and there, and everywhere were Chadwick's young crusaders, the Assistant Commissioners, scouring the country in stage-coaches and post-chaises, or beating up against the storm on ponies in the Weald, returning to London, their wallets stuffed with Tabular data so dear to philosophic Radicals," wrote the great historian of the Victorian age, G. M. Young, describing the period. Everywhere also were the new inspectors. There were factory inspectors from 1834. Soon there were also prison inspectors, then school inspectors, railway inspectors, and mines inspectors. The great architecture of official calculation, still in place today, was taking shape—each inspector armed with definitions against which they tested the schools or factories, counting, tabulating, and assessing.

Before Chadwick it seemed almost immoral to count human beings, especially those in need. "Is this a subject for cold calculation?" asked insurance man Samuel Blodget in 1806 in his best-seller *Economics: A Statistical Manual for the United States*—underneath his neat table comparing the price of slaves and the estimated monetary worth of free men. "No, it is the cause of feeling! Of humanity! Of virtue!" But after Chadwick and his colleagues, the great inhumanities of society cried out to be numbered. The moral campaigners would count, make the numbers public, and shock an unfeeling world into action.

Chadwick's sanitary inspectors traveled the country measuring drains and cesspools, counting death rates, and the number of people with each disease, and the number of calories the poor needed to survive. But above all, he counted muck, which he believed was the source of all illness: Until his dying day in 1890, he never believed in germs. Other moral reformers saw filth rather differently.

There were the figures collected by the Massachusetts Society for the Suppression of Intemperance in 1816, which published regular statistics about the number of distilleries closed, the number of paupers, and—if it was possible—the number of "disciplinary measures" taken by pastors against members of their congregations. It was this Society that calculated that "half of all sin" was caused by drink. They didn't seem very interested to discover what caused the other half.

Another Boston society tried to quantify the religious feelings of schoolchildren in the city by counting the number of hymns they had memorized in the year to 1818 (1,899). The New York Moral Reform Society counted the number of brothels in the United States (12,000), the number of prostitutes (120,000), and the number of shops selling naughty pictures—which they described as the "paraphernalia of destruction" (50).

The figures joined those for the number of gallons of oil used in the lamps of Philadelphia, certainly by staying up too late (14,355), and the number of New England brides with advanced pregnancies at the time they got married (30–45 percent). Sometimes they completely overstretched the limits of pantometry, like the book of moral statistics that tried to count the number of tears shed by the wives of drunks since 1790—"supposing drunken husbands 15,000 a year, enough to float the U.S. Navy."

They counted what they were interested in—as we still do now—and then it was drink and sex. The self-portrait painted by any society isn't so much the figures they collect but the categories they think are important. Societies count what they fear, want, and need the most. In that sense, moral statistics mean more than the amoral ones.

VII

"The sign of a truly educated man is to be deeply moved by statistics," said George Bernard Shaw, and he was probably right. But Malthus and Chadwick were using them to appeal to those very educated people to shock them into activity. The trouble with moral statistics was that people soon realized they could believe them or not according to taste. They could even bend them selectively to their will, like the pro-slavery campaigners after the 1840 census. They weren't nearly as scientific as they seemed.

For one thing, the figures entirely missed out on "context"—as numbers always do. They always pretended each situation was simple. When Malthus saw that the population of America was doubling every generation, that was because there seemed to be no context at all. For Malthus, who never visited the United States, it was limitless space. The population of his own land had only quadrupled between 1550 and his own time—and that was far faster than it had in mainland Europe.

Whatever they're measuring, numbers never take place in the vacuum they imply.

For another thing, Malthus's hypothetical figures measured a theoretical extreme that could never be reached. When Victorian doomsters predicted that the streets of Paris would be four foot deep in horse manure by the end of the 19th century, they were simply extrapolating trends. Everybody knew that situation would be impossible. Malthus was obviously right—the population of the world would never expand beyond the means of feeding it—so one thing you also knew was that anyone claiming gigantic figures for the future population were bound to be wrong.

Ah, well, said the spiritual followers of Malthus—the moral statistics were describing a trend, a pressure on humanity. That's true, but then the figures weren't objective. They were a gesture, a colored argument, a moral exhortation, but nothing more.

Malthus had the equivalent of horse manure heaped on his head in his lifetime and long after his death. Chadwick had the same. Moral statisticians aren't popular with everybody. But then people don't like to be warned, and they absolutely hate being shocked into action. Most of us also don't like the thought that everything is running out—though in some ways it clearly is.

The Age of Malthusian Pessimism made a dramatic reentry a century and a half after his death with the Stanford population biologist Paul Ehrlich, whose 1968 book, *The Population Bomb*, took moral statistics to a whole new level. "While you are reading these words," said the cover of the paperback edition, "four people will have died of starvation. Most of them children." Ehrlich explained that the population of a city of one million was added to the earth every four and a half days. "In the six seconds it takes to read this sentence, there will be another 18 more people on the earth," he said.

Looking at his more recent writings, it is astonishing how much Ehrlich echoed Malthus with his emphasis on moral disapproval. "Showing at least mild disapproval of irresponsible reproductive actions can also help influence others," he wrote with his wife in *The Population Explosion*. "Our society must evolve to the point where it would be disgraceful for one's daughter to marry a real-estate developer who has turned a piece of Arizona desert into a sub-division with an artificial lake, helping to increase southwestern water deficits—or a man who owns a 'muscle car' and makes an extra contribution to global warming."

It was scary stuff, and it attracted attention—but it didn't win the argument. Ehrlich also lost a high-profile bet with the economist Julian Simon over whether the price of metals would go up or down. The problem was that, as so often with numbers, price wasn't a very good measure of scarcity.

It was the same four years later in 1972, with the highly influential book *Limits to Growth*. Once again, the world seemed to be running dry. It depended on what you measured, of course: It always does. *Limits to Growth* was written by a group of twenty-something scientists from the Massachusetts Institute of Technology, led by Donella Meadows, and it told the story of the virtual computer-model planet called World3. The growth of human need and population, time and time again, in scenario after scenario, saw the planet's ecosystem collapse—just as population reached between 12 and 15 billion. It was frightening. A population that grows at 2 percent a year does, after all, double in 35 years.

To the authors' surprise, the world paid attention. The book launch even attracted the father of the Hitler's V-rockets, Wernher von Braun, though it wasn't really his department. Even President Nixon talked about the book's importance. Columnists all over the world solemnly explained the implications of exponential growth, just as Malthus had a century and a half before. But again, the numbers didn't convince: "an empty and misleading work," said the *New York Times Review of Books*, talking darkly about "technical chicanery."

A generation later, we know some of the predictions were wrong. World population is now six billion, not the seven billion they predicted. Instead of running out, resources like oil and copper actually got cheaper because new technologies and rising prices meant it was suddenly economical to look for more deposits. Meadows and her colleagues were clearly right about the basic problem—just as Malthus was. It was just that their figures didn't convince people anymore. Moral statistics had run out of steam.

Whatever you felt about their figures, there clearly was a problem—it was just that the world's governments didn't stop in horror and go into emergency session to do something about it. They carried on their own sweet way negotiating trade deals and fighting happy elections. The hole in the ozone layer now engulfs part of Latin America, and the climate-change negotiations seem languid in the extreme. So despite all those frightening numbers about global warming, why is that? Probably for the reason summed up in a Hartford newspaper headline, quoted in a famous recent article by Annie Dillard: HEAD-SPINNING NUMBERS CAUSE MIND TO GO SLACK.

Here we all are, with our minds "slackened" by screeds of terrifying statistics, apparently powerless to rescue the world—or to distinguish the important figures from the unimportant. Maybe that is the most terrifying Malthusian legacy of all: He created the debate, and he did so because he cared about the poverty he saw around him, but the path he mapped out has made us immune to moral statistics. Maybe, on the other hand, they were never very effective in the first place.

VIII

For the brave new utilitarians, dry statistics and moral statistics all merged into one. "The first and most essential rule of its conduct is to exclude all opinions," said the first prospectus of the London Statistical Society. The new measurement only dealt with facts.

If you open the issue of *Illustrated London News* that described Chadwick's work on the Health of Towns Commission in 1848, you can find the precise number of Christmas parcels brought into London by railway (17,209); the number of children in the Clapton Orphan's Asylum (168); the length of the cane used to hit Queen Victoria on the head in Piccadilly (27 inches); the amount of tobacco imported (26 million pounds); and the number of Americans christened "George Washington" in the previous half century (more than 30,000). You can find the amount of rancid butter seized, the number of evictions in Galway, the number of potatoes eaten at the annual meeting of the Royal Agricultural Society, and on and on. It is the symptom of a scientific age, confident that it can control the chaos around it with the unrelenting application of facts and measurements.

The problem for the pantometrists was that, however much they counted, it still wouldn't give them the answer. It didn't tell Malthus how to restrain the population, any more than it told Bentham how to make everyone happy. It could tell William Sanger that there were twice as many prostitutes in New York in 1855 from Maine as there were from Virginia—even though they were equally far away—but it couldn't tell him why. That was the big mistake the utilitarians made: They still had to use their judgment and imagination. And a diet of nothing but facts and figures, without those things, was really rather horrifying. It gave you fake knowledge, the clipboard and laboratory definitions, but it didn't give you answers. And it didn't give you real life.

5

THE FEELGOOD FACTOR

*By psychology's "mortal" sin, I mean the sin of deadening, the dead
feeling that comes over us when we read professional psychology,
hear its language, the voice with which it drones, the bulk of its
textbooks, the serious pretensions and bearded proclamations of new
"findings" that could hardly be more banal, its soothing anodynes
for self-help, its décor, its fashion, its departmental meetings, and its
tranquilizing consulting rooms, those stagnant waters where the
soul goes to be restored, a last refuge of white-bread culture,
stale, crustless, but ever spongy with rebounding hope.*

Dr. James Hillman, *The Soul's Code*

*Where is the wisdom we have lost in knowledge,
and the knowledge we have lost in information?*

Dr. Richard Smith, paraphrasing T. S. Eliot,
in a *British Medical Journal* editorial, 1991

I

LESLEY FALLOWFIELD, A psychologist, sat through the final illness of her friend, who died of leukemia in her early thirties, then blasted the medical profession for its failure to consider people's emotional needs. The therapy had been unsuccessful with unpleasant side effects, and to make matters worse, the two could only communicate through a disconcerting plastic window. "Thus one of the most intelligent, sensitive, warm, and generous-hearted people I have ever known spent some of her final weeks cut off from physical contact with most of her family and friends," she wrote. "I am still haunted by the last conversation we had, when she asked why I had not tried to dissuade her from a therapy with poor chances of survival, but a high chance of destroying the quality of whatever life she had left."

Both medicine and psychiatry are fully blown sciences with risk and return ratios. They exist in a world where measurement somehow seems to belong. They weigh evidence, count blood cells, test hypotheses, and wire you up to machines, just as they used to read the charts at the end of your bed. You can hear them shouting out the figures on *ER* as they push the patients into hospital on their trolleys. Psychiatrists will often now use their own psychometric diagnoses, sometimes without even looking you in the eye while they tick the checklists. Single symptoms, blood counts, heart rates can all be measured.

The trouble is that, while medicine and psychiatry are sciences in themselves, they are applied to individuals with their own peculiarities and complex combinations of symptoms. The problems of distinguishing causes from effects in each symptom are precisely the same kind of problem that policy makers or economists have to face as well. Like economics, they are professions that have become more reliant on figures over the past century, and—like the early accountant James Anyon—there was a time when wise doctors sometimes put the numbers to one side because they obscured the basic underlying truth. There were hazy eras in the past when a reassuring bedside manner and an intuitive understanding of the human temperament were the *most* important attributes a doctor could display. Not anymore, and probably that's a good thing too. The problem is that the figures will always leave something crucial out. And those professionals most wedded to the idea of measuring an answer often shy away from important things that can't be measured. Like emotions, for example.

We know now, both intuitively and by measuring it, that emotions can have an enormous effect on our immune systems. Yet some doctors ignore them, except as irritating disease-causing complications, just as economists do, even though—according to the figures—distressing emotions have a similar risk to health as smoking or eating oily butter and greasy chips stuffed with cholesterol. According to some research, we are five times more likely to develop cancer if we are stressed, twice as likely to get colds if we are anxious, and five times more likely to die after a heart attack if we are depressed. Sometimes the numbers can take you by surprise like that.

Given that emotions are important, asked an editorial in the *Journal of the American Medical Association*, aren't there ethical reasons why doctors should at least try to get a handle on them? It would be silly to suggest that no doctors do so, but the profession as a whole has a poor recent record. Instead of understanding what each patient feels separately, modern medicine has insisted on measuring their emotions on a pseudo-objective scale. Lesley Fallowfield's search turned up what she called "ludicrously narrow" medical definitions of quality of life. The Karnofsky Performance Index of 1947 developed a way of working out how many nurses you might need on a ward, which scores people's health between 100 and 0. If you score 0, you're dead. Breast cancer patients score 80, whether they are bouncing with enthusiasm or crippled with depressive illness.

There have been many more attempts since then, from the Functional Living Index to the Rotterdam Symptom Checklist. There are other methods of getting patients to sum up what they feel, with tests of "well-being" from the SF-36 General Health Questionnaire to the McMaster Health Utilities Questionnaire, and with every year that passes there are more. Each one, of course, comes up with slightly different answers and slightly different categories, but they tend to beg the real question. Whose categories are these one-dimensional figures which can only measure on one scale from better to worse—trying to measure? Are they the health economists', the doctors', or the patients'?

Health economists tend to use QALYs—the so-called quality adjusted life years—to work out how to distribute their resources. But when you look more closely at the basis for the research, you wonder whether these are actually the kinds of trade-off people make in their own minds. Or whether they would really trade a relatively painless death for a painful, isolated life extension for a few more months with a bone marrow transplant. People would often actually trade a shorter life for better health. QALYs also tend to be based on interviews with relatively few patients, who are asked to rank different states of illness and what they feel about having them. Small differences in the sample make big differences in the preferences, which are then generalized and assumed to apply to everybody. And in any case, who ever heard of the fire department or the lifeboats checking up on people's QALYs before turning on the siren?

The counting obsession has caused the same crisis among doctors as it has everywhere else, as the supporters of "evidence-based medicine"—cold hard measuring followed by logical diagnosis—slug it out with their critics. Trisha Greenhalgh, from the Royal Free Hospital Medical School in London, is one of the most avid proponents of intuition-based, individualized medicine. She tells the story of "Dr. Jenkins' hunch," breaking off his Monday-morning surgery because a mother called to say her little girl had diarrhea and was behaving "strangely." He could never normally break off from a busy surgery. How could he know, using the available evidence, that the girl had meningitis? But she did. Maybe the word "strangely" alerted him. Maybe he knew the family and they rarely complained. But it wasn't the cold facts and risks that told him—it was the story.

Medical students can write long learned essays about the risks and competing treatments for high blood pressure, but that's not enough, says Greenhalgh. "When I ask my students a practical question such as, 'Mrs. Jones has developed light-headedness on these blood pressure tablets and she wants to stop all medication; what would you advise her to do', they are puzzled. They sympathize with Mrs. Jones' predicament, but they cannot distill from their pages of close-written text the one thing that Mrs. Jones needs to know." Who can blame them? Which of us can distill from the piles of research figures about health risks what we should embrace and what we should avoid?

Even outside the medical profession, there is a growing feeling that you can't treat patients as if they were average risks, in the same way you can treat cattle or buy stock. You can't offset one risk with another; you have to listen to each patient as an individual and get at the truth each time. Greenhalgh calls this listening to patients' stories "narrative-based medicine," because their complex experience comes in the form of a story that can't be reduced—as it is by researchers—to one little dot on a statistical scatter diagram. Why do they use a word like 'strangely'? Sometimes a single word like that can warn a doctor that the symptoms are serious. Computers can't do that.

Of course doctors need to count. They need to confirm hunches and, of course, to make sure their drugs won't have weird side effects—which is why the average new drug requires 100 research projects, takes between 12 and 24 years to bring to market, and costs at least $475 million to develop. Though they should also remember that one of the other peculiarities of the paradox of the Quantum Effect (see chapter 3) is that, what you look for in research you tend to find. But then doctors have been running up against the same mismatch of measurements as the economists have. People might be rich and healthy, so there shouldn't be anything wrong with them. But there is.

They're not happy. Numbers can point to this notion, but they can't solve the problem. In fact, they often only make it worse.

II

Doctors and economists have tried but never quite managed to measure happiness. Whether they use a checklist questionnaire or search for a mythical single "happiness gene," or whether they just count people's money, they still have the same problem. Happiness is a complex and often paradoxical state. For one thing, it's so difficult to compare—especially when, according to one Danish study, "the life of the average Dane is to a large extent confused, stressful, alienated, and isolated." For "Dane," read "most of us"—though actually, the massive Global Happiness Barometer project in 1999 found that 49 percent of Danes were happy—making them the happiest in the world, right up there along with the Australians (48 percent), the Americans (46 percent), and miles above the Russians (67 percent unhappy). The figures are pretty meaningless, especially as another study counting happy years of life expectancy put Iceland top and Bulgaria bottom, and another put Mexico top and the U.S. bottom. The point is just how difficult it is to pin happiness down. When the economists get involved, it's even more meaningless. Witness the recent findings by Dartmouth College that a good marriage makes you exactly as happy as an extra $100,000 a year.

The other problem with measuring happiness is that, physiologically anyway, happiness and misery are not opposites. They are dealt with by different parts of the brain and have to be measured in different ways. There's the problem of the Dutch proverb: "An ounce of illness is felt more than a hundredweight of health." Happiness and unhappiness are qualities that are so paradoxical that they slip through your fingers every time you get out the ruler.

Take the example of the writer and concentration camp survivor Primo Levi, who described how people found something to sustain them emotionally even in Auschwitz. Even at their lowest point, with nothing to look forward to, he says, they told themselves they could stop it raining just by running over to the electric fence. That sense of choice—that they could end it all whenever they wanted—was sometimes enough to keep them going in the face of devastating adversity. But try measuring happiness in that kind of laboratory. You can't.

Nor can we take the statistics of *un*happiness too seriously. According to the National Institute of Public Health, about a quarter of all Americans will suffer from depression sometime in their lives. That's what the figures say, and there's no doubt that an awful lot of people do. Why, as Oliver James puts it, do "winners in society now feel like losers"? Is depression really increasing or is it that drug companies are looking for a market for antidepressants? The whole idea of antidepressants was nearly canned by marketing experts in the 1960s because depression was such a rare disorder. In those days, they were developing Valium to tackle anxiety instead. Now anxiety is unfashionable and we're awash with Prozac and Xanax.

It was the same with obsessive-compulsive disorder. In 1980, the estimates were that people obsessively washing their hands or checking their front door accounted for less than 0.01 percent of the population. Now, experts estimate it affects one in 50 of the U.S. population at any one time. Are those enormous shifts really to do with a tidal wave of misery? Or is it something to do with subtle marketing, journal supplements, and conferences on the subject, sponsored by drug companies? Is it because we have only just become sensitive enough to see what was always under our noses and define these things correctly when we didn't before? Or is it the peculiar Quantum Effect: that we create what we count, and reality follows the model? Whatever it is, we wouldn't necessarily learn anything from the statistics, but we can still recognize an underlying sense of unease.

III

Happiness isn't just a problem for doctors; it's a problem for politicians too. One measure of success doesn't calculate in all the others. Money, for example, doesn't calculate self-esteem or well being. And for politicians on both sides of the Atlantic, it was a problem that dates specifically to the early 1990s, because the usual measures of success seemed to have let them down. People were having two foreign holidays a year, the value of their homes was rising fast, but people just weren't happy. The political press dubbed what was missing as the "feelgood factor."

This elusive, immeasurable, indefinable factor became one of the key issues of the Clinton campaign. Commentators discovered, as if for the first time, the terrifying numbers of "feelbad," the rising divorce and male suicide rates, the concern about parenthood, the gargantuan appetite for antidepressants.

People seemed to be so angry at the end of the 20th century. It wasn't just stories like that of Marlene Lenick, who shot her husband with a .38 because he wanted to watch the Philadelphia Eagles game when she wanted to watch the news. People were also needy. Bookshelves bulged with the weight of self-help titles like *Feel the Fear and Do It Anyway*. And when the marriage guidance organization Relate opened an office in a doctor's surgery in the middle of London's commuter belt, at South Woodham Ferrers in Essex in 1991, there was a sudden enormous demand for free 45-minute sessions with a psychologist for stress or loneliness. Within two months, the office had been so overwhelmed that it had to close altogether.

Maybe it was always thus. Maybe nobody had noticed before. But the emotional toll on the richest people in the world seemed to be landing most heavily on children, all with new-sounding labels—attention-deficit disorder, anorexia, even the inexplicable fatigue—whatever it was called—that resulted in long-term absences from school.

Then there were the diets. Suddenly girls of just eight or nine were worrying about their weight. Some scientists blamed Barbie dolls and their ultrathin bodies. "Why pick on Barbie?" asked a spokesman for the toy manufacturer. "An eleven-and-a-half-inch piece of plastic is not responsible for the ills of today's society."

But who was? Step forward the three main contenders—school pressures, rising divorce rates, and the consumer society.

School pressure is an international phenomenon, as the divide between the children under pressure from parents and exams and truants grows ever wider. In some affluent schools, children as young as eight have an hour's homework every night and formal tests in each area of schoolwork every week—and where they have such busy schedules filled with résumé-building after-school activities that "windows" for play are often a week or so apart. One study in England found that young pupils doing the most homework did worst at school, probably because they were so stressed. The homework was designed to get them through specific government tests that would determine the schools' place in performance league tables. They were and are dangerous figures.

Which brings us to the second contender. The chances of divorce for married American couples reached 67 percent by 1990. A decade later, it now takes only 20 minutes to produce the papers needed for a divorce through the U.S. QuickCourt interactive computer system. Yet divorce can have a devastating effect on children. According to the figures, children of divorced parents are more likely to get into trouble, perform badly in school, get stress-related illness, and get divorced themselves.

Which leaves us with the third contender—the pressures of a consumer society. By the time they are seven, the average American child will see 20,000 advertisements a year on television. By the time they are 12, they will have an entry in the massive marketing databases used by companies. And as corporations realize the spending power of children, so the efforts to get at their money increases. Advertising to children increased by 50 percent between 1993 and 1996, with movies, sneakers, and hamburger wrappers all linked together as part of the elaborate child marketing system. By 2000, partly thanks to *Star Wars* and Pokémon, up to half the spending on toys went on those licensed for TV or films. The numbers look extreme.

According to the poet Robert Bly, children have to develop such a powerful critical sense to resist all this wanting that they eventually turn it on themselves. No wonder they are miserable. But the awful thing is that the different measures of success actually contradict one another. Society is "successful" if you use the conventional measure—money. But there is more money being spent because of the breakup of family life. A Ford executive recently admitted that divorce boosts car sales. Broken families also need two houses instead of one, so it pushes up house prices. And the toy trade certainly benefits: Many children need duplicate toys—one for each home. Some measures of success hide other kinds of failure.

The communitarian Amitai Etzioni tells the story of truck driver Rod Grimm, delivering his truckloads from Los Angeles to Maine. His work keeps him on the road 340 days a year, so his wife moved into the cab with him, their friendships have been reduced to occasional encounters, and their relationship with the daughter to a cell phone link. Yet the economic measures see all the money he's earning and register this as a success.

Despite all the measures of success that are dashing off the scale, showing that our children are richer, smarter, and healthier than any generation before them, the present generation in the West is also more lonely, angry, miserable, aggressive, and depressed. We demonstrate that mismatch with the use of figures—of depression, suicide, and alienation—without which we would carry on our own sweet way regardless. When you break away from one solitary measure of success, you do get closer to the truth.

Maybe the numbers crunchers will one day prove exactly where the problem lies, but I doubt it. Real problems about real people don't usually have one single root. And even if they do, you can measure the causes next to the effects—as we've seen—but it's extremely hard to disentangle them enough to see which is which. Not without falling back on good old-fashioned common sense and intuition.

The point is that success and happiness can't be measured. They just have to be experienced. Or as the French aviator Antoine de Saint-Exupéry wrote in *The Happy Prince*: "It is with the heart that one sees rightly. What is essential is invisible to the eye."

IV

John Vasconcellos, chairman of California's Ways and Means Committee, is one of the first to take the feelgood debate somewhere political, taking it a little further than the usual clichés about "family values"—pioneering an attempt to measure what's really important—but to do so without recourse to numbers. If lack of self-esteem lies behind a range of intractable social issues, he reasoned, how can we hammer out a political program to do something about it?

Nobody had asked the question before. Coinciding with the angst on both sides of the Atlantic about why people were wealthier but more disturbed, Vasco's initiative has fed into a whole new way of thinking about how institutions like schools and prisons succeed—and how we can judge whether they do, according to their success in building the self-esteem of the pupils and prisoners in their charge. And the point about self-esteem is that it is just as complex a concept as happiness: Measuring it in numbers would be no less complicated. But then he wasn't intending to measure it.

Vasconcellos is difficult to categorize. Some dismiss him as a refugee from the '60s—though he also represents Santa Clara, including Silicon Valley, which makes him bang up to date. They dismiss him as a shaggy branch of the New Age movement too, but as chairman of the committee responsible for balancing the state's budget, he has also had to be pretty down to earth. The local media has always gone heavy on his appearance, more like a cross between a rock star and a drug smuggler, according to one magazine. "I mean worn loafers," wrote one interviewer about his shoes—this is, after all, a nation where politicians' shoes are as carefully coifed as their hair. "I mean, I got a higher shine on my worn loafers than he's got on his loafers and the last time my loafers shined, the Village People were still going strong."

Vasco began as a good Catholic. "I was the best Catholic boy in the entire world," he says now. In his valedictory speech in college he promised to devote his life to furthering the work of Jesus Christ. It was the time of the film *Man of La Mancha*, of dreaming the impossible dream—just to add to the Don Quixote impression—and Vasconcellos set up the La Mancha Fund to beat the impossible foe.

The trouble was, he didn't like himself, as he later put it. In fact, he had such low self-esteem that he lost the first election he ever fought—for eighth-grade president—by one vote. His own. Even as a politician he was going through a period of disillusionment. The same year he was elected also saw Ronald Reagan take the reins of power as governor of California, with a remit to dismantle everything Vasco held dear. Soon he was storming out of meetings at the Assembly.

Throughout the '70s, he grew his hair—at one stage refusing to cut it for three years. He got angrier and went through periods of heavy depression. Then he suddenly found himself in a process he described as "cracking open." It was the start of a long struggle with himself under a protégé of the great humanistic psychologist Carl Rogers and the bioenergetics therapist Stanley Keleman. "If I carry on we're going to open up your rage," Keleman told him. "It may end your political career." But the political capital he had built up got him through. A committee of colleagues was set up to calm him down every time he exploded during a debate. When he went public about his personal demons, he became a national figure.

California was in crisis by the end of the 1980s. The voters were poised to cut back the state's budget, but the prison system was 175 percent full and two out of three arrested in Los Angeles were testing positive for cocaine. Drug abuse was costing $235 million in medical expenditure, $4 billion in lost work, $2 billion in law enforcement, $235 million in prisons, and $280 million in premature death—in California alone. And nobody seemed to have anything new to suggest on the subject beyond lower taxes, tougher sentences, and family values. But even these weren't what they were. Not when half of California's children will live in single-parent households before the age of 18, and when 8 percent of them live in traditional families where the fathers work full-time and the mothers stay at home.

It didn't add up. This was one of the richest states in the richest country in the world: The normal methods of measuring such things didn't seem to provide any answers. But what if the problems were symptoms of something so fundamental that the measurements for them simply didn't exist. Vasconcellos consulted his friend, the self-esteem guru Jack Canfield, later to become immensely successful by selling seven million copies of his book *Chicken Soup for the Soul.*

Together, they put together the proposal for an official task force about self-esteem, which would make the case of "feelgood" as a personal and political issue and suggest what could be done about it. The first attempt in 1984 passed through the California Assembly in Sacramento by 55 votes to 22, but while Vasco was recovering from triple heart bypass surgery, it was defeated by the Senate. Next year it got through both houses but was thrown out by Governor George Deukmejian. "I do not agree that the creation of an additional quasi-governmental body as the appropriate way to address this problem," he said.

Next year, Vasco was back, broadening the remit to include "personal and social responsibility." The senators nodded it through and he went to see the governor himself. "Why not just hand it over to a university to study?" asked Deukmejian.

"Because by spending a few tax dollars, we can collect the information and get it out. If that helps even a few persons appreciate and understand self-esteem and how they can live their lives and raise their kids better, we may have less welfare, less violence and drugs—and that's a very conserving use of taxpayers' money."

"I've never thought of it that way before," said the governor, and signed it into law. The task force would have a budget the same as sending one person to prison for 14 years.

In May 1988, Vasco went to San Francisco for a brainstorming session with M. Scott Peck, author of *The Road Less Traveled,* and began advertising for task force members. A record number applied. They appointed an unusual mixture ranging from a gay therapist to a captain in the LA sheriff's office, the vice president of a poultry farm, a poet, musician, and the chairman of the board of the Evangelical Free Church. As chair they appointed David Brooks, coauthor of *How to Be Successful in Less Than 10 Minutes a Day,* as chair.

It ran into trouble with the media straightaway. "As if they needed to reinforce Sacramento's credentials as the kook capital of the world," said the *San Francisco Examiner.* "The taxpayers had the right to hope that such silliness left the state with Governor Moonbeam," said one Republican assemblywoman, referring to the great days of the semihippie governor Jerry Brown.

Nonetheless, the task force report, *Toward a State of Self-Esteem,* hit the streets on January 23, 1990. It hit the front pages right across the United States, dismissed by the Right as a waste of money and by the Left for obscuring the issues of poverty and deprivation—but it sold 60,000 copies. Similar task forces were set up immediately in Maryland, Louisiana, Illinois, and in 50 of California's 58 counties. Rhode Island senator Claiborne Pell drew up plans for a national task force on "human resource development," which was withdrawn after a battering against it from the Christian conservatives.

The report wasn't signed by the whole task force. The evangelical refused unless the definition of self-esteem included the words "accepting myself as the image-bearer of God," the gay therapist refused unless it included a model program for lesbian and gay youth, and the turban-wearing yoga teacher refused unless it included some simple yoga exercises to reduce stress.

But the report was finally out, packed with figures and inspiring little quotations, and it had an effect. Slowly, fitfully, government attention shifted toward Vasco's three Rs: responsibility, self-respect, and relationships—especially in small ways. Hillary Clinton even began keeping toys around the White House in case anyone needed to bring their children to work. The self-esteemers began drafting new laws for California—teaching art and creativity in prison, setting up parenting classes, putting self-esteem at the center of the school curriculum, and measuring the success of institutions by the self-esteem they created. The governor designated February 1992 as Self-Esteem Month.

"Self-esteem amounts to a social vaccine," said Vasconcellos. "It provides us with the strength not to be vulnerable to dropping out or getting pregnant too soon or getting violent or addicted. It's a new strategic vision for the development of human capital. We need to give people material things but also encouragement to become able to protect themselves and take charge of their lives."

Similar ideas had already succeeded in reducing delinquency figures, including truancy and teenage pregnancies. Some states already believed they could save $6 in welfare spending for every dollar spent backing self-help programs to boost self-esteem. There have also been some spectacular successes in schools, led by the superintendent of one school district, in San Jose, that gave all pupils 40 minutes of self-esteem training a week. Average attendance increased to 97.7 percent and achievement scores shot up 10 percent a year. You may not be able to measure self-esteem, but it feels effective.

Self-esteem has become an American industry in itself. So why did the political movement for self-esteem not capitalize on its momentum? Maybe because of the difficulty with one of the task force's recommendations—the so-called California "self-esteem czar" was never appointed. But then, as one local paper put it, "Who's got a sense of self-worth strong enough to step into the role? Big enough to deflect an entire stable of gag-writers?"

Vasconcellos practices what he preaches. "The government doesn't bestow it," he told me. "Its role is the assessment of institutions. But there is a *bottom* bottom line and that is whether I have self-esteem. If I just talk about it and just measure it and never experience it, then I'll never appreciate it." It's an exciting and innovative approach to take a leap at what's really important, knowing that it can't be measured. It means that, in the end, however much policymakers may demand the figures, the fundamental question can only be measured intuitively. "Do I have self-esteem?" is a pretty fundamental question, and one I answer differently for myself every time I wake up. That's the bottom line. The leap in the dark is to extend that to anyone else.

John Vasconcellos remains as convinced as ever of the vital importance of self-esteem but frustrated by the criticism and the problem that people try to measure it. "Measuring it, knowing how it's destroyed and created, takes a lot more knowledge than we have so far, because there is so much involved in being a human being," says Vasco. Even so, the movement he gave birth to had worked, he said. "Most people now take it for granted," he said. "It's aspired to, talked about, written about, designed into programs for kids. It's become so widespread, in fact, that it has created a backlash."

What made things even more difficult was that, as well as finding it hard to quantify and so almost impossible to measure how much self-esteem was being built in institutions like schools and prisons, there was also hardly any research being carried out on the idea. Worse, some academics brought out papers saying that self-esteem was the same as egotism. The report defines it as "appreciating my own worth and importance and having the character to be accountable for myself and to act responsibly toward others." When you're going to count something, it has to be defined. When it's as complex a definition as that, it's pretty hard to count.

Next the cartoonist Garry Trudeau—who had lampooned the task force for months—went public about research that showed that North Koreans were best at math but thought they were the worst, while for

Americans it was the other way around. Was U.S. self-esteem actually getting in the way? Or is that defining it in the wrong way again? Then there were the seven professors the task force had commissioned. They admitted that the links between self-esteem and the social issues Vasco had been committed to tackling remained unproven. However much they stacked up the statistics and talked about common sense, they just couldn't prove that crucial link.

Vasconcellos defended the idea: "Just because the causality chain is incomplete with regard to self-esteem, it does not mean that it is implausible."

The problem of cause and effect keeps coming up when you rely too much on quantification. Are people on drugs because of low self-esteem, or is it the other way around? Four out of five studies show a link between self-esteem and teenage pregnancy—"Anti-social teenage girls don't get violent," said Vasco, "they get pregnant"—but can you be absolutely sure they don't have low self-esteem because they're pregnant? Are the schoolchildren improving because of the self-esteem training or just because people are paying them more attention? Or even more centrally, are people successful because they have self-esteem, or do they just like themselves because they're successful? Once again, it has to come down to common sense and intuition.

Then two things happened to blunt the growth of the self-esteem idea. The first was the California budget crisis, after the electorate voted to seriously cut taxes. The second event was "emotional intelligence."

Daniel Goleman, a journalist on psychological matters on the *New York Times*, published his book with this title in 1995, and it was an immediate best-seller, selling approximately three million copies around the world. Goleman tells the story of an elderly Japanese man on the Tokyo metro that calmed a large and aggressive drunk who was threatening the passengers. The last thing they saw was the drunk in tears, laying his head on the lap of the old man and telling him about his dead wife. "That is emotional brilliance," said Goleman.

Writers like Jack Canfield and Nathaniel Brandon had best-selling feelgood books out. Corporations were organizing humor workshops for their staff. There were even cartoons poking gentle fun at families standing outside in their gardens, feeling the warm night breezes instead of sitting indoors watching the final episode of *Falcon Crest*. It has been enormously influential, though slightly embarrassing to Europeans to have children made to wear T-shirts saying "If it needs to be done, I'll be the one." Even so, self-esteem bumper stickers can occasionally give you a jolt. "Commit Random Acts of Kindness" even reached Europe.

What Goleman tried to do was to turn the toe-curling aspects of self-esteem into something respectable for policy think tanks. *Emotional Intelligence* did just that. Emotional intelligence, he showed, helped people to work better. It meant they were able to defuse tension, deal with racial diversity, work in teams, and handle criticism—at a time when many premature deaths are caused because young men are completely unable to deal with shame. But that wasn't all. Goleman argued that emotional intelligence also made you healthier. Breast cancer sufferers, for example, found that a weekly meeting of emotional support doubled their period of survival.

Lay self-esteem and emotional intelligence side by side, and you won't see much difference, but the advent of the latter drove out the attention self-esteem was getting. "Culture has this curious awful fascination with novelty," Vasconcellos told me, with a slight edge to his voice.

But the problems of measuring emotional intelligence are exactly the same as measuring self-esteem. And when Goleman talked about the concept of "flow"—that sense of letting go in the moment that athletes or artists feel at their most creative and victorious—it gets even more difficult to measure. It may be possible to start measuring such states of mind with electrodes in the brain, but in practice it's not going to be an everyday tool to check each other's pulses. Let alone the success of our schools.

Then there is hope, which he describes as a crucial element of emotional intelligence. To measure hope, you have to define it, and Goleman does it like this: "Believing you have the will and the way to accomplish your goals, whatever they may be." Try putting a stethoscope up to that one. But then just because measuring what's really vital is extraordinarily hard, it doesn't make those elements any less important.

V

"What we are doing is deeply political and seriously radical," said Gloria Steinem, the leading feminist, dressed in what looked like fetching leopard-skin trousers. "The truth is there is already at birth a unique fellow human being—someone with all the human qualities in a unique combination, which has never happened before and will never happen again. Any process of child-rearing which isn't devoted to finding out exactly who that child is, is not proper education. Emphasizing what goes in during education, rather than what comes out, will convince a child that in order to live safely, they must become someone else."

It was the second international conference on self-esteem, and speakers from as far afield as Poland, Ukraine, and Australia were in Cambridge, England to take the story on further. Steinem has been the most articulate modern promoter of self-esteem, describing the moment when she meekly accepted being thrown out of a hotel lobby before interviewing a celebrity because she was an unaccompanied woman—before going back the next day and clearly and confidently making things clear to the manager. She is also an exponent of a healthily unpragmatic and nonutilitarian social philosophy: that we are not all numbers and we all have something individual that counts. "Most of all we have to have faith that everything we do matters," she told us in Cambridge. "And understand that the end doesn't justify the means." Bentham wouldn't have liked it.

Anyone who believes that every individual is unique, as every individual surely is, has trouble with the categorizing and defining that goes with counting them. One of the healthy aspects of the self-esteem movement in the United States is that it has, generally speaking, understood this and turned its back on the whole numbers game. Unfortunately, it has also paid the price of this—because we live in a numbered society. Unless self-esteem could be quantified, numbered, and tracked, the technocrats didn't want it, didn't believe in it, and couldn't recognize it even if they did.

The conference where Gloria Steinem spoke was organized by the UK Self-Esteem Network and held in Cambridge, the same year that the British organization Antidote was founded by film journalist James Park in order somehow to bridge this gap. He had been advised by therapist Susie Orbach that, if he wanted there to be an organization working for more "emotional literacy," he would have to start it himself. The economic case was already being made—legal costs related to marital breakdown and alcoholism were rising, anxiety and depression were resulting in a third of all sick leave—but they felt that somehow it required a different kind of counting. They wanted to measure "emotional and social well-being."

"We keep on using economic data when it comes to talking about the causes of crime or well-being, when it really doesn't tell us any-thing," Park told me in their offices in London's Barbican. "The idea is to bring the reverence for economic data down a few notches and showing how little it actually reveals, and allowing emotional 'indica-tors' to be used alongside." Emotional "indicators"—like economic or environmental indicators—are supposed to be those parts of the com-plex elusive business that you *can* measure.

But isn't that just swapping one set of bizarre measurements for another, I asked?

"No, we don't want indicators for that. We want emotional indica-tors to give us a revised basis for hypotheses about what might be going on. It's not about saying that the reason why crime has gone up is that the emotional indicators have gone down by 0.2 points. That would be absurd. But at the moment, one element in the equation lacks the spu-rious credibility that the figures give it." The really frightening thing about being director of Antidote, Park told me, was meeting economists who really couldn't see the point.

The problem for the self-esteemers is that they all suffer from the same very practical problem: How do you convince a world obsessed with measurements that you are right? "If you don't measure it, it doesn't count," said the economist John Kenneth Galbraith. It remains a problem, and it means that exponents of self-esteem as a basis for measuring the success of institutions will have to rely on convincing the world via gut feeling and shock value.

The reactions to media appearances on the subject by Susie Orbach herself were more convincing than any facts she brought to bear. No media interview with her can go by without reference to her author-ship of *Fat Is a Feminist Issue*, or the fact that she was Princess Diana's long-suffering therapist. Having got past that—and putting the case for emotional literacy on a BBC panel discussion in 1996—she was greeted by an assortment of columnists and politicians who reacted with a sniggering mixture of cynicism and alarm. "We don't want to encour-age people to let everything 'hang out'!" said a leading ally of Margaret Thatcher's. You could almost hear his little shiver of British revulsion at such things—though all Susie Orbach was suggesting was that society needs to help people learn how to deal with their emotions better. Somehow his reaction—and her insistence that they were aiming for exactly the reverse—was a better confirmation of her arguments than anything else she could have said.

But the message does seem to be getting through, despite the impossibility of measuring emotional literacy directly. Business is showing more interest in emotional indicators than any other sector, and this is no coincidence. Nor is it that Vasconcellos happens to represent the new emerging information economy from Silicon Valley, paying a critical role swinging them behind Bill Clinton in his original bid for the presidency in 1992. Even if politicians still insist on measuring school pupils in a one-dimensional way, businesses are increasingly looking for people who are a little bit broader.

The search for feelgood in companies made many discover they had been measuring it the wrong way all along. The UK bank Midland, now HSBC, was spending £6 million on a staff reward scheme but found that actually what most employees really wanted was for their manager to say "Well done" occasionally. They managed to save two-thirds of the money by teaching managers how to do so.

Businesses are also learning that happy, well-balanced staff is more productive, though to convince any of their contemporaries, they have to express this in figures. According to one study of UK manufacturing companies in 1999, in fact, cultivating a better corporate culture can result in a 10 to 29 percent difference in profits—whatever that means. Another study at Bell Laboratories in Princeton showed that their star performers were not those with the highest IQ, but those with the most successful interpersonal strategies. That's the attraction of employing more women, and it's why businesses are urgently researching how to build trust.

The full flowering of this idea is probably appearing—rather shockingly in its surprise value—in the courses run in American corporations by the British poet David Whyte. "Continually calling on its managers for more creativity, dedication, and adaptability, the American corporate world is tiptoeing for the first time in its short history into the very place from whence that dedication, creativity, and adaptability must come: the turbulent place where the soul of an individual is formed and finds expression. . . . The sound and the fury of an individual's creative life are the elemental waters missing from the dehydrated workday." Whyte said in his book *The Heart Aroused*—with the tremendous subtitle *Poetry and the Preservation of the Soul in Corporate America*.

Poetry at work, art in prisons, stories in the surgery, they are all an alternative approach to the dry analysis of numbers, and they have all emerged from the self-esteem movement. Their advocates say: "Forget the numbers for a minute. How do we inject humanity and life back into this situation?" Their answers are intuitive, disturbing sometimes, and impossible to measure directly. They tend to exalt creativity as a way of liberating the best in people. They are what would, in other circles, be called "holistic." Everything they stand for rejects the idea of chopping problems up into neat pieces, measuring them, and puzzling out what affects what.

VI

Blundering around in the fog while on holiday near the Santa Lucia Mountains in California in the early 1960s, the psychologist Abraham Maslow stumbled upon the retreat center where, a decade later, Vasconcellos would bring the battling legislators from Sacramento for a naked soak in the hot springs. The Esalen Institute was then attracting theologians like Paul Tillich, therapists like Carl Rogers, and mystics like Carlos Castaneda and was fast becoming one of the founding influences on the Summer of Love and the New Age movement.

It was an argument over Maslow, and the whole issue of whether there are different kinds of needs—from shelter to spiritual—that caused Vasconcellos and the new governor Ronald Reagan to fall out over dinner the first time they met. And it was Maslow's relationship with the Esalen Institute before he died in 1970 that popularized his so-called Hierarchy of Needs—now the basis of a great deal of modern marketing. He argued that you can't just measure people's needs and desires—they have lots of different ones. They start with food and clothing, and then when those are satisfied, they move up the hierarchy to shelter. And so on to needs like keeping up with the Joneses, and beyond that to some of the sophisticated consumers of today, in control of their needs for the lower steps of the ladder, who want fitness, education, self-improvement. Different aspects of their personality need different things at different times of their lives. You can't measure needs as if they are a simple issue you can put on a scale, even if people *really* want what they say they want. They don't, of course. They measure different aspects of their life differently, and see things differently at different periods. What makes them happy sometimes just doesn't work other times, and when five things are going well and one small thing remains wrong, they tend to focus on the final problem. There's no balance, no one scale, and there's certainly no bottom line.

Self-esteem, emotional intelligence, emotional literacy, all are ways of measuring the success of schools, which don't reduce human individuals and which can inject life, spirit, and significance back into the business of education—and medicine too. They are all symptoms of a shift away from too many numbers, which amount to the first glimmerings of a new kind of ideology. The danger is that, once the number crunchers get their hands on them, they are reduced again to technocratic and simplistic measures that leave the basic problems untouched. We can't escape from the basic problem, however much we might want to. There are no two ways about it: The best recruitment policy focuses on individual jobs and individual applicants. The best education policy focuses on each pupil individually. That may not be achievable in the short term, but it will always be true.

The idea of tailoring education policy to every pupil seems like a revolutionary idea, but something similar has been going on in business for years with the idea of what business guru Martha Rogers first called "mass customization"—that companies can customize products for each individual customer. Businesses are telling customers—as they say on the Levi Strauss Web site: "There's only one rule. Be original. Other than that, just be your self. Hopefully you're both." Wouldn't it be so much more effective if school or prison management could give up all these aggregated numbers and do the same?

In the meantime, ideas like self-esteem have managed to escape from the old closed-minded ideologies of the past, which forced the facts to fit the frame, providing a structure that brings common sense to bear on the dead world of figures, so we can see patterns again. We may not be able to measure trust—or feelgood or self-esteem—but we know what it is when we see it. That requires human institutions that make people happy in the round, and humans to run them. It doesn't need schools like factories that define learning in such a narrow way that it is sucked dry of all joy.

You can't measure these human attributes directly, but that doesn't mean they're not important. Quite the reverse: They are a different kind of bottom line altogether—one that doesn't reduce people or squeeze the truth. Or as Vasconcellos puts it: "*We* are the bottom line."

6

FREDERICK TAYLOR'S
TIME MACHINE

*Well, I can't prove it,
but I can smell it.*

Henry Ford

*As long as measurements are abused as a tool of control, measuring
will remain the weakest area in a manager's performance.*

Peter Drucker

PHILADEPHIA, 1878

I

WHEN A 25-YEAR-OLD machinist gets a promotion and suddenly
decides he is going to boost the output of his former peers, you can
expect that he won't stay popular too long. When he uses them to test
out his theories of time and efficiency, as guinea pigs on which he
would build his career as a management guru, there are really only two
things that can happen—abject failure or stunning success. In the case
of Frederick Taylor, it was the latter. It is said that nobody except Freud
and Darwin influenced the 20th century as much as he did.

By the end of Taylor's three-year battle with his coworkers' working
habits at the Midvale Steel Company in Philadelphia, most had been

sacked, others had finally succumbed to his definition of a fair day's work, and several had threatened his life. His youthful intransigence would stamp itself onto the coming century in the idea of "efficiency." It has led to the practice of measuring in factories and offices that has lasted ever since, to incentives, bonuses, and output ratios so complex that a whole army of middle managers would have to be recruited to police them. Half a century later, the ideas that he formulated at Midvale—attaching numbers to the way people worked—had been embraced by Henry Ford and Lenin alike.

II

Taylor had been promoted to subforeman in the machine shop at Midvale in 1878. It was his first managerial position. In those days, foremen were the lynchpin of American industry—strutting around in frock coats with the power to hire and fire at will. He had been a clerk in the accounts department before, but he hated it and asked to be moved onto the shop floor. For two months he worked alongside the others as a lathe machinist.

"Now, Fred," said one of his colleagues when he got his promotion, "you're not going to be a damn piecework hog, are you?" It was a reasonable question: Was their former colleague going to force more productivity out of them by manipulating the amount they were paid per job? The answer was that it was precisely what he was going to do. He was now part of management, Taylor explained, and—although he would react the same way in their place—they now had to knuckle down and do it his way.

For Taylor, that way meant the rite of the stopwatch. There had to be a scientific way of measuring exactly how much work a trained machinist—or any worker—could achieve each day. If that could be measured, and productivity increased accordingly, then the most productive workers could be paid more. As a result, there would be more leisure time and society could relax into a happy sense of efficiency and puritanical delight at a good day's work. That was the big idea: It was all about measuring and precision.

And so began the titanic struggle. If they didn't work hard enough, he had their wages cut. If they still didn't, he had them sacked—and these were the days of the 1870s depression, so jobs were hard to come by. If their machines broke down—it was common practice for workers to sabotage their own machines to demonstrate the strain of extra work—he made them pay for the costs of repair. If there was a scratch on their lathes, he fined them too. He fined one man $64, then as much as two months' pay—and when he broke his own machine, he fined himself. Soon he was getting death threats, but wandered home happily along the deserted railroad tracks oblivious to the danger. "They can shoot and be damned," he told his family, letting it be known around the factory that, if he was attacked, he wouldn't fight fair.

Decades later in 1912, he naively told a congressional hearing investigating his method that nobody really minded. "My anger and hard feelings were stirred up against the system, not against the men," he told them. "Practically all of those were my friends, and many of them still are my friends."

But by then he was a controversial prophet of what he called "scientific management" and people believed him. The late Victorians on both sides of the Atlantic thrived on precision and embraced Taylor's philosophy wholeheartedly. The great statistics they generated were recited with pride. When they weren't out measuring ants' nests or butterflies' wings, they would be reading their illustrated newspapers with articles packed with the most ridiculously precise numerical information. Darwin's nephew Francis Galton had even invented a series of hidden machines that could measure the dullness of meetings by noting the number of times a person fidgets, and he was testing out a statistical study on the effectiveness of prayer. The proud citizens of Philadelphia, for instance, knew that their population in 1880—during Taylor's struggle with his workforce—was precisely 847,170 and that in the previous financial year, the city had exported $49,649,693 worth of goods down the Delaware and across the oceans. Probably some of them even claimed the credit for the extra three dollars.

These were the great days of the city that had played host to William Penn and the Declaration of Independence, then the second biggest in the United States. Not only were those export figures more than 5 percent of the exports of the whole nation, but Philadelphia had recently hosted the enormous Centennial Exhibition, celebrating the first century of the Union. It's working population could be seen streaming off the dirty black ferries of the Delaware in the early mornings or onto the horse trams, bound for the great smelters, locomotive works, and carpet factories that were the source of the city's new wealth. Its affluent population could be seen strolling in the magnificent Fairmount Park, scene of the recent exhibition, past the zoo and sparkling new waterworks—pumping 100 million gallons of water into the city every day.

When Taylor moved from browbeating his staff to experimenting on them in the early 1880s, the American engineer Hiram Maxim was putting the finishing touches to his gun and the Scottish writer Robert Louis Stevenson was putting the finishing touches to *Treasure Island*. And on the opposite side of the Delaware River from Frederick Taylor, who lived in the Philadephia suburb of Germantown, lived the poet Walt Whitman—busy on his latest edition of *Leaves of Grass*, banned by the district attorney in Boston but embraced enthusiastically by a publisher in his own city.

On the face of it, the bearded author of "Song of Myself" and the inventor of time-and-motion study had nothing whatsoever in common. Whitman was receiving writers like Oscar Wilde on pilgrimage from Europe, while Taylor was dreaming of the vaster potential of his lathe. But actually there *was* something, and it was summed up in the word *democracy*. While Whitman was dreaming of a sturdy poetic democracy of the soul—something way beyond voting, let alone arithmetic—Taylor was dreaming about democracy of another kind: changing the economics of work so that ordinary workers could share in the spoils of time and money. He wanted to create factories so efficient that they set the people who worked there free—to earn more and to play more.

They were great men of entirely different kinds, but both dreamers and both ever so slightly hypocritical in their way. Whitman always was a loner, never a politician of any kind. One thing Taylor never did was play. But if Whitman created a kind of democratic dream that molded the 20th century, Taylor molded the new century in much more concrete terms. He also created the workplace of the future: timed, tested, measured, production-lined, ever striving for greater efficiency.

It wasn't just Taylor, of course—it never is. He happened to be born into a moment in industrial history when change was in the air. The 1880s was the first era of the great mergers by titanic corporations, as the so-called "robber barons" battled to consolidate their power, like medieval Machiavellian princes, discarding the old idea that business was subject to ordinary morality. "He must be able to glide over every moral restraint with almost childlike disregard," wrote John Rockefeller, describing the kind of employee he would be willing to pay a million dollars, "and has, besides other positive qualities, no scruples whatsoever and be ready to kill off thousands of victims—without a murmur."

Not surprisingly, this kind of amoral drive led to massive economic change. After the Civil War, two-thirds of American factory workers were employed in textile and shoe factories. In Taylor's time it was steel and shipbuilding and railways, and soon it would be cars. The first precision machines were appearing, and the first electric lights meant machinery could be run without shafts and moving belts driving the machines, which in turn meant airier factories and more natural light. In the six years before Taylor went to work, 3,000 miles of new railroad had been laid and opened across the United States.

Bentham's counting helped make the Industrial Revolution possible. Counting was used by Malthus and Chadwick to calculate its effects. But it was Taylor who first took numbers into industry itself, at least with precision, in an attempt to control the processes that went on there so mysteriously in the half-light behind the conveyor belts. As a result, he has been held responsible for the production line, for consumerism, for the gas chambers, for class warfare, and also for the final defeat of communism—and probably he was in a small way responsible for all of them. But if he was, he used an extremely simple tool: the stopwatch. It was Taylor's stopwatch that defined his life and, as we shall see, his death as well.

III

Frederick Winslow Taylor was born on March 20, 1856, into a prominent family of Quaker "aristocracy," in an upper-middle-class suburb of Philadelphia. His father had a private income: One contemporary described him as "born retired." His mother was an early feminist and abolitionist. As young Fred was growing up, it seems likely that they were harboring escaped slaves. By the time he was six, he was taking part in home-guard practice during the Civil War. Soon a brand-new monument to the Union dead would find its way into their home suburb.

As a teenager he spent time with his parents in Europe and was entirely indifferent to the art his father demanded that he should enjoy, a characteristic he shared with Bentham. But he was bitten by the European obsession with collecting and measuring birds' eggs and by the English obsession with cricket—which, as anyone who has played it will know, is so slow-moving that the statistics and batting averages are more interesting than the game. Cricket was popular among the well-to-do in Germantown those days.

But like Bentham and Chadwick, Taylor was at heart an inventive utilitarian. By the end of his life he held 40 lucrative patents. At a frighteningly early age he had invented a brake for a bobsled, a special tennis racket with a spoon-shaped head and—to the fascination of his biographers—a special harness to stop him from having nightmares. He discovered he had these "disturbing thoughts" only when he rolled onto his back at night, so he designed the gadget to dig into his dorsal muscles until he woke. For the rest of his life, he used to sleep sitting up. Like Bentham, he used to go through the most bizarre rituals before actually going to bed, and seemed to resent losing control of his highly disciplined mind the moment he fell asleep.

He never smoked or drank alcohol, tea, or coffee. When he went to dances he drew up strange charts classifying all the girls into attractive and ugly and calculated his time so he spent precisely half conversing with each. It sounds awfully like his nightmares were sexual dreams, which fell foul of what he called his "whale of a New England conscience," and he was subduing the flesh to force his mind back into control.

But if he wasn't subduing the flesh, he was subduing the spirit. He never rested and he never played. Even his golf was a series of experiments with special long-handled golf clubs of his own invention. When it came to the point of relaxing, he could never quite see why. There were things to do, gadgets to invent, calculations and experiments to be made, and a reputation to be won.

He was accepted into Harvard and dropped out without even taking up his place because of fears that his eyesight was failing, but that didn't seem to stop him from coming home and joining the Enterprise Hydraulic Works as an apprentice. Nor did it stop him from studying at night while he held down a full-time job. For four years, he would start at the factory at 6:30 A.M., work there until 5:10 P.M., walk two miles home—occasionally do a bit of volunteer work—then go to bed. But then he would set his alarm on for 2:00 A.M., dress in his work clothes, and study until 5:00 A.M., catch half an hour's sleep, then the 6:00 A.M. train to work. It was a punishing schedule: It probably wasn't surprising that his colleagues laughed at him for it, but it seemed to improve his eyesight.

He didn't get his engineering qualification until 1883, which meant this schedule continued throughout the battle of wills with his workers and the start of his long experimentation with lathes and a stopwatch to spread his ideas to the plant as a whole. Midvale's president, William Sellers, also promoted the young Taylor before he graduated.

Taylor absolutely worshiped Sellars for his bluff ways and violent remarks. "Now, young man, I know that you are a fool," Sellars told him when he asked to start the lathe experiments. "But I'm going to let you go right ahead and spend that money to prove you are a fool." And he let him carry on doing the highly inconvenient experiments—continually turning the machinery on and off through the day as he measured and timed. Taylor had the freedom to analyze which tools were most effective and what kinds of steel were most productive in order to calculate how much work each employee should do each day. Scientific management entails regimented experimentation, and Taylor's experiments went like this:

First, you break down any job into its component parts—as far as it would go, to the basic movements.

Next, you time each of those parts with a stopwatch to find out just how quickly they can be achieved by the quickest and most efficient workers.

Next, you get rid of any parts of the job that aren't necessary.

Then you add in about 40 percent to the time for unavoidable delays and rest. This bit was what he used to call "rule of thumb" before the idea of scientific management required that there be no such thing. It was always one of the most controversial parts of the package—a clear example of Counting Paradox #5 (see chapter 3), that the more accurately we measure, the more unreliable the figures.

Finally, you organize your pay system so that the most efficient people can earn considerably more money by meeting the optimum times, while the average have to struggle to keep up.

Of course there was much more to it than that. Taylor later argued that it was about scientific recruitment too, appointing the most efficient people in the first place. There were also his systems to centralize authority into one office, keeping track of the timings on every job, allocating costs job by job, and—above all—standardizing timings, machine tools, systems, and people. That was the core.

It helped that Taylor was the kind of man he was. He responded favorably to the great arrogant bullies who used to run factories in those days. He smiled all the time, and he was also probably the most willing and determined employee Midvale had ever had. When a large drain was blocked in the factory, and a team of men with rods failed to clear it, Taylor crawled in himself, narrowly avoided being drowned in black slime, fought past the obstruction, cleared it, and forced his way out again. His skin was stained the color of the slime for a week afterward.

And he swore. Apart from his habitual blue suit and his trim 1880s mustache, Taylor's swearing was the most noticeable thing about him for the rest of his life. He did it for effect and always when you least expected it. He never swore at work. Instead he swore in front of his puritanical mother, or during his lectures at Harvard. It was human and slightly shocking for those who couldn't categorize him—but then of course Taylor had invented a whole new category for himself. He was the very first "knowledge worker," according to the great management pioneer Peter Drucker. Nobody knew then how management gurus or knowledge workers were supposed to behave. Maybe the new breed would swear all the time.

Taylor's swearing was partly for effect, and it was about as emotional as he got. But it was also an attempt to demonstrate whose side he was on. Because whatever they said about him—and his opponents said a lot—he didn't see himself on the side of the factory owners, and he certainly wasn't on the side of the financiers, whom he despised. He saw himself on the side of the workers. That was why he spoke like that, and why he tried—and failed—to learn how to chew tobacco. That was why there were no strikes at Midvale for 14 years, he claimed: because the workers there were able to use his system to earn high wages. Yet the workers never regarded Taylor as being on their side: It was as if he was trying to "rescue them from themselves." They regarded Taylor's stopwatch not as an aid for earning more money but as a tyrannical instrument of control.

The trouble was that Taylor's ideal worker wasn't really a human being at all. He was a cog—an automaton that did what he was told. "Every day, year in and year out, each man should ask himself over and over again, two questions," said Taylor in his standard lecture. "First, 'What is the name of the man I am now working for?' And having answered this definitely then, 'What does this man want me to do, right now?' Not, 'What ought I to do in the interests of the company I am working for?' Not, 'What are the duties of the position I am filling?' Not, 'What did I agree to do when I came here?' Not, 'What should I do for my own best interest?' but plainly and simply, 'What does this man want me to do?' "

Yes, it was obedience Taylor wanted, and as he got older he got angrier when he didn't get it. Taylor never really grasped that people could never be as efficient as machinery—especially not if you measured efficiency in the way he did, which meant keeping up with the speed of the machines. It was an absolutely basic mistake and it had far-reaching consequences.

IV

Soon Taylor was putting his new techniques into practice all over Mid-vale, applying the same system of measurements to unloading pig iron or changing lightbulbs. When Midvale was sold and Sellars pushed out, Taylor ran a disastrous paper company in Maine and tried far less suc-cessfully to do the same there. He tried to rescue an equally disastrous bicycle ball-bearings factory in Massachusetts. He carried out his famous measuring experiments with shovels and as a result designed a new shovel with the optimum carrying capacity. He measured the Link-Belt Company, a machine-engineering company that became his showcase, until everyone was blue in the face. It was all fiddling until he got his big break.

Taylor's grand culmination came in 1898. The steel industry was under investigation at the time because of the way it priced armor plate for the new generation of ironclad battleships shooting down the slip-ways all over the world. Bethlehem Steel, just outside Philadelphia, turned out to be selling it to the Russian navy for $250 a ton and to the U.S. Navy for $600 a ton. When Congress dug a little bit deeper, it turned out that European manufacturers had been "squared" by their American colleagues so that they didn't tell Congress about prices. The resulting battle over how far the price should drop threatened to under-mine the cozy understanding between Bethlehem and its rivals at Carnegie, led by steel magnate Andrew Carnegie's Machiavellian lieu-tenant Charles Schwab. Somehow the steel mills had to cut the cost of production, and that's where Taylor came in.

He started characteristically by making a major enemy of Bethle-hem's machine shop superintendent, Harry Leibert—who made it his task from then on to frustrate Taylor at every move. And there were a lot of moves. The plants had to be shifted around. The tools had to be tested and replaced with standardized models. The new tools had to be measured in place so that the piecework rates could be calculated. It all took time, Taylor's most valuable commodity.

So to avoid the unwelcome attentions of Leibert—who seemed to be winning over Bethlehem's boss, Robert Linderman—Taylor decided to try out his science first in the plant yard. And it was there that he met the man he used for the rest of his life as the model for his tech-niques.

The work in the plant yard involved lifting pig iron. It was work so crude, as he put it, that it could have been done by an "intelligent gorilla." And that was just the way Taylor liked it. After working with a gang of 20 Hungarians and a stopwatch, he worked it all out—the "best men" could lift 75 tons of pig iron a day, six times the previous average. If you allow the usual "rule of thumb" of 40 percent for rest and necessary delays, that came to a total of 45 tons a day. Anyone who managed that would be able to earn 46 percent extra, but most of them probably wouldn't make their usual rate of $1.15 a day.

The experiment started in earnest on March 16, 1899, with the "best" men, who immediately refused to work on that basis and were sacked. Taylor then tried Dutch and Irish workers. They wouldn't budge either and went the same way. By offering higher wages there and then, Taylor and his assistants managed to attract volunteers, but by the end of May he reckoned he could really describe only a miserable 3 out of his team of 40 as "first-class men." It was another frustrating example of people's failure to emulate machinery. "Most of the rest break down after two or three days," he exclaimed with disgust.

It soon became clear that even the three strongest men could manage to carry weight only for exactly 42 percent of the day. Any more, and they got exhausted. It doesn't seem to have occurred to Taylor that, when even the strongest human beings were pretty different, you couldn't standardize them in this way either.

But one of those three just carried on. He was called Henry Noll—or Knolle, according to which account you read—and Taylor named him "Schmidt" in almost everything he wrote, describing him as "stupid and phlegmatic." Or, with just a hint of excitement, as "an ox." Noll was Taylor's great example: He was what he really wanted working men to be—focused, uncomplicated, and compliant.

"If you are a high priced man, you will do exactly as this man tells you tomorrow, from morning to night. When he tells you to pick up a pig, and walk, you pick it up and walk," Taylor told Noll, sounding like a strange perversion of one of Christ's healing miracles. "And when he tells you to sit down and rest you sit down. You do that straight through the day. And what's more, no back talk."

Yes, it was tough to talk to people like that, Taylor agreed in his lectures later, but Noll or Schmidt was "the mentally sluggish type"—just the way he wanted it. He was the model worker. Noll lived until 1925, and history doesn't relate whether he appreciated this kind of fame.

By 1901, the workforce at Bethlehem was handling three times as much material as before and their wages were 60 percent higher. One of their workshops was probably the most modern in the world. But Leibert had encouraged management to doubt the whole enterprise, and they were anyway angry with Taylor for all his sackings. As well as running the steel plant, Bethlehem needed workers to rent their local homes, and Taylor seemed intent on emptying the company villages of tenants.

Taylor was also getting frustrated at having to fight every step of the way. He was becoming prone to violent outbursts if anyone questioned his orders, and—overworked and unstable—he gave Bethlehem an ultimatum to stop interfering if they wanted him to stay. He popped it in the internal mail and unwisely left for a golfing holiday. When he came back he found the following letter waiting for him on his desk. "Dear Sir," it said. "I beg to advise you that your services will not be required by this company after May 1st, 1901. Yours truly, Robt. P. Linderman, President."

A month later, Linderman sold Bethlehem to Schwab. The great experiment was over.

V

Taylor never worked for anyone else again. He lived off his patents and set up as the first management consultant, earning the then massive fee of $35 a day, traveling around the country giving his standard two-hour lecture—with Schmidt as the model worker—and sending disciples out as consultants in his place.

By the time he left Bethlehem, Taylor was already well known. His inglorious end there didn't diminish his fame. Nor did the consistent—and insistent—complaints of the workers. When he read a paper to the American Society of Mechanical Engineers in Saratoga Springs in 1903, it was hailed as the "most important contribution ever presented to the society and one of the most important ever published in the United States." Eight years later, in 1911, everything seemed to be coming together.

That year saw the publication of Taylor's book, *Principles of Scientific Management*, one of the most influential management books ever written—and probably also one of the shortest: It was basically Taylor's standard two-hour speech. It was serialized in *The American Magazine* and was acclaimed an enormous success. "It is no small matter when a man arises who can show us new ways of commanding our environment," wrote editor Ray Stannard Baker, breathlessly. It wasn't the last time Taylor would be hailed in such messianic terms.

The same year, he was contacted by the campaigning lawyer Louis Brandeis—later a justice of the Supreme Court—who was working for a group of East Coast trade associations trying to fight higher transport fees from the railroad companies. The companies said they had put up wages and therefore needed to put up prices. Brandeis sensed that Taylor's expertise could provide an alternative. Together they dubbed it the "Million a Day Savings Plan" and it made Taylor into a national figure.

Suddenly Taylor was demanded at platforms all over the world, hailed as a leader of a new technocratic age—a sort of John the Baptist for the coming Great Efficient Leader, who would be able to measure the nation objectively and make it efficient. This dream was to remain a fascination among technocrats for the first half of the century, until Hitler emerged as just such a leader and the world drew back in horror about what numerical efficiency too objective for morality might mean.

VI

Like so many of the great quantifiers, Taylor's numbers and timings were about control. Taylor's systems meant moment-to-moment control by managers of everything going on in the factory, just as—four centuries before—Pacioli's bookkeeping allowed merchants to have day-by-day control of their finances, even though their stock might be on the high seas. It meant that a central management office in every factory could control every aspect of the work, job by job, in a flurry of paperwork and cost allocations—a revolution in time study but also in accountancy. From the center of their web—like the jailer in Bentham's Panopticon prison—Taylor's managers could watch the numbers changing in the factory.

It wasn't just Taylor, of course. It was also the spirit of the time. But it was Taylor's measurements that were having the most profound changes on the way factories were run. When he took the train to downtown Philadelphia for his first job, his colleagues at Midvale were craftsmen who brought their own tools and their own ways of working to the factory gates in the morning. They learned on seven-year apprenticeships where they wrote nothing down but learned by doing. The true authority, the bottom line, in any factory was their know-how and skill. By the time Taylor had taken early retirement as a consultant—thanks largely to his own work—tools were becoming standardized and provided by the factory, and every aspect of skilled work was subject to measurement. It wasn't skilled anymore. The managers knew better than the workers did how to do the workers' jobs.

When Taylor started, the foremen were usually rather unbenevolent despots. Usually they were the only ones in the factory who knew how many they had personally hired and fired that week. The personnel policy of the foreman of one Philadelphia factory at the time meant throwing apples at the crowd by the gates in the morning and hiring the people who caught them.

It was brutal system of happy inefficiency. The foreman was in charge of ordering materials, and most ordered just a little extra to help with odd jobs around the place. By the time Taylor had finished, every job had an order number and exactly enough material for the order assigned to it—ordered by the new middle managers, who hired, fired, calculated, and decided. All the foreman had to do was to make sure the workers understood what they were supposed to do and did it.

It wasn't just a factory revolution; it was a social revolution too. Taylorism meant a new class of middle managers between the factory owners and the newly unskilled workers. There they were, filling the new upper-middle-class suburbs of the great centers of American manufacturing—Chicago, Cincinnati, and Philadelphia—with their respectable white collars, making Taylor's new administrative machines work. The social distinctions were exploding. No longer could a wealthy young man like Taylor go into the factory as an apprentice without eyebrows being raised; he would be a middle manager instead—though Taylor himself would have hated it.

The irony was that Taylor missed the foremen. He didn't want to work with the fastidious new middle managers, and he certainly didn't want to work for the financiers. He wanted what he called a "large-minded man" like Sellars. But the middle managers, trained to be focused and conservative, were only the first to replace men like Taylor's hero. Whether he liked it or not, Taylor had succeeded in reengineering the whole business world. It took a long time for anyone, with the possible exception of the workers themselves, to acknowledge that Taylor only had one-half of the equation.

VII

It was a meeting in New York City in 1907 that turned "scientific management" into a movement beyond Taylor. None of their biographers agree exactly where it was, but either in a lobby of an engineering building or at his colleague Henry Gantt's flat, he finally met Frank Gilbreth, the motion expert who matched his own time expertise.

Gilbreth was a vast, flamboyant former bricklayer turned contractor, turned advertiser, turned consultant. By careful analysis, Gilbreth had managed to reduce the number of movements you need to lay bricks, increasing his output from 1,000 to 2,700 a day. It became the basis for his success. By the age of 27, he had offices in New York, Boston, and London, a yacht, and lots of cigars. Two of his 12 children wrote an affectionate portrait of him in *Cheaper by the Dozen*, later a Hollywood film showing Clifton Webb as Gilbreth—with his stopwatch out—checking how long it took each of his kids to welcome him home from the office, urging them to shave another few seconds off their kissing time.

Gilbreth was obsessed with measuring, breaking down every manual operation into what he called "therbligs" (Gilbreth spelled backward). He buttoned his vest from the bottom up because it took four seconds less than buttoning it from the top down. He cut 17 seconds off his shaving time by using two brushes. Using two shavers cut 44 seconds, but then he cut himself and had to spend another two minutes looking for a plaster. He took most of his children with him on business trips and around factories, armed with pens and pads, but their home in Montclair, New Jersey, sounded a bit like Taylor's factories:

> Dad installed process and work charts in the bathrooms. Every child old enough to write—and Dad expected his offspring to start writing at a tender age—was required to initial the chart in the morning, after he had brushed his teeth, taken a bath, combed his hair, and made his bed. At night each child had to weigh himself, plot the figure on a graph and initial the process charts again after he had done his homework, washed his hands and face, and brushed his teeth. Mother wanted to have a place on the chart for saying prayers, but Dad said as far as he was concerned, prayers were voluntary.

Taylor and Gilbreth together were a powerful combination: Taylor provided the stopwatch and Gilbreth and his wife, Lillian, provided the photography. Time-and-motion study was their joint baby. The trouble was, Taylor and Gilbreth never really agreed. Gilbreth's work wasn't primarily about counting, it was about analyzing movements. His "micro-motion" study involved cameras as much as stopwatches: as much to do with judgment and imagination as measurement. He also handled people better. There were no big disturbances at plants where Gilbreth worked—unlike the pandemonium that was beginning to break out the moment Taylor walked through the door of a new factory.

But Taylor's associates were deeply suspicious of Gilbreth from the first, describing him as a "great bluffer." They finally fell out over Gilbreth's work at the Hermann Aukum Company, where Gilbreth showed them how to cut the number of movements folding handkerchiefs from 150 to 16, and Gilbreth charged $35,000 for what Taylor called "trifling work." Taylor accused him of being in it "solely for the money"—ironic, since that was normally the only motivation he would accept or understand in his workers.

The Gilbreths counterattacked. Although Gilbreth had set up the Taylor Society—meeting once a month in Keen's Chop House in New York City—by 1920, he and Lillian were attacking time study as unethical and "absolutely worthless."

If Taylor was the father of the production line by breaking functions and decisions down into basic units, the Gilbreths were the parents of expert systems—and therefore of modern software. And although Frank died as early as 1924—maybe it wasn't a coincidence that the time study pioneers didn't tend to live long—Lillian became one of the great names in industrial psychology and lived long enough to witness Neil Armstrong on the moon. Time, in that sense, was on the side of the Gilbreths, although micro-motion study had since evolved into other arenas.

Taylor was destined to leave a more potent legacy, but his personal record of success was dwindling. Trouble really started when he took his methods into the most unionized factories in the country, the enormous government-run arsenals. The Machinists Union at the Watertown Arsenal, just outside Boston—which made gun carriages out of 4,500 different components, responded to time study with a weeklong strike in 1911. They were followed shortly afterward by the Rock Island Arsenal, even though nobody had even uttered the word "stopwatch" there. Soon congressmen were trying to have the whole idea investigated.

Taylor had to face two lengthy congressional inquiries into his methods, gathering evidence, lobbying, and giving evidence himself—just as Louisa began to suffer from serious depression and need his almost constant attention. Under heavy questioning from union leaders during one congressional hearing, he lost his cool completely. Presumably it was his famous swearing that led to his remarks being stricken from the record.

By then, Taylor was under enormous strain—leading the movement and caring almost full-time for his wife, as well as looking after their three adopted children. He never had time to prepare new lectures. At meetings he seemed abrupt and bad tempered. He never was very good at dealing with people who questioned his thinking; now he was downright bad at it. Worse still, the trade union opposition was still rising. In 1915, Congress passed a law that banned stopwatches from government factories. It stayed on the statute books until 1949. Factory workers the world over were beginning to fight back.

French factory owners had taken to the logic of Taylor's ideas like the Japanese would to Deming a generation later, but the Renault car workers responded immediately by going on strike too. Taylor had no patience: "If a man deliberately goes against the experience of men who know what they are talking about, and refuses to follow advice given in a kind but unmistakable way, it seems to me that he deserves to get into trouble." It was the number crunching philosophy laid bare, and it wasn't very attractive.

By the winter of 1914, when the European armies were beginning to slug it out at Mons and Ypres—the scale of slaughter made possible by industrial mass production—Taylor was mentally and physically exhausted. He caught a chill lecturing in Cleveland the following March and caught pneumonia while he was visiting his sister in Philadelphia. The doctors carried out rigorous tests and confidently predicted he would recover.

Every morning in hospital, he would get out of bed briefly at the same time and wind his precious watch. On her rounds at 4:30 A.M. on March 21, the nurse noticed that he was winding his watch hours earlier than usual, and vaguely wondered why. When she came back half an hour later, he was dead. It was the day after his 59th birthday.

VIII

When Taylor died winding his watch, his book was already available in eight languages. He wasn't the first to break work down into its elements—Adam Smith and the computing pioneer Charles Babbage had done the same—but he was the first one to do it so rigorously and to measure it so precisely. His work led to a whole new class of number crunchers and specialists with clipboards. As late as 1991, one GM assembly-line worker was referring to them as "techno-cretins," whose annual presentations he described as "one long lullaby of foreign terminology, slides, numerology, and assorted high-tech masturbation." Workplaces would be the same until Bill Gates encouraged his staff to come to work in jeans.

Taylor's ideas caught the imagination at the start of the century. Before the First World War, Theodore Roosevelt was calling for "national efficiency." Immediately afterward, the French prime minister Georges Clemenceau and the Soviet leader Lenin were both urging their factories to adopt Taylor's methods. Soon the ideas had spread to offices. New personnel departments were created within companies that put Taylor's ideas into effect—with batteries of intelligence and aptitude tests, trying to recruit the "best" men and women, trying to approach work in a measurable, scientific way. Consultants around the world struggled to find the atomic units of movement, reaching, turning, moving, and grasping. Every manager had a thick tome called *The Manual of Standard Time Data for Offices*. Clerks and secretaries were timed for their dictation, letter writing, form filling, and procedure. Offices became like factories—like the fearsome desks stretching away into the distance in *The Apartment*, as Jack Lemmon struggles with the figures to get the key to the executive washroom.

Soon there was the first modern management consultant, James McKinsey—he of the fallacy—putting Taylor's idea that you could measure anything into practice. There was Cyril Burt, the first industrial psychologist, trying to find one measure of intelligence that could apply to everyone—whose discredited IQ tests condemned a generation of British children to lifetime success or failure determined at the age of 11. But the greatest of Taylor's followers claimed never to have heard of him. In Detroit, the pioneer car maker Henry Ford had been watching the moving conveyor belt of dead cows in a Chicago slaughterhouse when he hit on the idea of the assembly line—the ultimate tying of the workforce to the rhythm of the machines.

The results were astonishing. Before the production line started at Ford's River Rouge plant, each Model T Ford took 12-and-a-half hours to build. Eight months later, with the line plus Taylor-style standardization, it took just 93 minutes. Soon there were six lines roaring away.

And although the first Model Ts came in blue, red, green, and two shades of gray, Ford realized that mass production and mass consumerism meant absolute standardization. In the end it had to be "any color you like, as long as it's black."

Ford and Taylor were two of a kind. Both despised Wall Street, both prided themselves on their practicality, both successfully managed to raise basic wages, yet they spent their later lives battling trade unions. Neither of them liked books much. "They muss up my mind," said Ford. For Ford, as it was for Taylor, labor wasn't supposed to be about skills. People's skills were supposed to be available for their community *after* work; at work they should be cogs in a giant machine that set the pace and forced them into line.

Yes, Taylorism was the first management fad. Its critics point at the worst excesses of 20th-century inhumanity—the slaughter of the First World War, the hideous efficiency of the Nazi gas chambers—as results of the standardization of people. When Taylor's follower Morris Cooke urged that the First World War should be "managed scientifically," that isn't quite what he meant—but that's what happened. Of course, it depends what the military commanders were being efficient with, what resources simply couldn't be sacrificed. Unfortunately, on the western front, it was the machines. The men were disposable.

But while Ford was pushing Taylor's ideas to one extreme in the United States, a particularly hideous perversion of them was appearing in the Soviet Union, as the artists of the new regime tried to develop a "pure proletarian" culture. There was the bizarre Symphony of Labor, performed in 1922 by workers and soldiers from Baku, with instruments including aircraft engines, cannons, and factory sirens. Or, even worse, there was the enthusiasm of poet Andrei Gastev—a great admirer of Taylor's and author of "Factory Whistles, Rails and Tower"— for "the idea of subordinating people to mechanisms and the mechanization of man." The new regime approved so much that they made him director of the Central Institute of Labor. Or worse still, the new Soviet acting school inspired by what Taylor called "biomechanics," where every movement was supposed to be simplified, rational, and without any kind of intuition. Biomechanics was supposed to be the kind of acting that workers could take up in their spare time. It received its premiere in 1922 with a tedious play called *The Magnanimous Cuckold*.

IX

Managerial science isn't like that anymore. Modern management gurus are mysterious types, theologians almost, whose theories and practices go beyond number. They know the numbers don't really add up anymore. They are the witch doctors of modern times, but we're now in a very different climate from the one where Taylor hammered out his stopwatch measurements. Taylor's efficiency doesn't work now. His hierarchies of control became too slow moving, so the downsizing of the early 1990s got rid of them. His office workers and unskilled laborers are disappearing from Western factories, replaced by robots in the North and highly unscientific sweatshops in the South. In a world where an Internet venture could be worth more than the biggest aircraft manufacturers in the world, production doesn't matter in quite the same way.

It still matters, of course. Somebody has to deliver what you've bought online—as the failing e-commerce ventures discovered to their cost—but it isn't the first problem on the minds of the financiers or the share traders.

But in a sense, we still have Taylor's spirit with us. We still search for best practice, benchmark it, and subdue our outlying organizational empires to the same figures. We still redesign the business processes; we still reengineer a couple of corporations before breakfast every morning. But in the Internet age, the old measures don't work anymore. That's the counting crisis for you.

In a way, they never did work very well. The grand old man of management wisdom, Peter Drucker, hailed Taylor as the first knowledge worker—increasing wealth with the application of know-how alone, and far more influential than Marx. But he also pointed out his fundamental errors.

Most important—and unfortunately—Taylor measured human beings like machines, which is why he always felt they were malfunctioning. Like Bentham and Sherlock Holmes, Taylor wanted to remove emotion entirely. Like Gradgrind, he wanted nothing but facts—but the world just isn't like that. The important aspects of it can't be measured. Part of the problem was that, like other number crunchers, Taylor was determined his methods should be seen as "scientific." He retraced his steps and cut out any reference to "rule of thumb." There should be no value judgments at all in scientific management.

The trouble was, without the rule of thumb, it wasn't very accurate.

Nobody, however oxlike, can work at full tilt all day, and there has to be a rule of thumb somewhere, simply because everybody is different. The *l'homme moyen*—average man—just doesn't help. It's the wrong mold.

The second fundamental mistake, according to Drucker, was that Taylor divorced planning from doing, when they should have been part of the same job. It was like separating swallowing from digesting, he said. No wonder the workforce was resistant to change: They were being given only part of a job to do. The truth was that, although Taylor could push up productivity in their present job, he did so by undermining their ability to work well in their next job—let alone the one after that—because he didn't train their minds or allow them to use their imagination or initiative.

The great weakness of Taylor's world was that workers weren't supposed to use their imagination or initiative. He wanted them like Noll, "stupid and phlegmatic"—and in the end that wasn't very efficient. It took more than half a century for management to grasp that this kind of centralized control made organizations lumbering and stupid themselves. But by the late 1980s, competition was about speed and imagination—not production and authority. A staff with no initiative was too much of a luxury.

His cult of the technocrat meant that experts were supposed to change not just the workplace but the whole of society. By 1907, Taylor had come to believe his approach could be applied to the nation as a whole. He thoroughly shocked Harvard president Charles Eliot in a lecture there attacking the new business schools: Graduates in industry should be subject to the same rigid discipline and same hours as the men they were about to manage, he said. On the contrary, said Eliot in his reply. Harvard wanted to encourage "men having personal initiative and the faculty of independent thought." He could raise to power a whole cadre of technocrats to tinker with the way it all worked, measure it, and make it efficient. Or as Ross Perot put it nine decades later, "get under the hood."

This was the third fatal error that Drucker never mentioned. Taylor may have allowed the free market to beat Marxism by working "smarter," but if he did, he also made 20th-century offices just a little like totalitarian regimes. "When the Berlin Wall fell we instinctively knew that the nearest we had to an East European dictatorship was the workplace," said the poet and business consultant David Whyte. The cold war battled against a system of mind control that had its echo in the free-market office: There wasn't any democracy, but they'd look after you if you did what you were told.

Taylor's revolution led to the standardization of things, but it also led to the standardization of people—and that could never work. The less it worked, the more frantically the management accountants tried to measure it. The more they measured, the more customers and staff leapt out of the measurements and went their own sweet way. And thank goodness for that.

X

Toward the end of his life, even Taylor became aware something was missing. As well as everything else, he was also a tragic mixture of Henry Ford and Lord Baden-Powell, and he didn't really believe in fun. He read the occasional adventure story, about clean living, strong-limbed young men. His favorite character was Hopalong Cassidy. He saw sport as a branch of work, urging his adopted sons out to "get into the game" by playing baseball with much older boys. Like other pioneering utilitarians, he would stand in front of pictures and wonder what made them great. He would try to puzzle out the scientific laws behind ethics and religion. By his late fifties, his thoughts had become so obsessive that he could work for only half a day at a time. John Stuart Mill's old malaise was reaching out to him.

What are you trying to save time *for*? one of Gilbreth's children asked their father. "For work, if you love that best," he replied. "For education, for beauty, for art, for pleasure. For mumblety-peg, if that's where your heart lies."

But for Taylor, none of that made sense. He despised art, took no pleasure, and seriously doubted the value of education. In a world that does nothing but measure and count, you save time so you can save time. The modern world is a little like that, and in our heart of hearts—as we struggle to slice a few minutes between traffic lights—we know it.

TOWARD AN ETHICAL
PROFIT LINE

*Grown-ups love figures. When you tell them that you've made a
new friend, they never ask you any questions about essential
matters. They never say to you "What does his voice sound like?
What games does he love best? Does he collect butterflies?"
Instead they demand "How old is he? How much does he weigh?
How much money does his father make?" Only from these figures
do they think they have learned anything about him.*

Antoine de Saint-Exupéry, *The Little Prince*

First comes fodder, then comes morality.

Bertolt Brecht

I

INFORMATION IS THE new money. Torrents of it flow through the
world's computer networks every day. It's the flow of global information
rather than money—information about value, facts, measurements,
and indices—that makes the world go round. It's information that lay
behind the gigantic instantaneous fortunes of the Internet billionaires.

Our current perception of information goes back to 1959, which is
when management guru Peter Drucker published his book *Landmarks of
Tomorrow*. In it, he coined the powerful phrase "knowledge workers" to
describe the footloose, innovative people whose business is the manip-

ulation of information or the creation of world-beating ideas. It is strange to think that within those four decades since Drucker's prediction, knowledge workers have already come to make up more than a third of the whole U.S. workforce.

Drucker later described how one of largest U.S. defense contractors did a survey in the 1980s to find out what kind of information was needed to do the job effectively. "The search for answers soon revealed that whole layers of management—perhaps as many as six out of a total of fourteen—existed only because these questions had not been asked before," he wrote. "The company had data galore. It had always used its copious data for control rather than for information."

It was a familiar pattern and it still is, because information and knowledge mean different things. You can have too much information. But apart from the futurists who think our brains are about to explode with future shock, nobody believes you can possibly have too much knowledge.

There's another difference too. You can put information into figures, tables, and graphs, but you can't necessarily do the same with knowledge. Ironically, most organizations and bureaucracies very much prefer information, which they know as "data." Knowledge, often simply informal know-how that people exchange over coffee or a cigarette, often gets ignored because it can't be measured. Often the people who hold it are the first victims of downsizing.

This fascination for measuring "knowledge" and "learning" is the latest in a century-long struggle by business to isolate the figures that determine success. Time-and-motion pioneers like Frederick Taylor measured efficiency, realizing how much this know-how could improve the profitability of a factory, but he missed out on a key asset. His colleagues had no interest at all in the knowledge, wisdom, and skill locked up in the heads of their human cogs. Only in the knowledge of the men in white coats.

Half a century later, it was the advent of Total Quality Management, an attempt to measure quality by the American business guru W. Edwards Deming, that launched the modern business dash to measure the immeasurable. It was a matter of counting the production mistakes, instead of just throwing them away and forgetting them, then finding out why they were happening and eliminating them completely. Deming was also one of the first of what became a herd of trampling American management gurus, but in those days he was ignored by his compatriots. Only the Japanese took any notice.

"Why is it that productivity increases as quality improves?" he asked on the first page of his book *Out of the Crisis*. It is hard to remember that, until recently, most Western companies were obsessed with how much it might cost to make sure their services and products were good enough. They were afraid that too much effort put into improving quality would cut their profits. They ignored Deming's answers to his own question, which were: "less rework" and "not so much waste." Yet the Japanese businesses that adopted them found that, just by counting these things differently, a whole world of greater profitability opened up.

Deming's idea took flight after Japanese engineers studied the quality-control literature from Bell Laboratories. The company had seconded some of their engineers to General Douglas MacArthur's staff occupying Japan. And by 1950, every top management meeting in Japan had this "less rework" mantra up on the blackboard behind them. So when Deming went out there the following year to give a lecture tour on his statistics, they were so pleased to see him, they created the Deming Award in his honor. It soon became the most coveted industrial prize in Japan.

Deming had a rival Total Quality guru, J. W. Juran, who took a similar idea and applied it to any business at all—from manufacturing to offices. Both were understood only in Japan, and they managed to carry on the feud between them well into their late '80s. Perhaps this was because they were so similar: Both grew up in tarpaper shacks, Deming in Minnesota, Juran in Wyoming—though he had actually been born in Romania. Both were influenced by the Bell Laboratories physicist Walter Shewhart, the man who turned statistical ideas into a manufacturing discipline. Both also rose to such eminence in Japan that they won the Order of the Sacred Treasure, Second Class. Goodness knows what you have to do for the first class.

Total Quality had given Japanese industry a powerful edge by the competitive 1980s, before a combination of Japanese banking mismanagement and the sheer economic power of Wall Street pushed the Americans back in front. By then, Western manufacturing had caught on. Toyota was getting 5,000 quality suggestions a day from employees, but their rivals at Ford were offering over half their executive bonuses for contributions to quality. Sometimes, you will notice, it is hard even to describe these things without resorting to numbers.

By the late 1980s, the big management idea was "reengineering," which in practice meant sacking staff by the thousands, but in theory—

according to one of its gurus, Michael Hammer—it meant making the company "easy to do business with." Trying to measure this elusive concept, which Hammer turned into an acronym, ETDBW, led to a disturbing discovery for big manufacturers. They found that most orders went through 15 to 20 departments in the average American business before they were actually fulfilled. Each department provided an excellent opportunity for mistakes and delay. It was an expensive process too. One company found it cost $97 to fulfill an order for batteries worth just $3. One soft-drinks company found that only 55 percent of its invoices were correct.

Hammer revealed that something was missing from the equation: know-how. The problem wasn't simply that companies need to be "reengineered." That kind of thinking implies that the *numbers* are more valuable than the *people*. A company that dumps 100 delivery vans before they are worn out has to record them in their books as a loss. But if they dump 100 employees they have trained they don't have to record it anywhere. The experience and knowledge of employees have no value on conventional measuring scales, because what they represent is hard to measure, except in terms of salaries.

Swedish business writer Karl-Erik Sveiby contemplated this dilemma when he joined Sweden's oldest business magazine, *Affarsvarlden,* as a managing partner. He had been a commercial manager at Unilever's Swedish toiletries company, so in his new job he was given the task of balancing the books. This was difficult because the magazine outsourced almost everything. They had almost no assets to put in the books, apart from their brand name, which Sveiby put down in the books as worth one krona. "I kept forgetting to put [the one krona] in, so the books wouldn't balance," he told *Fortune* magazine. "Then I would reflect that our brand was really worth much more."

Out of that thought emerged the Konrad Group—named after St. Konrad's Day in Sweden—of Sveiby's management thinker colleagues, trying to work out how to measure know-how in a company. Soon Japan's business guru Ikujiro Nonaka was also studying how business can create knowledge, *Fortune's* columnist Thomas Stewart was starting to write about intellectual capital, and the "knowledge management" movement was beginning to grow.

Sveiby's insight has turned into a major business trend, and European companies are now spending about 5 percent of their revenues on applying Sveiby's theories. Bizarre and unexpected new job titles are popping up around the corporate world, like "Learning Manager," "Knowledge

Engineer," "Intellectual Capital Controller," or "Chief Knowledge Officer." Soon Coca-Cola was selling off its tangible assets altogether in a bid to become just the sum of its brand and its management ability.

The knowledge management movement teaches us that knowledge is wealth, in fact, so the old measurements don't work anymore. Count up the value of companies' fixed assets and you come up with a figure wildly different from their actual value on the world markets. Securities analysts now believe that 35 percent of the market value of the stocks they follow is not covered anywhere on the balance sheets. "How ironic," says the American business professor Baruch Lev, "that accounting is the last vestige of those who believe that things are assets and that ideas are expendable."

Lev is an academic accountant who believes the whole profession is going to have to change, because the way we measure the economy is suddenly so out of date. His research shows that American business now invests almost as much in their intangible assets as they do in old-fashioned buildings and equipment. Microsoft is an extreme example. Its balance sheet lists assets that amount to only about 6 percent of what the company is worth. "In other words," says the futurist Charles Leadbeater, "94 percent of the value of this most dynamic and powerful company in the new digital economy is in intangible assets that accountants cannot measure."

This is not just an interesting but useless theory. Knowledge may be intangible but it creates "real" money. Microsoft has created tens of thousands of millionaires among its own employees, not to mention its investors—and provided goodness knows how much wealth to its founder, Bill Gates. Then there was the odd story of the media company DreamWorks SKG. It was formed with capital of just $250 million but was mobbed by investors who quickly drove up its value to $2 billion, purely because of the intangible and unmeasurable value of its founders, Steven Spielberg, David Geffen, and Jeffrey Katzenberg.

Now, if you were to take that intangible difference between the measurable and the unmeasurable and put it under a microscope, what would you find? The first thing would be the mildly intangible—those legal fictions like intellectual property and copyrights—but let's put those aside for the moment because they don't actually make up the gap. The rest is the seriously intangible, like the skills, capabilities, and expertise of the workforce—or maybe even the team of outside consultants they have gathered around them—plus the value of the brand name and its future sales potential, and the reputation of the company.

Fortune's Thomas Stewart defines intellectual capital as the sum of everything everybody in a company knows that gives it a competitive edge:

> It is the knowledge of a workforce. The training and intuition of a team of chemists who discover a billion-dollar new drug or the know-how of workmen who come up with a thousand different ways to improve the efficiency of a factory. It is the electronic network that transports information at warp speed through a company, so that it can react to the market faster than its rivals. It is the collaboration—the shared learning—between a company and its customers, which forges a bond between them that brings the customer back again and again.

"Reputation, reputation, reputation," exclaimed Othello, noticing something similar. "I have lost the immortal part of myself, and what remains is bestial." But how do you measure such things?

The short answer is that it is impossible, but that's not good enough for businesspeople who see their rivals making enormous profits simply from their ability to measure intangibles and sell them. Or to boost the value of their companies: Coca-Cola believes its brand name is worth $39 billion. And there are all those high-tech companies that have never made a profit, like the Internet bookshop Amazon.com, but which still made its owners billionaires as the belief in their value shot them thrillingly up the Wall Street markets. Suddenly a Web site like @Home was worth the same as Lockheed Martin, or the Internet sharetrader E*Trade was worth the same as the giant American Airlines. The point was that, even if you couldn't put a value to your intangible assets yourself, the markets would measure it for you. Precisely.

As the old-fashioned measuring systems break down—those tried and tested columns invented by Fra Pacioli—the divisions between the real and the hyped begin to go fuzzy. If enough people believe it, the hyped can become real. "Do you believe in fairies?" asks Peter Pan, and Tinkerbell recovers if the audience does. It's the same with the modern world of high-tech stocks.

So measuring the unmeasurable matters, which is why there has been such a flurry of business gurus, all of them trying to corner the market by naming the missing factor. Should we call it knowledge management or "Intellectual Capital" like Thomas Stewart, or "Working Knowledge" like James Brian Quinn, or "Managing Know-how" like

Karl-Erik Sveiby? In fact three books with the title *Intellectual Capital* came out in 1997 alone. But they all agree on the main point: that easily measurable money is no longer the most scarce commodity in the world. Information, know-how, intelligence is—get hold of that and the money will pour forth. All the old-fashioned balance sheets could do was give a vague idea of what you might get for a company if you bought it, chopped it up, and sold it. As one management writer said, you might as well say a human being is worth $3 because that is what our various chemical components might be worth.

And so it was that the Swedish company Skandia published the first annual report supplement on intellectual capital, and another Swedish company, Celemi, published the world's first audit of its intangible assets. Soon the idea had spread so completely to the U.S. business world that they were convinced they had thought of it themselves, christening the whole phenomenon the "new economy."

"I have seen the new economy and it works!" exclaimed Al Gore in 1997. But it wasn't quite clear, even then, whether it does. The Dutch engineering business Kema put a price tag of more than $400 million on its highly intelligent staff, but then found that their $12 million profits in 1994 looked rather small in comparison. The board member responsible for IT joked that maybe they should file for bankruptcy.

Other companies missed the point by sinking vast sums into their computer systems, then ignoring their staff altogether. The result was that their "intellectual capital" often decided to look at the job pages and drifted away. ING Barings bank lost half of its most successful Taiwanese team when it just got up and walked out the door to Merrill Lynch. This never used to happen in the good old days of measurable bricks and mortar. Suddenly an accounting problem became a serious personnel headache. There was the strange story of the sacking of advertising guru Maurice Saatchi from the company that bore his name. Saatchi forced the board to dismiss him, but he was followed out the door by some key staff and two crucial accounts—Mars and British Airways. The stock halved in value, and the Saatchi & Saatchi shareholders found they actually owned only half of the company. The rest of the value had seeped away almost overnight.

"In the knowledge society," writes Peter Drucker, "the most probable assumption for organizations—and certainly the assumption on which they have to conduct their affairs—is that they need knowledge workers far more than knowledge workers need them." If you can't measure your assets and you don't know where they are, then you may not notice when they disappear. It's not a healthy situation for a cut-throat company.

So what could they do? What they have done is to try to empower their workforce, open up information inside the company, and measure anything that moves, mining the tons of resulting data for patterns and strange parallels. And that's just the start when you are trying to measure what counts. Accountants PriceWaterhouseCoopers called it the "K Factor." Remember, urges the business manual *Blur*, "every sale is an economic, informational and emotional exchange." That means extending "the emotional experience of your customers to every aspect of your organization." If you thought intellectual capital was difficult to measure, try empathy.

Jeremy Bentham would be turning in his grave, if he had one. Yet businesses still have to make the attempt if they are going to measure their progress, and the difficult fact is they will probably find a way—and stake their future on it. What makes the new world of numbers different from the old is that no two companies, and probably no two people, would measure it in the same way.

II

Now try ethics. While the business world has carried on in its own sweet way looking at the bottom-line figures, the profits and losses, the earnings per share, a whole sector of the financial services industry has emerged to measure companies in a different way. Not according to how much they make, but how nice they are—or how ethical—and then to invest in them accordingly. It's called ethical investment.

Ethical investment is suddenly trendy in financial services. Expensive conferences are held on the subject. Enormously expensive software is used to track the ethical performance of companies around the world. Rival tables are produced and pored over. Even Dow Jones has launched its own "Sustainability Index." And well over $100 billion is claimed to be invested ethically in the United States alone, with pacifist money avoiding the companies that deal in arms, and environmental money pouring into businesses that either avoid damaging the planet, or positively try and improve it. Christian investment goes into antiabortion companies, and even Scientologist investment goes wherever these things go.

The whole idea began with the investment fund Pax Christi during the Vietnam War, and it grew from there via disinvestment in South Africa in the 1980s into an industry that even the biggest pension funds have to take seriously. It also took strength from disastrous revelations of corporate greed, like *Exxon Valdez*. Or like the Bhopal disaster in 1984, when a Union Carbide gas leak killed 2,500 people and injured 200,000 after the company misrepresented its safety record.

Now the British government has ruled that every pension fund must not just reveal its profits but make an ethical "statement of investment principles." Most preferred not to say they had none.

It's a new world. Only a generation ago, General Motors chief Charlie Wilson—later U.S. Defense Secretary—could say in public: "What's good for the country is good for General Motors, and what is good for General Motors is good for the country." These days we don't see "good" in such clear-cut, easily measurable, utilitarian terms. Instead we try to give our lives more of a moral coherence, a kind of joined-up self-government, so that we don't spend our lives campaigning for tropical forests only to find our pension money is invested in logging companies. And we don't pray for peace only to find our hard-won savings are invested in boosting arms exports to unsavory regimes.

Quite what we do next is still argued about, but we start by measuring the moral efficacy of our investments. We ask about interest rates less and about human rights policies more. Then we invest in the companies with the cleanest or greenest record. It's rather a strange shift, especially for hard-nosed businesspeople who had never looked anywhere but the bottom line before.

As the years have gone by the fashions have changed. Should we be avoiding what's downright wrong or should we be seeking out the good and investing in it—or some strange combination of the two? The return of what they call "positive criteria"—measuring the good in companies rather than the bad—has been steady over the past few years, with ethical investment researchers like Washington-based IRRC, New York–based Council on Economic Priorities, or London-based EIRIS starting to screen companies according to their positive employment and environmental policies.

As always, measuring something like ethics depends on how you define it. It's the screener's job to define exactly what we mean by human rights, or "involvement in genetically modified food," and to scour the media for the growing bundles of stories where companies get caught out in "unethical" activity. They get paid to do this because— now that the ethical investors are flexing their muscles across the world—then dumping an oil rig on the bed of the North Sea (as Shell did) can cost you a lot of money. So can teaming up with an American TV evangelist who vilifies homosexuals (as the Bank of Scotland did).

This is the strange paradox of ethical investment. It began as a way for people to accept a lower return for their money because they were keeping their consciences cleaner. But now there are so many of them that the money seems to be going their way too. Generally speaking, and in the long-term, ethical companies seem to perform just as well. There are now so many ethical investors that sustainable strategies can raise a company's share price by 15 percent, according to the latest study. Two American academics worked out that winning an environmental award boosts your share price by an average of 0.82 percent. Bribery or corruption accusations cut it by 2.3 percent. That is—I suppose—as precise a measurement of the money value of morality as it's possible to get. But when an animal-rights protester secretly filmed in laboratories owned by Huntington Life Science a few years ago and showed what she shot on the UK broadcaster Channel 4, the company's share price slumped to less than one-sixth its previous worth and stayed there.

In other words, ethics has gone from an obscure way of measuring corporate success to something as vital as it is undefinable. By 1998, there were 15 companies in the FTSE 100 with over 5 percent of shares owned by ethical investors. That's enough for serious leverage. In fact, it's probably enough to mount a takeover bid. So watch out, major corporations—the ethical corporate raiders may be coming.

With a collective shudder, the business world has begun to realize that the rules are changing. EIRIS is busy measuring their morality, and shareholder activists are irritating them with questions at their annual general meetings, asking directors to justify their pay packets. "Justify? Can you justify YOUR salary?" bawled an enraged Lord King, the former British Airways boss, at the 1999 AGM of a small company called Aerostructures Hamble, of which he was nonexecutive chairman.

"With respect, sir," said the questioner, the shareholder's representative from Abbey Life. "This is not my AGM, it's yours." Not surprising, perhaps, that some Japanese corporations have responded by hiring Yakuza gangsters to stop people asking difficult questions at shareholder meetings. It doesn't work, because slowly but surely the secrets that traditional balance sheets ignore are coming out in the open.

There was the Chentex factory in Nicaragua where, in 1997, Wal-Mart, Kmart and JCPenney were sourcing their jeans and where workers made $0.11 for sewing each $14.99 pair. There was also the Mexican factory subcontracted by Walt Disney where there was no drinking water—workers had to bring their own. It all suddenly becomes public under the close attention of the new auditors. So does the truth about where our money is invested. Suddenly the Church of England turns out to be investing in the Playboy Channel, Shell in BP, and BP in Shell. It's a strange shadowy world, where, without ethical investment researchers, antismoking campaigners could find their pension money is invested in Philip Morris.

Hot on the heels of the ethical revolution is a demand for honesty, openness, and standard definitions. No longer are colored photos of smiling children in the annual report enough to demonstrate a commitment to charity or community investment. Ethical investors want to know how much, whether it works, what local people think, whether it's gender specific, and the answers all go into the league tables. It's an exhausting process to measure it, and even then there are some knotty problems.

Here's one. If a small company gives a large proportion of its profits to charity, and a large company gives much more—though it happens to be a smaller proportion of its profits—which of them is the most ethical? Ethical investors don't know the answer, though whole conferences and reports are devoted to finding out. Those of us familiar with the Gospels might recognize it as the Parable of the Widow's Mite, where the widow is praised for her tiny gift to the poor because it was all she had.

III

You don't manage a football team by looking at the score, says one management consultant. In the same way, it's not a very good way of managing a company if all you're doing is looking at one simple measure of success—the profit line. The world is now much more complicated.

Many companies still believe the only purpose for their existence is the one they measure and nothing else—shareholder value. Critics say that profit became the main corporate goal for companies only as recently as the middle of the last century, that the original purpose behind the charters for the East India Company or the Hudson's Bay Company was public benefit. Even a century ago, a robber baron like Cornelius Vanderbilt kept his profits secret. He kept all his figures in his head because he didn't trust anybody.

Since then, business writers would quote the old economic warhorse Milton Friedman with approval: "A corporation's social responsibility is to make a profit." Not anymore. Even Henry Ford realized there was more to it than that. "Business must be run at a profit, else it will die," he said. "But when anyone tries to run a business solely for profit . . . then also the business must die, for it no longer has a reason for existence."

If you have well over half of your customers measuring your products by how ethical you are, then you are already living more in Ford's world than Friedman's. The old measures don't work: How can they when between 25 and 40 percent of shoppers admit to boycotting unethical companies? One study in France found that 71 percent of consumers would choose a child-labor-free product even if it was more expensive. And if measuring everything by the bottom line worked—and corporations were the great hope for the world—then how come the world is in such a mess?

That still leaves us with the question of how we can measure these various ethereal qualities that seem to lie at the heart of business success. Either you try to put a price on them, like intellectual capital. Or you measure them all in a completely different way, like ethics. Both are impossible to do with any accuracy, which is why companies are trying to knit the whole equation together. What they need, say the Harvard business gurus, is a new kind of scoring system. They call it the Balanced Scorecard.

For some reason, most companies prefer to divide this scorecard into three different measures. At Skandia it is human capital, structural capital, and customer capital. Ben & Jerry's ice cream has a three-part mission statement: economic mission, product mission, and social mission. Du Pont goes for shareholders, environment, and society, and its rival Dow Chemical slips another one in unexpectedly, measuring four kinds of success: economic, environmental, social, and health. For John Elkington of the influential London-based consultancy SustainAbility, it is what he calls a "triple-bottom line"—financial, environmental, and social.

Elkington cut his environmental teeth by rescuing Egypt's largest delta lake from a series of massive development projects and spent the next decade or so writing some of the first corporate environment "statements." But it was his runaway best-seller, *The Green Consumer Guide*, in 1988 that made his name and reputation, and unexpectedly brought the big companies rushing to employ him—even though Monsanto and three separate sections of ICI were also trying to sue him at the same time. His follow-up *Supermarket Guide* was based on the answers to a 99-page questionnaire: The process of measuring the green-ness of companies was beginning. Then in 1990, he produced a report on environmental "auditing."

"Within days, 45 or 50 companies had called up saying 'We'd like an environmental audit—by the way, what's an environmental audit?'" he said later.

That was the second bottom line, but what about the third one—the social dimension? Companies were already starting to measure some parts of their effect on society. Some were trying to measure their reputation. Some, like Marks & Spencer, were measuring their suppliers' creativity. Most were trying to measure customer satisfaction, though often the wrong bits—the booking staff was polite, but the train was still late. A social audit went even further, trying to measure the impact companies have on what are now generally described as their "stakeholders"— which can include anything from neighbors to employees' families.

The audits were developed by a range of organizations and pioneers like Richard Evans of the ethical trading company Traidcraft and Simon Zadek of the London-based New Economics Foundation, known to its friends as NEF. The result tended to be an extremely complex audit report, packed with numbers and measures but no bottom line.

Shell was one of the key companies in the trend. They realized that if their public antenna had been a little more sensitive, they could have predicted the outraged reaction to dumping the Brent Spar oil rig— including having bullets sprayed across their gas stations in Germany. If they had worried a little more about what the world thought of them, maybe they could have prepared better against the execution of Ken Saro-Wiwa in Ogoniland. Nike was another: Its "Just do it!" slogan led to accusations about the conditions in their Asian factories. Nike responded by inviting in independent inspectors and social auditors, just as Shell did, and both began the painful process of peering in the mirror at themselves long and hard.

When the Shell Values Report was published, it carried this piece of unexpected corporate honesty in the front: "We had looked in the mirror and we neither recognized nor liked what we saw. We have set about putting it right. . . ."

Measuring your corporate success in terms of a social bottom line can be a laborious process. It sets yardsticks by which you can measure your progress, and then measures it—and that can mean judging your success by some unusual ideas. Like the ethnic diversity of your employees (Co-op), your wage differentials (Happy Computers), your spending on internal training (Body Shop), customer complaints (Ben & Jerry's), trust in the company (BP), number of employees dismissed for taking bribes (Shell). None of those will give a complete picture—in fact you might get more complaints if your reputation is high—but they are no longer the rigid business of looking at the profits and nothing else.

IV

I first came across Simon Zadek when he was at the New Economics Foundation, developing the idea of social auditing to the point where it was suddenly embraced by the big accountancy firms. He wore, as always, a strange brown hat with a wide brim and talked with animation in frighteningly complicated sentences—like a cross between Indiana Jones and a crazy English professor. By the end of the 1990s he had established the idea enough for his Institute of Social and Ethical Accountability to attract some of the biggest names in business to their annual conference. Over the same period, he spread inspiration and irritation in almost equal measure—he was even threatened with legal action at one stage for using the phrase "social auditing" at all.

Trained as an economist, Zadek cut his auditing teeth with Coopers & Lybrand, working in developing countries with the World Bank. But he had also done a Ph.D. in the economics of utopia. "Science fiction writers know more about development than economists," he told me. "They take a systems approach without even thinking about it. In economics, all the emphasis is on simplification, but in fiction the whole emphasis is on nuance."

Zadek's heroes were writers like Ursula Le Guin and Marge Piercy—and Jurgen Habermas, the unintelligible Frankfurt philosopher of ethics. He was also a Buddhist; he wasn't your average auditor. Still, there he was writing reports for the government of Saint Lucia, working with VSO and other development organizations. By 1992 he was at the New Economics Foundation, working with the ethical trade organization Traidcraft Exchange and developing a method for audits without a bottom line, spelled out in their joint pamphlet *Auditing the Market*. "In practice that was what we now understand a social audit to be," he told me later. "It means understanding how an organization thinks and breathes and acts, from its procedures it has and its inner thinking. It means looking at it not from one perspective but from many perspectives."

You might say their social auditing relates to financial auditing rather as Picasso's modernistic paintings relate to classical ones. You have all the perspectives at once crowded onto the one canvas. This is "cubist" auditing.

Simon Zadek wasn't the first ethical auditor by any means. There were methods called "constituency accounting," developed by the radical accountant Rob Gray in 1973. There were ethical accounting statements developed in the late 1980s in Copenhagen. Even the phrase was coined by Charles Medawar when he launched Social Audit Ltd. in 1971, a joint venture with the founder of the Consumers Association, Michael Young. There was also a collection of Marxist journalists called Counter Information Services who carried out a series of "audits" in the 1970s. They didn't pretend to be unbiased. The CIS "audit" of GEC had a photo of bomb damage on Vietnam on the front. Their report on Ford carried a big picture of the Spanish dictator General Franco.

Social audits have to be as objective as financial audits, of course. It's just not clear how. When Medawar and his company carried one out on the UK Alkali Inspectorate, which was supposed to be checking things on behalf of the public, it proved to be such a secretive organization that auditing of any kind was impossible. But when they carried out a more cooperative audit on the Avon Rubber Company, the company withdrew its support the moment it caught sight of the draft. "A detailed correction of the report would in our opinion result in a document as voluminous as the draft report itself," the company said.

How could social auditors be objective? You can't do it without the cooperation of the company, but if you cooperate can you be objective? But as so often happens, practical demands overrode the logical problem. "I would love it if every shareholder of every company wrote a letter every time they received a company's annual report and accounts," wrote Anita Roddick of The Body Shop in 1990. "I would like them to say something like 'Okay that's fine, very good, but where are the details of your environmental audit? Where are the details of your accounting to the community? Where is your social audit?' "

Where indeed? But by 1995, she had one of her own, conducted with the help of Zadek's team at the New Economics Foundation, and then a full-blown Values Report commissioned partly as a response to the transatlantic campaign against The Body Shop started by the American journalist Jon Entine, who accused the company—bizarrely—of being "the most evil company in the world," mainly for what he claimed was hypocrisy. The Body Shop's first social report, *Measuring Up*, meant interviewing nearly 5,000 people. It even involved Zadek flying out to New Mexico to ask the views of the Santa Ana Pueblo Indians who supply the blue corn for The Body Shop's face washes. Then there was Ben & Jerry's, the hip ice cream manufacturers from Vermont. By 1995, when they commissioned a social audit from NEF, they were turning over more than the entire Russian economy and giving away as much as 7.5 percent of their profits to charity. They were hardly an average company. The results of both were impressive.

One of the great advantages of getting socially audited is that it can stop companies from deluding themselves with their own public relations. But the other side of the coin is that it can be embarrassing to make the results public. When Ben & Jerry's received their report in 1995, it showed that employee morale—admittedly very high—had dropped during the year. It also showed staff complaining that the company's commitment to the Children's Defense Fund conflicted with their own struggles to juggle family and job.

The idea of social audits arrived just as companies had finished their massive clear-outs of staff—known as downsizing. They had flattened their hierarchies and outsourced their services, and found that their success now depended on building relationships of what Zadek calls "intimacy, understanding, and trust." The old hierarchies didn't work anymore, just like the old measurements. There was no hierarchy to order around, just relationships with outsiders or valuable staff. Social auditing seemed to be a way of measuring them.

Zadek's model was based on the idea that stakeholders have the right to be heard, which gives social audits a kind of objectivity which simple market research doesn't have. They deserve a voice in big organizations that affect them. So the auditors just go out and listen—just as conventional auditors were found to have overlooked the peculiar finances of BCCI or Robert Maxwell's pension funds.

Yet social auditing is still measurement. "Five years ago, those organizations were completely blind," says Zadek now. "Certainly the more progressive companies now have a far better knowledge, far more sophisticated understanding, and therefore a far more sophisticated ability to explore into civil society before it becomes part of the problem—for them. What made us a Trojan horse for the business community was our argument that this is not an evaluation. It's helping you count what counts, we said. The sales pitch was—you've obviously got an asset because you want to manage it, and that's all we're doing."

Of course, that wasn't all the social auditors were doing at all, which may be why there is a continuing grumbling from the old guard, clinging to the bottom line. Suppliers also reported being fed up with being audited by their customer companies over and over again. One magazine editor even dismissed the intellectual capital gurus like Thomas Stewart as "business Bolsheviks" for their "justification of irrationally overvalued companies."

"Why we bolshies want the market to be high, I don't know," replied Stewart.

But does social auditing work? As Chairman Mao said about the effects of the French Revolution, it's too early to tell. But the early indications are that measuring how effective it is could be yet another nonrational, uncountable business. It works if companies approach it with honesty and enthusiasm. If they don't, it doesn't. And like any other counting system, it may not be that accurate.

Simon Zadek tells the story of the successful completion of a social audit for a leading South African company. At the end of the board meeting, the chief executive took him out onto the balcony to congratulate him for a job well done. But social audits can't see the whole picture, he said. "Every company has a killer story that they're not disclosing," said the chief executive, looking out across the other corporate headquarters below. "And just to prove it, I'm going to tell you what ours is. . . ."

By 1999, social auditing was all the rage. PricewaterhouseCoopers was offering the service. KPMG had bought up The Body Shop's social audit department lock, stock, and barrel—a prime example of buying intellectual capital—announcing that the social audit "market" would soon be worth $30 million a year. One New York consultancy was reporting 50 inquiries a day from companies wanting social audits. Suddenly ethics were big business. "In a pinch? Thinking about re-tooling your company's ethics training?" said a full-page advertisement in 1999 from the Ethics Resource Center in Washington, D.C. Or, as the PricewaterhouseCoopers advert put it: "We'd like to be ethical, aware and responsible. But what's in it for us?"

What's in it for us sounds like a contradiction when we're talking about measuring ethics. The answer is that social auditing is about measuring your reputation—not according to what it's worth to put it on the balance sheet but to show where it's wanting. It's not so much a matter of measuring how organizations perform, it's about listening and distilling what people say about you. It is as close to a way of measuring without using numbers as it's possible to get.

V

Business has faced the counting crisis by changing what they count, and counting even more. They are taking their attention away from the bottom line just a little, but enough to look at what they call the company's "balanced scorecard." In doing so, they have shifted from narrow financial reporting to something more broadly economic.

As long ago as the British Companies Act of 1985, companies were told to calculate the value of their "cumulative goodwill." Most ignore this on the quite reasonable grounds that it is impossible to work out. But the realization that the old measurements just don't measure those vital intangibles has led to a new multiplicity of counting systems to choose from. There is an "emotional bonding" measure to measure customer loyalty. There is "lifetime value modeling" to work out what customers might be worth throughout their buying lives. There is Customer Value Management, lead indicators, lag indicators, Total Asset Utilization, People Value-Added, even Calculated Intangible Value. There is a new generation of horrendous acronyms: GIPS, TOMAS, EFQM, or BREEAM (Building Research Establishment Environmental Assessment Method). There are the new social auditing standards SA8000, GRI, and AA1000. It's a number cruncher's paradise. There is even a measure of culture, devised by North West Water and Manchester School of Management, with 11 "metrics," including a measure of "internalization"—or how much your staff believes all the rhetoric about values.

And behind the measurements there is a vast amount of data and whole offices full of "data miners"—with their picks and Davy lamps—digging through computers to come up with bizarre correlations in the figures. It's done so quickly: "Every month, I'd receive three cartons of paper that I spread out on the floor in my office," said Skandia's sales statistics manager Per Kingfors. "I also received files on disks and faxed reports. It took days, weeks even, to put all the data together. Now we sit and drum our fingers if we wait more than 20 seconds to get a report."

But behind all these figures, you get the feeling that somehow it isn't working. The more they all measure, the more it all slips through their fingers.

Of course, the measurements are not exactly what they want. Screeds of data about customers and how often they buy from you is not the same as a real measurement of "loyalty." "If you want loyalty, buy a dog," said the chief executive of a UK chain of hardware stores when research showed that most people out DIY shopping didn't know whose store they were buying from.

Even the bottom line figures are behaving oddly. "If you want to look at regular stock, you go either to a financial analyst or an economist," said online information giant Michael Bloomberg, as the value of the Web site Yahoo! overtook that of British Airways. "If you want to value an Internet stock, you go to a psychologist or a publicist."

Even the investor magazine *Fortune* has included a rant against the rising tide of measurement. "If information is a strategic asset, does that mean more and more must be good?" asked columnist Michael Schrage in 1999. "Just because single left-handed blond customers who drive Volvos purchase 1,450% more widgets on alternative Thursdays than their married non-blond, right-handed, domestic car-driving counterparts does not a marketing epiphany make."

In one slightly complicated sentence, Schrage has put the problem in a nutshell. Measuring is easy these days, but the world is too complicated for figures. That's why the originator of "reengineering," Michael Hammer, now believes that three-quarters of all business reengineering processes fail—because of the unscientific, uncountable human factor. "It's easier to count the bottles than describe the wine," says Thomas Stewart in *Intellectual Capital*.

It doesn't seem to matter how many figures you have laid out in front of you, they will not interpret. They will not give you cause and effect. For that you have to make a leap of intuition. Which of all the millions of figures that most companies have at their disposal are the ones making them succeed—or is it just the business cycle? Or will they find themselves praised for their astonishing performance one moment, like Apple Computer, and the next moment find themselves dropping down the markets like a stone.

Companies now have vast data banks of information about their customers, segmentable in every possible direction. They know precisely how they behave and what they buy. *Why* they behave like that remains as elusive as ever.

Which is one reason why it's so difficult to come to a clear conclusion by calculating a better bottom line. Zadek makes no attempt to add up all the figures in a social audit. "It would be meaningless," he says. And how do you balance up the triple bottom line?

"I don't know," says Elkington. "The point is that there are at least three different dimensions to valuing performance that we need to address. The best companies can integrate all three and scarcely be aware of it—like walking. For several years I felt it was better to separate them out and give them a bit of oxygen, but sometime over the next five to ten years, all of them must be collapsed back together and integrated."

This is the great-unanswered question, like the search for the yeti. Is there such a thing as one number at the bottom that really says it all? As far as I know, this is the impossible dream—single numbers don't seem to be able to live up to the complexity of life—but you never know.

There's an echo here of the days before any kind of auditing. Before Pacioli invented his bookkeeping methods, medieval merchants had no books to balance. Instead they kept a kind of diary that listed transactions together with birthdays, battles, and other social events. "The Italians called this a *ricordanze*," wrote the historian of such things, Alfred Crosby. "But how does one balance a diary?" Social auditing is simply a return to the ricordanze: You can't balance it.

For the time being, anyway, imposing single numbers seems to distort. Managing by them tends to lead to lower morale, worse service, and higher costs. The fact that management has moved a little further on from there is definitely progress. We have come a long way from the 1970s, when fearsome executives would appear with their printouts at far-flung edges of a corporate empire to grill local managers about figures and nothing but figures. No longer is one of the biggest companies in the world so committed to getting a 20 percent return on investment that it issues all their executives underwear bearing the words "ROI 20%."

In the end, even after all those measures and highly paid Knowledge Managers, the difference comes down to people, their instincts, and their intuitions—those business pioneers who can do things as automatically as walking. Perhaps that's why the most successful manager in the world, General Electric chief executive Jack Welch, spends the vast majority of his valuable time interviewing people for the top 500 jobs in his company. "My whole job is picking the right people," he said. And if you wonder how he has time for anything else, he probably doesn't.

Given that, is it possible to make a difference to these great corporate machines without counting? Social auditing suggests that a compromise might be possible, and the work of business guru Tom Peters—so often a critique of conventional measurement—seems to suggest so too. That's probably what he meant by the great noncounting management technique MBWA, or "Management By Walking Around." But perhaps the most hopeful sign is the success of the biggest used-book chain in the United States, Half Price Books. They have successfully built themselves into a major chain by expanding city by city not according to financial calculations, marketing projections, or anything else that requires a calculator. They decided where to open next according to wherever their employees happened to have family reasons for wanting to move.

I'm sure Half Price Books employ accountants, but they don't let that get in the way of making sensible decisions. That's the future.

8

THE FINE BALANCE OF
JOHN MAYNARD KEYNES

He keeps a lady in a cage
Most cruelly all day,
And makes her count and calls her "Miss"
Until she fades away.

G. K. Chesterton, "Song Against Grocers"

It is astonishing how many foolish things one can temporarily
believe if one thinks too long alone.

John Maynard Keynes

SCOTTISH COAST, 1916

I

IT WAS JUNE 5, 1916. At the river Somme on the western front, the Allied armies were gathering for the battle they believed would finally cut through the German trenches. To the north of Scotland, it was a cold, stormy evening as the British cruiser *Hampshire* set sail from the anchorage of the British Grand Fleet at Scapa Flow. Her four funnels belched smoke as she sailed past the sheer cliffs of Marwick Head, taking the western route past the Orkney Isles to avoid the worst of the buffeting wind. At 7:40 P.M., a mile and a half from the coast, an enormous explosion almost cut the ship in two. She had sailed straight through a minefield laid by U475 with great precision, but in the wrong place. Within 10 minutes the ship and crew had disappeared. Only 14 survived. One of those never seen again was the British secretary of state for war Horatio Herbert Kitchener. He was 19 days short of his 67th birthday.

Kitchener had presided over the last cavalry charge of the British army. He was a national hero for his conduct against the Boers. As secretary of state for war, he was instantly recognizable from his poster campaign—with a pointing finger and the words BRITAIN NEEDS YOU— which succeeded in recruiting two and a half million volunteers. About 19,000 of them would be killed on the first day of the Battle of the Somme, just 25 days after his icy death. He may not have been a great man, said Margot Asquith, the prime minister's wife, but he certainly was a great poster.

In this sense, Kitchener embodied the casualty figure. By the end of the war there would be as many as 22 million Allied forces killed, captured, and wounded. By December 1915, the official British kill target was 200,000 Germans a month, but approximately the same number of British soldiers seemed to be dying in the process of achieving that target. The generals saw no further than the numbers. "We are like a gambler who must always call his opponent's bluff," said General Sir Henry Rawlinson about the horrendous casualties. "Whatever chips he puts down, we must put down more."

Kitchener's death belongs in this story not just because of the numbers but because British prime minister Lloyd George had been planning to accompany him on the Arctic journey and changed his mind at the last minute. Had he joined Kitchener on the ship, Lloyd George would have taken with him a brilliant young Treasury economist named John Maynard Keynes.

The day Kitchener met his end was also Keynes's 33rd birthday. At the time he was also a fellow of King's College, Cambridge, an active homosexual, and a central member of the Bloomsbury set, which had already begun its revolution to exorcise stuffy Victorian religion and morality. He was a recognized expert on Indian currency, and politicians and civil servants alike increasingly sought his views. If we had lost Keynes on the *Hampshire*, he would not have been there to lay the foundations of modern economics, the world financial system, the IMF—and gross national product, the system whereby we can count up the wealth of a whole nation, and see whether it is rising or falling in one figure.

Although his history-changing, *General Theory of Employment, Interest, and Money*, would be packed full of equations and statistics to prove his contentions, and although he spent eight years before the First World War writing a treatise on probability—pausing on the task during the war years, Keynes didn't like statistics very much. Numbers fascinated him, but then so did myths and fairy tales—especially the story of Midas, who could turn anything he touched into gold. He was skeptical of the whole idea of econometrics, which meant applying numbers and statistics to economics. He saw economic problems as basically moral crises—not the old-fashioned kind of morality, urging thrift and careful saving—but all because of people's fatal love of money. Keynes described this love as "a somewhat disgusting morbidity, one of the semi-criminal, semi-pathological propensities which one hands over with a shudder to the specialists in mental disease."

"The truth seems to be that numbers were for him simply clues," wrote his latest and most voluminous biographer, Robert Skidelsky, "triggers of the imagination, rather like anecdotes are for the non-mathematically minded." Keynes was not, at first sight, in the league of the great number crunchers. How could he be, as the central intellectual figure in the Bloomsbury revolution? He was among those urging a new individualism—urging people to use their intuition and creativity and abandon the dead hand of Victorian pomposity.

And the person he blamed more than anybody else for this stuffiness was the counter-in-chief, Jeremy Bentham, whose tradition he described as "the worm that has been gnawing at the insides of modern civilization and is responsible for its present moral decay." Keynes was fascinated by that which couldn't be measured, like creativity or poetry. He fell in love with an artist, married a ballerina, and spent part of the Great Depression financing and supervising the creation of the Cambridge Arts Theatre. "If I had the power today," he said in 1933,

I would surely set out to endow our capital cities with all the appurtenances of art and civilization on the highest standards . . . convinced that what I could create I could afford—and believing that money thus spent would not only be better than any dole, but would make unnecessary any dole. For what we have spent on the dole in England since the war we could have made our cities the greatest works of man in the world.

He didn't believe in the reduction of the grandeur of human life to money, or to numbers. So how come he is in this book at all? The answer is that it was, ironically, Keynes's national accounting system, which would sum up everything in an economy in one gigantic number, that kept millions alive during the darkest days of the Second World War, consistently outperforming the Nazi economy that everyone thought was so efficient.

As the finest economist of the century, Keynes used figures every day to win his intellectual battles and conduct his highly successful speculations on the world's stock exchanges. But he never used numbers to pin down life. It was the generation that came next that took his national accounts and turned them into an absolute description, one that reduced whole nations to a single tyrannical figure. By the time Keynes was dead in 1946, his invention of national accounts had become a little like Frankenstein. It had a life of its own.

II

On June 5, 1883, the day Keynes was born, Karl Marx was three months under the turf at Highgate Cemetery, Frederick Taylor was conducting his early experiments at Midvale, and it would be 33 years to the day before the *Hampshire* would be sunk. Like Bentham, Keynes was a sickly child, coming down with rheumatic fever and heart pains around his sixth birthday. For the rest of his life he was obsessed with the idea that he was physically repulsive. He also soon realized he was homosexual—a nervous moment in history to discover that about yourself. "Gross indecency" was punishable by a year in prison with hard labor and had been since he was two years old—as Oscar Wilde discovered so tragically. There was no exemption for genius.

At the age of 20, he was elected to the elitist intellectual group known as the Apostles, a regular 12 of whom had been meeting since the start of the previous century. The Apostles met behind bolted doors at King's College, Cambridge, on Saturday nights, listening to endless learned papers from each other, eating anchovies on toast.

It was a brand-new century, and a new age seemed to be beginning—based on the individualistic ideas of the Cambridge moral philosopher G. E. Moore, who declared that morality couldn't be calculated; it had to come from within. It was "exciting, exhilarating, the beginning of a renaissance, the opening of a new heaven and earth," said Keynes. "We were the forerunners of a new dispensation, we were not afraid of anything."

The following year he came first in a whole spread of papers in the Civil Service exams, but only eighth or ninth in economics. "I evidently knew more about economics than my examiners," he wrote. Soon he was working in the India Office, spending his evenings working on what would eventually become his book on probability—linking it to intuition rather than anything directly measurable—and raging at the way government was run during his day job. It was "government by dotardy," he wrote after his first committee meeting. "At least half of those present showed manifest signs of senile decay, and the rest didn't speak." He kept the same tone, inside and outside government, for most of his life.

He was in love with the artist Duncan Grant, much to his friend Lytton Strachey's fury, and was already going to the ballet at Covent Garden twice a week, feeling his way toward his theories of Indian currency. Around him there was a flowering of Edwardian culture. Human nature changed in December 1910, said Virginia Woolf later. From then on the truth was to be found by intuition as well as reason. No more Benthamite calculus. No more tabular data as the source of all truth. No more obsessive collecting of figures. This was the age of Picasso, of leaps of daring imagination.

The Great War broke out over a holiday weekend. "Who is this Keynes?" asked Lloyd George the following day. As Chancellor of the Exchequer, he was furious about an interfering memo on the currency, and from that moment on "this Keynes" would become an increasingly important shadow in Lloyd George's life, sometimes as nemesis—at the peace negotiations in 1919—sometimes as savior. Keynes was soon working at the Treasury with a staff of 17 under him, and was so well respected that he would have accompanied Lloyd George on the ill-fated *Hampshire* had the chancellor not canceled.

It was a difficult position for a sensitive man like Maynard Keynes. It made him exempt from military service, which could well have saved his life, yet he found himself increasingly disillusioned with the war and its conduct. After conscription started in 1916, he was constantly battling to get his friends exempted too. As an act of symbolic protest, he even declared himself as a conscientious objector. He agonized about whether to resign his post in protest, only to come home to find an article by a well-known Liberal pacifist on his dinner plate. Attached to it was a note that read: "Dear Maynard, why are you still at the Treasury? Yours Lytton."

Keynes finally broke down at the Paris peace conference in 1919, resigning from the British delegation and struggling home in despair. Back in London, he denounced the disastrous peace treaty that was to impoverish Europe over the next decade, condemning Lloyd George for threatening the peace of Europe. He described him later, in a more forgiving mood, as "this goat-footed bard, this half-human visitor to our age from the hag-ridden magic and enchanted woods of Celtic antiquity." His book on the subject, *The Economic Consequences of the Peace*, made him a world figure but flung him out of his cozy position of influence with the establishment.

Keynes was brilliant, charming, rude, and peculiar. He judged people by the cleanliness of their hands and fingernails. He always wore silk underpants, though sometimes until they were so old that they barely held themselves together. He was also staggeringly efficient, holding down a weight of committee work and his teaching, writing laborious articles and newspaper supplements, as well as playing a leading role in a range of other projects from speculation to farming. Even so, he managed to find time to play bridge in college, go riding, and spend an hour or so gossiping in the Bloomsbury manner, and his stooping gowned figure would be seen throughout the 1920s dashing across the quadrangles, then ambling around the secondhand bookshops of Cambridge. Or into the little local stores that he described as "shops which are really shops and not merely a branch of the multiplication table." To Keynes, life was always more important than numbers.

In London, his life was at the heart of Bloomsbury, where the vermilion front door of his home at 46 Gordon Square proclaimed the fact that no ordinary people lived here. Upstairs the walls were covered by murals by Vanessa Bell and Duncan Grant. Downstairs was the high-pitched sensitive intellectual talk that made Bloomsbury such a powerhouse. Lady Strachey lived at No. 51, James Strachey at No. 41. Virginia Woolf's brother Adrian Stephen lived at No. 50. It was all a little incestuous.

It was also a home from home, though his increasing worldliness—and what his friends described as his increasing stinginess—divided him from it as the years went by. Especially when he shocked his friends by marrying the divorced Russian ballerina Lydia Lopokova, the daughter of an usher at the Imperial Alexandinsky Theatre. It wasn't so much his unexpected love for a woman that shocked them—the Bloomsbury set respected sexual choices no matter what—but she shocked Cambridge because she fit their category of chorus girl. She shocked his friends because she didn't talk the same language—"a half-witted canary," said

Lytton Strachey. "She has no head-piece . . . poor little parakeet," moaned Virginia Woolf, complaining that she threw her sanitary towels into the empty fire grate. But it was no marriage of convenience: They loved each other for the rest of their lives.

III

The world was changing fast. The next generation was embracing extreme politics, and the intellectuals were embracing a whole new philosophy of measurement, known as logical positivism. If you couldn't measure something, they believed it was meaningless. "What can be said at all must be said clearly, and whereof one cannot speak thereof one must be silent," said Keynes's mad friend, the philosopher Ludwig Wittgenstein. God was swept away. Mankind could take control by measuring and counting, and by sitting themselves down at the controls of a complex universe. There would be no more original sin, no more old men with their prejudices leading youth to the trenches. And by demonstrating that there were controls for an economy too, Keynes would only strengthen the mood.

Despite his disapproval of figures, counting, and statistics, he was inadvertently ushering in the world of the technocrat—the elite of intelligent men (it usually was men) who would take control of the forces shaping the world and make it work like a well-tuned machine.

The elite would run the machine. But to make the engine run correctly, economic statistics would have to take into account the "state of employment, the volume of production, the effective demand for credit as felt by banks, the volume of new issues, the flow of cash into circulation, the statistics of foreign trade and the level of exchanges," Keynes wrote in the early 1920s. He was well aware that, with all these screeds of figures, the new elite wouldn't be able to know which were most important at any one time. That's why he wanted an elite that was numerate but could still allow for what he called the "the play of judgment and discretion."

IV

"No Congress of the United States ever assembled, on surveying the state of the Union, has met a more pleasing prospect than that which appears at the present time," said President Calvin Coolidge in his State of the Union address at the end of 1928. Less than a year later, the Wall Street Crash heralded a worldwide economic disaster. Even Keynes lost a bundle.

Keynes hated international crises—they stopped him from sleeping. Throughout the depression he kept up an articulate and fiery bombardment to persuade the world's politicians that simply cutting back wasn't going to work this time. As he scribbled away in his study in Cambridge and unemployment rose, he became more and more optimistic in his public pronouncements—urging that the answer was to unbalance the budget and get life moving again. "It is often said by wiseacres that we cannot spend more than we earn," wrote Keynes in a letter to the *Manchester Guardian* in 1932. "That is, of course, true enough of the individual, but it is exceedingly misleading if it is applied to the community as a whole."

According to Keynes, there should be no more puritanical urgings for self-sacrifice. The whole idea of urging people to sacrifice themselves seemed horrific to Keynes after all those Kitchener posters. For Keynes, the whole idea of a healthy society wasn't about counting things, and it certainly wasn't dictatorship—it was about life. Encouraging people to save doesn't make anybody rich, he said. If we saved everything and spent nothing, we'd all die—leaving us simply "a peregrination of the catacombs—with a guttering candle." We are healthy children, he urged, so we should spend.

But economic sacrifice was the accepted wisdom. One economist back in 1899, who argued—like Keynes—that too much saving was bad for the economy, was told that he couldn't teach, not even to consenting adults in private. Even today, the Treasury copy of Keynes's pamphlet *Can Lloyd George Do It?* has been defaced by a junior mandarin with the words EXTRAVAGANCE, INFLATION, BANKRUPTCY scrawled over the front. It took a while for people to understand Keynes and realize that loosening their purse strings was neither extravagant nor sinful. "Over against us, standing in the path, there is nothing but a few old gentlemen tightly buttoned-up in their frock coats, who only need to be treated with a little friendly disrespect and bowled over like ninepins," Keynes said. "Quite likely, they will enjoy it themselves, once they have got over the shock."

The shock came with the war. It shocked the old guard into unbalancing its delicate budgets and it shocked Keynes into setting aside his usual dislike of statistics.

V

The year 1933 was a peculiar turning point in an unpredictable decade. The Apostles now included future Soviet spies Anthony Blunt and Guy Burgess. Hitler took power in January, and in March, Franklin Roosevelt took office as president. It was a moment of supreme crisis for the new government. About a quarter of working Americans were out of work, and on the early morning of the day before the inauguration, March 4, every bank in America locked its doors. Revolution seemed almost inevitable. Even Keynes was confused: "Even I would hardly think that I could know what to do if I were president," he told his wife. But Roosevelt inspired the world with his speech warning America that "we have nothing to fear but fear itself," thrilling Keynes as he listened to it on the radio at Lloyd George's country house.

Roosevelt's New Deal owed a great deal to Keynes's influence: Roosevelt had followed his career with interest, especially the thinking he had been carrying out with the now elderly Lloyd George. So, in their own way, did Europe's dictators, who were already enthusiastically unbalancing their budgets—and Keynes was already fearing the way they capitalized on economic collapse. He believed the First World War had destroyed the social connections that underpinned the economic system. Somehow it had to be rebuilt to "keep alive the possibility of civilization." Keynes was no revolutionary in any other sense. In encouraging nations to spend, he was trying to rescue the capitalist system from itself.

VI

When Hitler marched into Poland, Keynes was 56 and not very well. Battling to rescue the world from depression had seriously damaged his health, and in the month of the coronation of George VI in 1937, he collapsed with coronary thrombosis. He never fully recovered, but like so many others he was raring to help the war effort. He gathered around him a group of friends who had been involved in government during the First World War—including Sir William Beveridge, who had been in the ministries of Munitions and Food—and they met once a week in Gordon Square to discuss financial aspects of the war. Keynes called them the "Old Dogs." It was a frustrating time.

He sent a stream of notes to Roosevelt about how to finance the postwar reconstruction of Europe, but it was the problem of paying for the war in the first place that concerned him the most. Wars are an expensive business, after all. British finances were in no state to pay for one, and gigantic loans would soon be flooding into the British exchequer from abroad. Within the year, for the sake of national liberty, there would be no limit on borrowing at all. By default, the government was doing exactly as Keynes had urged for the past decade—they were unbalancing the budget and spending their way out of the depression because they had to.

The problem was that these vast sums would soon be swirling around the economy and there was no knowing where they might end up. With full wallets after 20 years of near poverty, and a U-boat blockade stopping luxury goods from appearing in the shops, anything could happen. It might not produce what the war effort desperately needed. It might produce rampant, morale-sapping inflation. Prices had more than doubled during the First World War—though they had barely moved before in the century after Waterloo.

What could be done? Precious little without a set of national accounts to sum up the whole intricate complicated web and show where there was spare capacity and when the economy was overheating. But there wasn't one. The Soviets managed their intractable five-year plans by plucking numbers out of thin air and enforcing them with death or Siberia. But Britain had no way of providing any kind of overview of an economy in numbers. In his *General Theory* in 1936, Keynes had complained that the economic figures for Britain were completely inadequate—and it was impossible to manage an economy along the principles he set out without a figure for what he called "aggregate real income." The British government in 1939 had no such thing, though Keynes's younger Cambridge colleagues Erwin Rothbarth and Colin Clark were struggling to produce them.

Luckily for the British, some of the work was already being carried out across the Atlantic. The U.S. Congress had called an urgent meeting of economists as they struggled with the depression in 1931, with the sounds of bank crashes in the not too far distance. To their horror, they found there were hardly any of the figures they needed either. The following year—the last year of the Hoover administration—the Senate finally asked the Department of Commerce to prepare a comprehensive set of national accounts. The department called in a quiet and unassuming young economist named Simon Kuznets from the University of

Pennsylvania. They set him to work on what turned out to be the start of a lifetime as the international guru of aggregate real income—or, or as we call it these days, gross national product or GNP.

Working out the aggregate real income of a nation means counting money flowing through its economy. Using GNP means you can sum up a whole country in one number—one figure pumped out of a machine called the economy. At last there did seem to be a possible answer to the critical questions economists ask in wartime—how much can we produce and what impact will it have on the economy as a whole?

Thanks to Kuznets, the American government had the first set of national accounts in the world as early as 1935, the year before Keynes's *General Theory* was published. And by 1939, he had managed to carry out statistical work on 33 other countries—though not Britain. It was Kuznets's idea, but it needed Keynes's special insight for it to be possible in the first place. It was Keynes who realized that money was a flow. One economist was to call Kuznets's work the anatomy for Keynes's physiology. The two bits came together as one of the crucial pieces of the jigsaw that would eventually stump Hitler. But, even at the outbreak of war, the pieces weren't yet in place.

While the Old Dogs were struggling through the winter streets—with the sidewalks and lampposts painted black and white to help navigate during the blackout—Keynes was applying his considerable intellectual resources to the problem of how to afford the war. Luckily there seemed to be a breathing space: "There is still an astonishingly general belief, or hope, or perhaps a mixture of both, that something will happen," wrote the columnist Mollie Panter-Downs in the *New Yorker*. Almost nothing did—it was the period known as the "Phoney War." So Keynes had time to set out his ideas on war potential to the Marshall Society in Cambridge. He turned the lecture into two articles called "Paying for the War." Together, they formed a blueprint for keeping inflation down during wartime.

Because of a leak, which has still never been fully explained, Keynes's articles were published in a German newspaper, the *Frankfurter Allgemeine Zeitung* of November 7—an extraordinary mistake given how important they would be for the war effort. The *Times* didn't get around to publishing them until November 14 and 15.

Keynes's blueprint in the articles was based on the idea of national accounting and using the crucial figures to plan how much to spend and where. It also showed how the government could take some of the spending out of the economy to avoid inflation—but at the same time pay for what people actually needed. He suggested a family allowance of five shillings a week per child up to the age of 15, paid directly to the mother, and a list of the basic necessities of life that would be kept at a level price by subsidizing them. He suggested a top income tax rate of 80 percent, and he had brilliant masterstroke—compulsory savings. Part of people's pay packets would not be taxed but would be saved for them, then given back with interest during the postwar slump when they and the economy would really need it.

The articles provoked an excited response. The right-wing Beaverbrook Press didn't like it because of the tax rate. The Labor Party and TUC didn't like confiscating people's wages—even temporarily. The National Savings Movement hated it. But then it's all too easy not doing anything about inflation, Keynes complained—nobody then has to take responsibility for it. Next he incorporated the debate into a pamphlet published in February 1940, called *How to Pay for the War: A Radical Plan for the Chancellor of the Exchequer.*

Suddenly in May 1940, Hitler launched his blitzkrieg attack on Western Europe. Money was suddenly no object and national counting was really urgent. Keynes shuttled from meeting to meeting, conserving his energy in between with long rests in his room with an ice bag. By the time France had fallen, he was suffering from chest pains. By the London blitz, he and Lydia were sleeping in the corridor at Gordon Square.

His life seemed to be unraveling. A land mine on the square in September broke every door and window in the center of Bloomsbury. Virginia Woolf was on the verge of suicide. But he was finally asked by the government to help them prepare the 1941 budget. On budget day 1941, the white paper was published setting out the national accounts and figures on which the budget was based. "It was," said Keynes, "a revolution in public finance."

And after all that, they only partially put his ideas into practice. Low interest rates were fixed on both sides of the Atlantic, as he suggested, and family allowances came in toward the end of the war. But his deferred pay scheme saved only £120 million rather than the £550 million he planned, so there wasn't much to plow back into the sickly peacetime economy. Even so, it was still a key foundation stone for the postwar welfare state.

If the British adopted his ideas for a wartime economy, that was nothing to the Americans. In the first six months of 1942, Roosevelt's government—urged on by Churchill and his aircraft production minister, Lord Beaverbrook, when they arrived in Washington—placed orders for more than $100 billion in war equipment, more than their entire GNP. Donald Nelson, the purchasing vice president of Sears Roebuck, was appointed to lead the War Production Board and was given unprecedented powers.

To make sure this didn't lead to inflation, the Americans raised their top tax rate to 91 percent. The economist John Kenneth Galbraith was drafted in to make sure prices didn't go up—a process, without the powers to enforce it, became known as "jawboning." The vast capacity of the United States was brought to bear on the war, and if the contracts were too generous, a fearsome committee of Congress—chaired by Harry S. Truman before his unexpected rise to the vice presidency—chased them like terriers. By the end of the war, the figures were staggering: 86,338 tanks had been produced in U.S. factories; 297,000 planes; 17.4 million rifles, carbines, and side arms; 64,500 landing ships. Cargo vessels were being laid down and launched within four days, and the Kaiser Yard in California even managed it once in 24 hours flat.

Large-scale manufacture seemed to be working in Britain too. By 1941, the UK was outproducing Germany in its main military requirements. Despite the fact that the Nazis were using slave labor and had all the resources of a totalitarian state at their disposal, Keynes's and Kuznets's economic tool had beaten the Nazi efficiency machine where it really mattered—in their productivity. Four years later, Galbraith dashed into Germany ahead of the advancing Allied troops to seize the relevant documents, interrogating Goering and Speer for weeks. He believed by the end that national accounts had been a secret ingredient in the war effort of equal importance to the Enigma Code or the Manhattan Project. Hitler's production targets were far lower because he had not been able to use sophisticated national accounting.

In fact, Galbraith discovered, the Allied bombing campaign of inefficient German factories in 1944 was the only thing that managed to speed up Nazi production. Military planners are wedded to figures more than almost anyone else, and especially—for some reason—when it comes to aerial bombardment.

VII

By 1944, Keynes was preparing for the final triumph of his life—the meeting at Bretton Woods in New Hampshire to set up a postwar world financial system, one that could manage the currency flows across the world safely and fairly, without the danger of another crash. He was as charming and as rude as ever at the conference, teasing the American delegation for their jargon—he called it "Cherokee"—negotiating sometimes from 9:30 A.M. to 3:30 A.M., holding the 730 delegates from 44 United Nations countries spellbound. Although it was not primarily his version of the plan that was adopted for the IMF and other powerful institutions we still have today, Keynes was the hero and it was Keynes who moved the acceptance of the final act. When he finished, the whole assembly rose and cheered him as he walked toward the door singing, "For He's a Jolly Good Fellow." "At such moments, I often find myself thinking that Keynes must be one of the most remarkable men that have ever lived," wrote the British embassy's economic adviser. "The quick logic, the wide vision, above all the incomparable sense of the fitness of words, all combine to make something several degrees beyond the ordinary limit of human achievement. Certainly, in our age, only the prime minister surpasses him . . . shot through with something that is not traditional, a unique unearthly quality of which one can only say that it is pure genius. The Americans sat entranced as the godlike visitor sang and the golden light played all around."

Keynes died of a sudden heart attack at the age of only 62, at his country home at Tilton in Sussex, over Easter weekend 1946. "I lost my everything," wrote Lydia. His father, John Neville Keynes, struggled to his memorial service in Westminster Abbey at the age of 93.

VIII

Keynes and Kuznets were not actually the first to try to sum up a nation in a number. Nor were they the first to argue about what should be counted and what should be ignored. The first attempt at a set of national accounts had been made more than two hundred years before Keynes was born—in the 1690s—by Sir William Petty, the great anatomist, chemist, musician, surveyor-general of Ireland, and inventor of the copying machine. He was trying to find out how much you could tax the nation. "Instead of using only comparative and superlative Words," he wrote, "I have taken the course . . . to express myself in Number, Wealth." The great thing was to count and to sum things up in numbers, he told Charles II. "By contemplating the universal posture of the nation, its power, its strength, trade, wealth and revenues . . . by summing up the difficulties on either side, and computing upon the whole . . . is what we mean by Political Arithmetic."

When the French kings used to count the riches of a kingdom, they measured only agriculture as national wealth. It took Adam Smith to include industry and factories, but even he refused to count entertainment, government spending, and lawyers because they were "unproductive of any value." Alfred Marshall, Keynes's teacher and the founder of neoclassical economics, included both lawyers' fees and car prices for the first time—it was money that counted, after all. Things without a price got left out. They still are.

Even so, Keynes and Kuznets between them ushered in a whole new world. Their bottom-line figure for a whole nation meant suddenly that economists could start forecasting how the overall figure would change. A confusing new world of input-output ratios and linear programming was emerging, with economists—like white-coated scientists—wandering with clipboards through the corridors of power. "They are to be called wise who put things in their right order and control them well," wrote Colin Clark quoting St. Thomas Aquinas on the first page of his 1940 book, *The Conditions of Economic Progress.*

After the war, a new priesthood of number crunchers no longer preached the gospel of thrift. It was now the duty of consumers to consume, and they measured their ability to do so. And with one number that summed it all up, nation by nation, suddenly the economic priests discovered the number could move. If it went down it was recession. If it went up it was "progress." "Progress is our most important product," said Ronald Reagan week in week out as the host of the TV show *General Electric Theater.* The phrase "economic growth" emerged.

But could you really measure something as complex as progress in this way? Should we be pleased *just* because there was more money going through the economy? What about those life-enhancing but priceless aspects of life that never got counted?

The first cracks in the idea of numbering whole nations were beginning to appear as early as the late 1940s. Some of the biggest proponents of GNP were listing what couldn't be counted. Like damage to the natural world: Even in 1940, Colin Clark could write in the introduction to his book on the subject: "It is, unfortunately, as yet impossible to give even the most approximate numerical valuation of the extent of this destruction of natural fertility in different parts of the world. . . ."

How right he was. The first meeting of the International Association for Research in Income and Wealth took place three years after Keynes's death in his old college in Cambridge. Kuznets was there, and one of the key issues was what to count. National accounts were just supposed to measure final products. But what was education? It was free, so it didn't get measured. What about taking a walk? What about professional killers? Not included because they were illegal, yet money does change hands. Then there was the question of prices. Are they really a very good measure of what something is worth—especially today? What about housework—an argument that has continued ever since? Not included, but Kuznets reckoned it could make up a quarter of all national income. How could you measure "growth" in developing countries where the most important products were prayer and monks? It was no idle question—the World Bank needed to be able to compare the "progress" of countries in the third world. They were busily measuring their success in Africa using GNP, even though most production there took place for free in the household. It was as if only big industry counted.

It all seemed so simple when the object was just to win the war, but when it was to make society a better, happier, and richer place, then one measurement wasn't very effective. "Though unable to measure them," warned Kuznets as he listed the exclusions, "we must recognize that their omission renders national income merely one element in the evaluation of the net welfare assignable to the nation's economic activity."

Kuznets had been having doubts since his first report to Congress in 1934: "The welfare of a nation can scarcely be inferred from a measurement of national income as defined above," he warned. Nearly 30 years later, writing in *The New Republic*, he went much further: "Distinctions must be kept in mind between quantity and quality of growth, between its costs and return, and between the short and the long run." Goals for "more" growth should specify more growth of "what and for what."

But it was too late. The future of Western nations was being bound to GNP and how fast it could grow.

IX

Did Keynes have doubts too? Remember that Keynes was also—and always—suspicious of measuring things, or of reducing economics to figures. To find a social system that worked economically as well as morally, he urged people to stop "counting the money cost at all," telling the future to "diminish, rather than increase, the area of monetary comparisons." But then he never liked counting much—the real source of new thinking was intuition and introspection. "He was not the first of the modern statisticians, but the last of the magicians of number," writes his biographer Robert Skidelsky. "For him numbers were akin to those mystic 'signs' or 'clues' by which the necromancers had tried to uncover the riddles of the universe."

Theories weren't calculated from piles of figures, said the necromancer. They begin as a "grey, fuzzy, woolly monster in one's head." Keynes was on the side of Pythagoras and Plato rather than the modern number crunchers. He believed that science, art, and magic were more similar than they were different. Yet he invented the tools by which his followers would sum up a whole country with one number. So perhaps it shouldn't be a surprise that the man he named as his successor devoted his career to a critique of "progress" and "growth."

When they corresponded during the war, E. F. Schumacher was still 30 years away from writing his best-seller *Small Is Beautiful*—the book that cast doubt on the habit of economists to go for more and bigger— but Keynes recognized in him a fellow magician. "If my mantle is to fall on anyone," he told a friend in the Treasury just before he died, "it could only be Otto Clarke or Fritz Schumacher. Otto Clarke can do anything with figures, but Schumacher can make them sing."

Despite the numbers, Keynes still believed the only purpose of economics was to increase "the pleasures of human intercourse and the enjoyment of beautiful objects." And these things, like Keynes's probabilities, weren't really measurable. In April 1933, in front of almost the whole Irish government at University College Dublin, he delivered a famous and slightly shocking address called "National Self-Sufficiency." Reading it seven decades later, it still echoes as a powerful indictment of anybody who thinks that counting money is the same as counting wealth:

We destroy the beauty of the countryside because the unappropriated splendors of nature have noneconomic value. We are capable of shutting off the sun and stars because they pay no dividend. . . . Today we suffer disillusion not because we are poorer . . . but because other values seem to have been sacrificed . . . and sacrificed unnecessarily. For our economic system is not, in fact, enabling us to exploit to the utmost the possibilities for economic wealth afforded by the progress of our technique . . . leading us to feel we might as well have used up the margin in more satisfying ways. But once we allow ourselves to be disobedient to the test of an accountant's profit, we have begun to change our civilization.

THE NEW INDICATORS

*If the chief of your local police department were to announce today
that "activity" on the city streets had increased by 15 percent, people
would not be interested. They would demand specifics.
Exactly what increased? Tree planting or burglaries? Volunteerism
or muggings? Car wrecks or neighborly acts of kindness.*

The Atlantic Monthly, October 1995

*"London is too full of fogs and . . . serious people. . . .
Whether the fogs produce the serious people, or whether
the serious people produce the fogs, I don't know."*

Oscar Wilde, *Lady Windermere's Fan*

I

DICKENS SEEMS TO have foreseen our crisis in counting. In his 1854 novel *Hard Times,* he poses the hard questions about national wealth. Here we are in this nation with 50 million pounds, the horrifically utilitarian teacher tells apparently naive schoolgirl Sissy Jupe: "Girl Number twenty, isn't this a prosperous nation, and a'n't you in a thriving state?"

Sissy doesn't know the answer: " 'I thought I couldn't know whether it was a prosperous nation or not, and whether I was in a thriving state or not, unless I knew who had got the money, and whether any of it was mine. But that had nothing to do with it. It was not in the figures at all,' said Sissy, wiping her eyes.

" 'That was a great mistake of yours,' observed Louisa."

A century after the publication of *Hard Times*, it still seemed rather a mistake. The figures were supposed to stand for absolutely everything. Armed with the concept of GNP or GDP, the politicians believed they could see a new era of prosperity stretching before them—all because they could "count" a nation's wealth in one figure and see how much it was growing. It seemed like a simple idea—you just count up the total value of goods and services exchanged in the nation—but it led to a powerful new phrase entering the political lexicon: "economic growth."

The idea was introduced in Britain during the Conservative Party conference in 1954 to a public exhausted by wartime rationing and postwar austerity. If Britain can "grow" by percent a year, then living standards could double by 1980, said Chancellor of the Exchequer R. A. Butler. He repeated the message over and over again during the 1955 general election. "It's not pie in the sky but a sober picture," he told the crowds that used to go to political rallies in those days. "Moreover we don't have to wait until 1980. Progress will come year by year if we concentrate on production and investment. The government will help with great new schemes. We will build roads and railways, develop atomic power and help with the reequipment and modernization of the whole of industry."

And so it was that a radical method of measuring that arose out of the battle to rescue the world from depression, and then from Hitler, was embraced by the establishment. And once they had embraced it, they never let it go. It seemed the perfect scorecard. Measuring national success by the amount of money changing hands seemed to fit neatly with the spirit of the age: increasing prosperity and increasing comfort.

The mantra of growth has been repeated with growing conviction ever since World War II, and with a kind of manic frustration as real life failed to comply with the figures. Growth has been gigantic, the technological innovations astonishing, and the living standards—if you measure them in terms of money—have shot up. Governments fell over themselves to compete for growth, sacrificing their wildlife, nature, and people's sanity—and sometimes even their populations—to make way for great dams or motorway projects. Enormous investment flowed as a prize to the countries where the growth was high. And within that, policy makers battled for supremacy over who had the most mobile phones or computers per head. Anyone who questioned whether it was a good idea to flatten this wetland for a road or that neighborhood for a tower block were told, fatuously, that you "can't stand in the way of progress." It was an irritating inversion of the meaning of the word.

And life wasn't actually better, as we all knew in our heart of hearts. In the 45 years since Butler painted his hopeful future of growth, there are more ill health and less creativity, fewer people on sports teams, less amateur dramatics, fewer learning musical instruments or painting. There are more people with asthma, depression, and cancer. There is more crime, more people in prisons. But the key measure of success used by politicians and economists recognized none of these things as important. By narrowing the definition of what constituted "wealth," we ended up narrowing all our lives.

The work we all do bringing up children didn't get counted and planned for; but work flipping hamburgers in McDonald's did. The first was ignored. The second was built into government policy for single mothers. Only money counted—it was like Jeremy Bentham's calculation, but far narrower. And if the whole of public policy was devoted to improving this one bottom-line figure, it was a kind of self-fulfilling prophecy. Things that money couldn't buy were driven out. "A country that cut down all its trees, sold them as wood chips, and gambled the money away playing tiddly-winks, would appear from its national accounts to have got richer in terms of GNP per person," wrote one economist in 1989. Some of them almost did.

Yet economics was by now firmly wedded to this simplistic measuring system. "Economic growth is the grand objective," said Keynes's sidekick and biographer Sir Roy Harrod. "It is the aim of economic policy as a whole." And overwhelmingly the establishment agreed with him—people whose wealth was considerable but whose lifestyles were probably increasingly exhausting. It was the tyranny of the bottom line all over again.

It wasn't a new discovery that wealth meant more than money. "To my big brother—the richest man in town!" says George Bailey's brother in *It's a Wonderful Life*, even though we know he has very little money.

But it's a lesson that has to be constantly relearned. "The sentence 'let's get out of this airy stuff and look at the bottom line' ends with one small phrase," wrote the poet Robert Bly. "And yet a whole civilization can disappear through that small hole."

II

The backlash to GNP has been a long time coming, even though the idea that life shouldn't have to "grow" at all is hardly new. John Stuart Mill certainly believed that "it is only in the backward countries of the world that increased production is still an important object." But over the past generation, it has begun to occur to people that there might, after all, be some difference between counting money and counting "wealth" or "progress," or "success." There *are* other things we want to achieve apart from money. But what could they do instead? The solution was, as always, to measure something else—and preferably a lot of different things: If you want to measure the unmeasurable, this usually seems the best solution.

It has been a revolution brought about by a long list of people, but four stand out. The first was the economist E. J. Mishan. Mishan's book *The Costs of Economic Growth* came out at the height of flower power in 1967 and four years before the green movement arrived with a fanfare of trumpets and the publication—within a month of each other—of *Blueprint for Survival* and *Limits to Growth*. It was also the year of the *Torrey Canyon* disaster, where an oil tanker split open off the Scilly Isles and covered the beaches of Western England with oil. It required an enormous cleanup operation—all of which counted as a plus in the national accounts. "The civilization of the West carries with it the seeds of its own disintegration," wrote Mishan, whose colleagues at the London School of Economics regarded him as an "amiable eccentric" as he railed against what he called the "mass flight from reality into statistics."

"Our environment is sinking fast into a welter of disamenities, yet the most vocal representatives of the main political parties can't raise their eyes from the trade figures to remark the painful event," he wrote. "We have become so preoccupied with the ups and downs of the indices that we fail to raise our sights to the larger issues that confront us."

Mishan was a prophet, but no revolutionary. Quite the reverse—he prefaced the new editions of his book with long rants about schoolgirl pregnancies, junk mail, gay hotlines, and one-parent families. "The suburbs were quiet and pleasant," he wrote nostalgically in 1993 about the days before economic growth. "Nobody's ears were assailed by low flying aircraft or the neighbors' stereos, nor indeed by screaming chainsaws and long-wailing lawn-mowers. In English seaside resorts it was still possible to smell the salt sea air. The Mediterranean coastline had not yet been wrecked by "development" and the waters were clear and fit to bathe in."

But as his analysis grew in influence, he became the target for more abuse. What about the costs of not growing, said his critics? What about the poor people who need economic growth? "Ministerial twaddle," said Mishan. What about the fact that raw materials haven't actually run out yet? "A man who falls from a hundred-storey building will survive the first ninety-nine storeys unscathed," wrote Mishan. "Were he as sanguine as our technocrats, his confidence would grow with the number of stories he passed on his downward flight and would be at a maximum just before his free-fall abruptly halted."

The freefall continues unabated. But help was at hand for Mishan from a completely different point of view. The New Zealand MP, Marilyn Waring, whose book *If Women Counted* was published in 1988, used the example of a tree. When it is chopped down and sold as wood it has a measurable economic value. But while it is alive and creating oxygen it doesn't. Surely we should start measuring in such a way as we can include the living trees as well, she said.

It was her time as chairman of the New Zealand public accounts committee that really opened her eyes to the problem. Waring noticed that many of the aspects of life that mattered most were completely ignored by the government, because officials counted only money. And one of these aspects of life was the work done around the world by women, often in the home—which had previously been regarded by economists as an infinite resource. She wrote a paper for the Women and Food conference in Sydney in 1982 and submitted it for comment to Australia's deputy chief statistician. "His memo of reply to me—a classic of sexist economic assumptions—was one of the major incentives to write this book," she wrote in the introduction. *If Women Counted* was a brave book to write, and she quoted her fellow New Zealander Katherine Mansfield at the outset: "Risk—risk anything. Care no more for the opinion of others, for those voices. Do the hardest thing on earth for you to do. Act for yourself. Face the Truth." It was a risky move for someone with a political career.

She dug out the lists of students who worked under Kuznets in the 1930s to develop national accounting in the first place. The names were all men, but at the bottom was an important note: "Five clerks, all women with substantial experience and know-how, assisted importantly in this work." These anonymous women—all with substantial experience apparently—had become nonpersons. And their invisibility had spread to the system they created, which still ignores women's work. In the UN accounting system, farmers' wives and daughters were excluded from the statistics of agricultural laborers because there was no money changing hands. When a man marries his housekeeper, said Waring, the value of GNP goes down.

In 1970, the feminist Lisa Leghorn used a survey by Chase Manhattan Bank to find out "what a wife was worth." By multiplying the figure by the number of housewives in the United States, she came up with a total figure of about half of U.S. GNP or twice total government spending. There have been endless studies since, all of them arguing about whether you should value housework at prevailing wages, at the cost of actually getting the hoovering done, or the cost of something else. Strangely enough, however it gets worked out, most studies seem to come up with a figure somewhere around half GNP.

III

The first step toward a more accurate indication of a nation's well being was to come up with an alternative to GNP or GDP. One of the best known was the Index of Sustainable Economic Welfare (ISEW), which measured money but also subtracted the "bads" from the total—pollution, disease, or depletion of natural resources. It was drawn up by the alternative economist Clifford Cobb, whose father, theologian John Cobb, teamed up with World Bank economist Herman Daly to publish the idea in their book, *For the Common Good*.

The ISEW reached a much wider audience as the Genuine Progress Indicator in a long article in *Atlantic Monthly* magazine in 1994. It was called "If the GDP Is Up, Why Is America Down?" The article was written to mark the foundation of a new think tank in San Francisco called Redefining Progress. It was written by Clifford Cobb, with the journalist Jonathan Rowe and Ted Halstead—the whiz-kid founder of Redefining Progress, then still in his twenties—and it had an enormous response.

The Redefining Progress article seemed to hit home. It was the period when politicians were searching for the elusive "feelgood factor," which explained why people were so stressed, unhappy, and angry with the government even though the numbers said they were wealthy. "There seemingly inexplicably remains an extraordinarily deep-rooted foreboding about the economic outlook," said the fearsome Alan Greenspan of the Federal Reserve. People had money in their pockets, but they weren't content. It was a mystery to the politicians. They hate that kind of complexity.

The article piled on the evidence against GNP. The *Wall Street Journal* had just worked out that the O. J. Simpson trial had cost the equivalent of the total GNP of Granada. Was that progress? Then there were the liposuction operations—110,000 of which take place every year in the United States, each of them pumping $2,000 into the growth figures. GNP seems to win both ways—there is growth-making people overeat the least healthy foods, then there's growth operating on them to make them look thin again. There's growth-making pesticides that cause cancer and growth selling drugs to cure it—often by the same company. People in Los Angeles spend a total of $800 million a year on just the gas they use up in traffic jams. Is that "progress"? Not only do GNP and GDP ignore the collapse of environmental and social underpinnings to the world, but they pretend it was a gain. Readers reached the end of the article sweating with statistics but doubting the measurements of success.

Of course, this wasn't anything new. A century before, art critic John Ruskin had urged people to distinguish between wealth and money spent making life worse—what he called "illth." But the Genuine Progress Indicator was something fresh. It showed that "genuine progress" had changed direction some time in the 1970s and was now back to what it had been in 1950. Rab Butler was wrong.

Cobb, Rowe, and Halstead attracted hundreds of letters from all over the country. Some of them were supportive and excited. "Gross National Product is Writ; the economists and statisticians its keepers," wrote one of President Johnson's former ministers in response. "A tranquillity index, a cleanliness index, a privacy index might have told us something about the condition of man, but a fast-growing country bent on piling up material things has been indifferent to the little things that add joy to everyday living."

It also attracted the rage of many economists. "GDP is not, and never was intended to be a measure of national welfare," wrote one senior government economist, warning that it was not his job to say what was good and what was bad. "Personally, although I enjoy arguments, that's one argument I'm going to stay 10 miles away from."

Jonathan Rowe popped into the meeting of the American Economic Association, just around the corner from the Redefining Progress offices in San Francisco's Kearney Street. He went to hear future Treasury secretary Larry Summers urging the media to distinguish between economic doctors and what he called "quacks." Even the great hope of the economic profession, Paul Krugman, described the people behind the article as "incompetents."

Rowe introduced himself as one of these incompetents to Krugman on his way out. "Well I'm sorry, but it's true," he mumbled, dashing off to do an interview.

IV

In 1961, Hazel Henderson was a newly naturalized American citizen, living in a small flat with her daughter. Like Cary Grant, she had made the transition from Bristol, England, to New York City and found it a thrilling place, bustling with new ideas in the first years of the Kennedy presidency. Unlike Cary Grant, who had come to America in 1920, the main thing she noticed was the smog and air pollution. "I was always getting bronchitis," she said. "I found that the city had an air pollution index but that nobody knew about it, and I thought it would be incredible if we could get it on the weather broadcasts."

So while her daughter was asleep during the afternoons, she started writing letters—to the newly appointed Federal Communication Commissioner and the heads of NBC, ABC, and CBS. When the commissioner wrote to say he liked the idea, she forwarded copies to the broadcasters, and five weeks later, the head of news at ABC phoned up to say they would do it. Soon the air pollution measures were in the *New York Times* and on the local radio stations, and they have been ever since in most American cities. "It was my first experience of the power of indicators," she said.

Soon she was organizing a radical environmental group called Citizens for Clean Air, releasing praying mantises into Central Park to cut down the need for insecticides, and learning about economics in her spare time. Her 1981 book, *Politics for the Solar Age*, made her one of the foremost critics of conventional economic measures in the world—but the air pollution index was an important step toward new ways of measuring success. Maybe we should stop measuring money altogether, she said, and start measuring the stuff that's really important. "Back then, I really thought that economics could be overhauled if we expanded the framework enough," she said. "That we could make all the necessary changes for GNP to reflect all the intangibles. When I finished the book, I realized that didn't work. A multi-dimensional society can't be measured using one discipline. Using money as the co-efficient would re-anoint economists and use their values to decide how to relate more clean air to more money. Why would we want to re-enthrone economists as philosopher-kings?"

But what should you measure instead? By the 1970s, the most popular alternative to measuring money was measuring "quality of life." The phrase dated back to 1939—about the same year somebody first coined the phrase "economic growth"—but in those days it meant the "good life," luxury, indulgence, and fun. It wasn't until President Eisenhower's Commission on National Goals in 1960 that it took on its present meaning, and for the next four decades, policy makers have been trying to define it and measure it. Quality of life has played the same role in government as intellectual capital has in business—the elusive Eldorado of measurement.

Then suddenly, cities began to wonder whether there was money in quality of life. Most cities used to think they could attract corporations to set up factories and headquarters by offering lucrative tax breaks or the chance to pollute happily and without fear. But then it became clear that, while the dodgy companies liked the idea of regulation-free zones, these perks were not that high on the priority list of others. Many decisions about where to move headquarters to were often influenced not by money at all but by where the chief executives and their families happened to want to live. Good schools, nice trees, and exciting theaters attracted more companies than low taxes.

The map publishers Rand McNally capitalized on this in 1981 by launching their regular *Places Rated Almanac*, which ranked 277 American cities in terms of their "livability." Atlanta came top the first year. Those at the bottom reached for their lawyers. In the second year, the *Almanac* staggered policy makers by putting Pittsburgh top. This was a city that had once been so polluted that it had to keep its streetlights on all day. At its best, measuring can shock people into realizing that something has changed.

British geographers were not far behind. A group of academics at Glasgow University managed to convince the Scottish Development Agency, and the regeneration body Glasgow Action, that they should try the same idea. But the UK almanac would be measured more accurately. Before anything else, they would do an opinion poll all over the country to ask people what they thought were the most important aspects of city life. Would it be good schools, low crime, cleanliness, or high art? Only if you measured that first could you find out how to weight the data. The public overwhelmingly rated low crime as the most important aspect of the good life.

The academics set to work. Alan Findlay was an expert in migration and believed that it was "quality" rather than money that was shaping where people were moving. Arthur Morris was interested in where industry wanted to move—and it wasn't a polluted crime-ridden hellhole with tax advantages. Findlay and Morris took on geomorphologist Robert Rogerson—an expert in movements of ice and continents—and over the next 18 months, they set about measuring everything.

Often that meant being on the road. Rogerson visited all the 97 places they measured in the next few years, talking to people at random in the streets and at bus stops to get a sense of place. This was no dry measuring project. Just as the shipping magnate and pioneering sociologist, Charles Booth hit on the idea of asking school board visitors first, Rogerson and his colleagues hit on the idea of asking real-estate agents. They gossiped to them about house prices and neighborhoods. Then there were all the other measurements: How long did people have to wait for operations city by city? How long did they get to spend with their doctors? How much violent crime was there? How big were the school classes?

It all went into the pot, and their first index was an enormous success. For three days, the university switchboard was jammed by reporters from all over the world wanting to cover the story. Birmingham came bottom because of the Bull Ring center, but the problem was that Glasgow didn't do very well either. Worse, their historic rival Edinburgh came top. It was the height of the "Glasgow's Miles Better" campaign that did so much to improve the city's image, and this was about the last thing Glasgow's leaders wanted to hear. They had helped fund the index, after all. The presentation to the city council was a stilted affair around a large oak table at Glasgow town hall. "They either printed the list of cities upside down or the interviews were conducted in Esperanto," the enraged city provost, Pat Lally, told the local press.

Rogerson moved the Quality of Life Group to Strathclyde University and extended the study to cover smaller towns. Most of them used the findings as the basis for improvement, but not all. The angriest confrontation was in the worst place in Scotland, according to their measurements—the notoriously corrupt town of Monklands. Red-faced with fury, one councilor called Rogerson an "upstart from Strathclyde University," shouting "I don't believe a word you say!"

A decade on, and everyone seems to be putting together tables of places that measure how good they are to live in. Most chose somewhere different for the topmost place. A Reading University study in 1986 put Frankfurt top. The pioneering "Booming Towns" studies in the 1980s put Winchester top. When they tried again taking house prices into account, they replaced it with Milton Keynes. *Fortune* magazine's best "foreign" cities for business put Toronto top, followed by London on the grounds that it is safe, friendly, and bustling. *Money* magazine in the United States chose the small town of Nashua in New Hampshire. The London office of the Swiss-based Corporate Resources Group publishes annual surveys of quality of life in different world cities to help companies work out what they have to pay their executives for working there. Using London as the base city of 100, their weighted index gives Moscow 52.

It depends how you work it out, of course. Especially when you start counting crime—because people's fears often bear no relation to reality. Two-thirds of shoppers from Leicester interviewed in the 1990s revealed that what scared them most was being killed by a terrorist bomb—which even then was pretty unlikely. Go to any city in the world, however safe, and the locals will tell you how careful you have to be. Even if you use the same measuring rod everywhere, local people perceive it differently, define it differently, and interpret it differently. Quality-of-life measures may be better than simply measuring the amount of money changing hands—but they are not exactly definitive.

This same argument was being played out in a series of angry battles behind the scenes at the United Nations. The Chapter 40 of Agenda 21, agreed on at the Rio Earth Summit in 1992, had committed all the signatories to measure progress toward sustainable development, using a series of what they called "indicators" of success. By 1995, they had come up with a working list of 134 of them they hoped all countries would adopt. The trouble was they all chose different ones. They collected data in different ways. They didn't want to subject themselves to some of the indicators—and some of them meant different things in different cultures.

But what should they measure? And who should decide? Would it just be the powerful Western countries all over again? What if one country wanted to measure its success by how energy efficient they were, but another wanted to measure progress by health statistics? The OPEC countries fought the environmentalists. The old-style statisticians who wanted scientific indicators fought the new sustainability professionals who wanted thrilling ones. The developing countries fought the developed. There was only one way forward—to let nations and communities choose their own measurements.

It was an important decision, and—although most countries have yet to put it into effect—there have been some countries that have. One of them has been the UK. And so, 160 years after Chadwick sent his assistant commissioners scouring the cities with their measurements and tabular data, their great-great-great-grandchildren set out again— this time by faster modes of transport than the post chaise—to measure the unmeasurable.

V

The early 21st century looks set to be dominated by the thousand miles or so of the North American Pacific coast. Not so much because of the Hollywood dream machine or the Los Angeles smog but because of the extraordinary outpouring of wealth and creativity associated with Silicon Valley. So it is no surprise that a book about measuring what is really important should keep coming back there. There was John Vasconcellos, Silicon Valley's representative in the California Assembly. There was Ted Halstead, founder of the Redefining Progress and now head of the Silicon Valley's own think tank, the New America Foundation, dedicated to providing a new view of the future of politics. There was the challenge to accountancy posed by measuring the value of companies like Microsoft.

The next part of the measuring story starts with Gary Lawrence in Microsoft's hometown of Seattle, home to coffee bars, Boeing, and the good life. Lawrence had been city administrator for Redmond, where Microsoft's headquarters is, before he was headhunted to be planning director of Seattle—after a nationwide search for a new kind of planner. The task was to create a plan for Seattle that would cover every neighborhood, would reflect what people actually wanted, and would cover not just issues like where the shops should be but health and education too. But since this was in the first flush of success after the Rio summit, the new Seattle plan would also measure progress against yardsticks set by the people who lived there. This was a system devised and promoted by the local group Sustainable Seattle, and it has spread all over the world.

It was a tough job and it was going to take years. The mayor was given his own weekly TV show where people were encouraged to phone in with suggestions and views. He and Gary Lawrence appeared on talk radio five times a week—this is, after all, the city of *Frasier*. Full-color brochures were delivered to every household; teenagers were hired by the city to translate the issues into language that other teenagers might understand. Lawrence himself did 400 presentations over two years. It was a gigantic exercise in local democracy.

Human cussedness being what it is—by the end of this unprecedented consultation, a third of the city had still never heard of the project. Worse, many of those that *had* heard of it said they hadn't been consulted enough. But they overwhelmingly supported the direction the plan was going.

Then there was the job of choosing their indicators of success, along the lines set out by Jacksonville in Florida, with help from Hazel Henderson. Seattle rejected conventional money measurements. They wanted to know how cultured, how educated, and how clean the city was. They agreed with John Kenneth Galbraith that "If it isn't counted, it tends not to be noticed." They wanted to measure their success by the number of books sold or lent out by libraries, by attendance at arts events, by participation in sport. They set out to measure the number of latchkey kids, the amount of blood donated, the number of hours people volunteered. They also wanted a series of ratios. They wanted to judge the city's success by the number of vegetarian restaurants as a proportion of the number of McDonald's. Or the amount of birdseed sold at local garden centers as a proportion of pesticides. They wanted to know the number of therapists per head of population—though I've never been clear if it was considered a sign of mental health if there were more of them or less.

That was 1993. Soon the same idea had spread to the UK, pioneered by the New Economics Foundation and UNED-UK, which set about encouraging a new generation of counters to get out there and measure. Once again, it was a question of how to measure what really matters. If you measure problems, you just get depressed. If you measure particular solutions, they might be wrong—they often are. You might, for example, measure how close the shops or bus stops are to people's homes—forgetting that the food could still be disgusting and the bus service scandalous.

No, you had to find what was most important—and you had to make it inspiring. "Few people feel passionately about spreadsheets," said Gary Lawrence. "For indicators to lead to change, there needs to be emotional content: people need to care in their hearts as well as their minds."

It was a revolutionary and enjoyably unscientific idea, and it led to the idea of "hot indicators." Hot indicators might not have been measuring the most important aspect of life. They might not be exact or scientific, but at least they could catch people's imagination. So Seattle now judges its success on the number of salmon in local streams. In the UK, Strathclyde Council chose to measure the number of breeding golden eagles. In Dundee it was the number of empty houses, and in Fife it was the number of fish landing at local ports. There was the amount of asthma in Leeds, the number of cars with only one occupant in Peterborough, the amount of local produce sold in local shops in West Devon, the number of streets quiet enough to hold a conversation on in Hertfordshire, the number of swans in Norwich, the number of people who have planted a tree in Croxdale, the number of stag beetles in Colchester.

Armed with their equivalent of tabular data, the new pantometrists stood at street corners collecting figures and bringing them back to the local council to collate. Sometimes it was local people doing the measuring, sometimes local officials, sometimes it was children. Naturally, the main object of the exercise—beyond science or calculation—was to create change. Perry Walker of the New Economics Foundation encouraged the idea because it was something schoolchildren could get involved in. "These are not scientific indicators," he said. "That's not how they achieve their impact. They do so because they're what people care about."

In another of his projects in Reading, in England, people were puzzling over how they could measure the amount of dog mess in local parks in a way that could excite people. They hit on the idea of planting a little flag by each small brown pile and then taking a picture of it. There were 900 flags in all, and the pictures were published enthusiastically in the local paper. Two weeks later they did the same, and there were only 250 flags. Counting had worked. Perhaps it should be no surprise that Seattle now has the highest life expectancy in the United States and more books are bought there than in any other U.S.city— you tend to get what you measure, after all.

By the end of the 20th century, alternative indicators were all the rage. The Canadian environmentalist William Rees has pioneered a method of counting the environmental impact of cities in terms of the hectares of the earth they need to satisfy their needs. The UN Human Development Index was ranking countries according to life expectancy, education, and purchasing power. The World Bank was working on its improved "Wealth Accounting System" that included environment and human measurements. Even Standard & Poor, the American financial touchstone, was rating municipal bonds according the quality of life of the city that issued them. And right at the end of the millennium, Hazel Henderson's Calvert-Henderson Quality of Life Indicators—measuring each country by a series of different measures of their environment, health, safety, human rights, and much else besides—were being sent out to 1,500 ethical investment brokers instead of their usual Christmas cake.

V I

So there they are, Bentham's new generation of counters around the world—peering through the smog in South American cities counting the number of days you can see the Andes. Or scouring the streets of Chicago measuring how many people can name their community police. The whole business of indicators began as a radical challenge to governments. One group called Green Gauge even bought the poster site opposite the hideous headquarters of the Department of the Environment in London and covered it with their own pollution and traffic measurements. But now everyone is doing it. As early as 1991, the Canadian government was measuring its success with 43 new indicators. The OECD was soon counting 150 indicators. A 1993 survey of England and Wales found that 84 percent of people wanted more environmental information from the government. And heavens—did they get it!

The new-look British environment department announced its 13 "headline indicators" in 1999, including the number of unfit homes, adult literacy, and more amorphous concepts like community spirit. Behind those 13 was another set of 150 subindicators—and they just covered one government department. For some reason, the official mind believes that if indicators are a good idea, then we should have too many of them. Soon every department of government was churning out figures of its own, each one backed by a battery of technicians and statisticians, publishing them all in screeds of tables.Why do indicators have such an appeal to modern governments? Partly because of the technocratic thrill of measuring the ebb and flow of cause and effect as if government was a gigantic, though not particularly well oiled, machine. It is the McKinsey Fallacy all over again. Yet cause and effect is the one thing it is quite impossible to measure—interpreting the burgeoning wealth of data to work out what causes what is always a matter of judgment, common sense, and intuition.

Yet governments still cling to their other dream—one number to sum up the whole caboodle. GNP and its partner GDP are alive and well. When the Clinton administration tried to add footnotes to the GDP figures that measured the depletion of natural resources, the whole idea was blocked by two representatives from coal-producing states. If national accounts showed air pollution, warned Alan Mollohan from West Virginia, "somebody is going to say . . . that the coal industry isn't contributing anything to the country." Quite so.

This fresh outbreak of measuring is one of the defining characteristics of our age. In politics the response to the wider counting crisis—that we need to measure what's really important—is to measure everything. But these bizarre local indicators are different. They are not intended to measure the world as much as change it. They are about inspiring people. It's the act of measuring that matters. Change happens when children go out measuring stag beetles in their back garden. It probably doesn't happen when the professionals do it with their precision and clever instruments. It happens when they ask people whether they feel well, but probably not when—as in Oldham—they measure the number of babies born less than the official healthy birth weight of precisely 6.1 pounds. This kind of measuring is more likely to suffer the same fate that most official counting suffers from. In alternative economic circles, it's known as MEGO syndrome. It stands for My Eyes Glaze Over.

What we count is important because it reflects who we are. Or as Hazel Henderson told the first alternative economics summit in 1984, "Reality is what we pay attention to." That explains why the contemporaries of Malthus spent so much time measuring people's religious feelings and why our own contemporaries are measuring allergies. Strange in a way that both generations counted stag beetles in their back gardens.

But it's more than that. We construct our own reality by counting it. "Indicators only reflect our innermost core values and goals, measuring the development of our own understanding," says Henderson. No wonder that when we measure what we fear the most—greenhouse gas or child abuse—the figures tend to get worse. At last, an explanation for the Quantum Effect.

Or as one Washington policy maker puts it at the foot of all her e-mails: "We are what we measure. It's time we measured what we want to be."

10

EDGAR CAHN AND THE
PRICE OF EVERYTHING

*If it cannot get beyond its vast abstractions, the national income,
the rate of growth, capita/output ratio, input/output analysis,
labor mobility, capital accumulation; if it cannot get beyond all this
and make contact with the human realities of poverty,
frustration, alienation, despair, breakdown, crime,
escapism, stress, congestion, ugliness and spiritual death,
then let us scrap economics and start afresh.*

E. F. Schumacher, *Small Is Beautiful*

*A man who knows the price of everything and
the value of nothing.*

Oscar Wilde's definition of a cynic

WASHINGTON, 1980

I

WHEN HE WOKE up in a hospital intensive-care bed after a massive
heart attack at the age of 44, Edgar Cahn had what amounted to a revelation. He realized he didn't actually like being waited on hand and
foot by a bevy of doctors and nurses attending to his every whim.

That was a bit of a surprise in itself. Nothing in his previous life had implied that he hankered after a life of luxury. He had spent his entire career raising hell, suing the government, writing inflammatory speeches for Bobby Kennedy, and battling for the rights of Native Americans. But we all imagine we might like that kind of care just a little if it happened to us. And as a successful law professor in a comfortable house in the plush Washington district of Friendship Heights, he might have expected to breathe a sigh of relief in hospital—to stop fighting a moment and relax.

But it wasn't like that at all. There was no sense that all that money on health insurance was finally going toward something worthwhile. Quite the opposite. He hated feeling useless.

It was 1980, and as he lay there attached to tubes—60 percent of his heart affected by the attack—he reflected on the recent news of layoffs and welfare cuts. He wasn't the only one feeling useless at the time. Older people and the unemployed were increasingly being defined in exactly the same way. "That's when it struck me," he wrote later. "All of those people I had read about in the newspapers were being declared useless too. And it occurred to me, I'll bet they don't like it any more than I do."

The whole experience changed Cahn's life. He went into hospital a conventionally progressive "liberal" lawyer, who had cut his teeth in the Civil Rights movement and the War on Poverty. He came out something completely different: a critic of conventional welfare, a radical who would shortly be taking up his cudgels against overbearing professions, but—most of all—determined to find a better way of measuring people's worth and contribution than simply measuring how much they earn.

In the two decades since then, Cahn has invented his own currency system based on people's time. He calls the new money "time dollars." He has pioneered the earning and spending of this by anyone from bedridden older people in Brooklyn to young criminals in Washington, and he has watched the idea spread around the world—first to Japan and now to England, France, Latin America, and eastern Europe.

Time dollars have become a way of measuring work by measuring people's effort rather than what the market will pay. They are a whole new way of rewarding people for doing those critical but unpaid jobs in the community that desperately need doing, from tutoring in schools to visiting seniors, which the market doesn't normally reward. They are a new way of measuring *real* work—including everything from bringing up children to helping out in the community—and rewarding it, but not valuing some people's work as more important than others'. Because actually, Cahn says, everyone's work is pretty important— otherwise it wouldn't be work. Time dollars have also become a whole new way of buying surplus equipment from the mainstream economy, like some of the 15 million computers that are thrown out and usually put into landfills in the United States every year.

With time dollars Cahn tackles the classic problem of measuring. To count something you have to define it, and thanks to the narrow thinking about GDP, we have defined "work" incredibly narrowly. We add it all up, count it, and measure it according to what it earns—and suddenly find that we're still missing something.

Why does this happen? Because we are living in the age of highly complex cost-benefit analysis, where almost anything—from the effects of accidents to the preservation of a species—is being reduced to monetary terms. Because although generations of romantics and social critics have poured scorn on the attempt to measure the money value of everything, nobody has ever really come up with a money system that doesn't just reflect back what the market says is important. And in the days when an Albanian orphan costs $6,000 and a reasonable house in San Francisco costs $2 million, the market probably isn't a very good measure of "worth." On the other hand, unless they are assigned numbers and monetary values in some cost-analysis function, they run the risk of being considered "worthless."

Cost-benefit analysis is both a way to protect what's important and an attempt to avoid value judgments, political acrimony, or disagreement of any kind over decisions. The more difficult the decision—from where to put a new airport to who pays for global warming—the more it seemed to need measuring and costing. It's a very modern dilemma: If you don't give an economic value to intangibles, they get ignored; if you do, there are dangers that people will believe you. However necessary it may be to try to work out what all the whales in the world are worth, there are dangers if people start taking it too seriously. As if you could *really* buy the view or the species. Or worse, as if you could really sell it.

Cahn's time dollars looked at the problem another way to try and avoid the dilemma altogether, and that meant measuring the effort people put in around their neighborhood according to the time spent and not the market value of their work. The idea has spawned a whole movement, and there are now more than 200 of these "time banks" operating in the United States alone. It's an upside-down kind of economy, where a bedridden elderly lady can earn an hour for an hour by making supportive phone calls to neighbors—on just the same basis as a lawyer or a brain surgeon. It's a whole different way of measuring value that seems diametrically opposed to the efforts of the cost-benefit economists, but it's as much a symptom of the counting crisis as they are. Time dollars emerged because money wasn't a good way of measuring people anymore.

It is hard to categorize Cahn in either the left or right wings of the debate about welfare and professionalism—which is, after all, just as he wants it. But the whole idea of a parallel measuring system, like a parallel currency, had—like him—impeccably radical credentials.

II

Edgar Stuart Cahn was born in New York City on March 23, 1935, the son of an eminent law professor who was best known for the legal concept of a "sense of injustice." People might not understand the law, said Cahn Senior, they might not be able to measure it—they might not even understand the detailed legal concept of justice—but they can recognize injustice when they see it. It's an important principle. Just because you can't measure something precisely doesn't mean it isn't there.

Edgar trained as a silversmith and worked in a factory making wire cords for telephones to pay his way through graduate school at Yale. The factory experience gave him an insight into the successors of Frederick Taylor. He watched the time-and-motion experts at work measuring productivity levels—setting targets for the workforce for every hour, week, and month, measured by how much wire had run through the machine. In fact, Cahn's fellow employees very soon learned how to fake the system while they nipped out to the bathroom for a cigarette. It took a much more worldly-wise foreman to make a deal with the workforce, agreeing on a real production total—a percentage of the figure the machines were sending to the head office to keep the production executives happy.

Cahn Junior was never easy to categorize, but he was plunged into radical hell-raising partly because he married young. He was Jewish and his wife, Jean, was black—and in Washington in the early 1960s, that was still considered a difficult combination. Often their neighbors wouldn't speak to them. When he worked for Attorney General Bobby Kennedy, Kennedy would occasionally call the recalcitrant neighbors and ask them to take a message around—enjoying the struggle inside their minds between racism and deference.

It was the start of a lifelong involvement with civil rights. Two decades later, a Washington magazine would have pictures of both on the cover, under the headline THE BRILLIANT ANGRY CAREERS OF JEAN AND EDGAR CAHN.

At one time, Edgar was working in the office of Attorney General Kennedy and his successor, Nicholas Katzenbach, writing speeches and working as "special counsel" assigned to particularly controversial projects. As Kennedy's speechwriter, Cahn penned his controversial address to the Alabama bar on their opposition to desegregation and his "swansong speech" on equal justice for the poor. But it was the other role that paved the way to the future.

As special counsel, he was loaned to the Department of Justice to help with the authorizing legislation for the War on Poverty, President Lyndon Johnson's massive attempt to create what he called a "Great Society." While he was there, he and Jean coauthored an article in the *Yale Law Journal* called "The War on Poverty: A Civilian Perspective." It was the blueprint for what would eventually become the National Legal Services Program, the free legal-advice service for disadvantaged people and communities—if necessary to sue the government to get their rights.

It was a revolutionary idea that government money could be used to take the government to court, and Johnson's response was a resounding No. It took what Cahn now calls "devious maneuvering to say the least" to persuade the American Bar Association and get the idea running anyway.

To do this, Jean was leant by the State Department to launch the program, and Edgar settled in as special assistant and speechwriter to the general charged with conducting the War on Poverty, Sargent Shriver. It was just the start. Having provided legal advice to the poor, the next step was to find ways that poor people could become lawyers themselves. The result was the Antioch Law School, now the District of Columbia School of Law.

Antioch was designed to turn out a new breed of lawyers committed to justice and trained in the first and only "clinical law school," where students from their first semester onward were both in the classroom and apprenticing in the school's own teaching law firm. From there the students would represent people who needed it, run test cases, launch major litigation—even try new kinds of community economic development.

Both institutions—the law school and the legal-services program—would turn out to be important later. But Cahn also plunged into an early shot across the bows of the number crunchers—on behalf of Native Americans. He launched an investigation of the Office of Management and Budget and the General Accounting Office, the central temple of measurement in the United States. Unfortunately the research disappeared in a suspicious fire at the law school and was never published.

He had actually chosen a moment in history where cost-benefit was suddenly extremely fashionable. By the 1960s, the new cadres of professionals in government were championing this kind of analysis—and nobody more than the U. S. secretary of defense during the Vietnam War, Robert McNamara.

McNamara, who was still president of Ford Motor Company, was about to take up the position in 1960 when he ran across a former Oxford don named Charles Hitch with bold ideas about how cost-benefit could be used in defense procurement. It was, they said, the administrators' equivalent of "love at first sight." Hitch was taken on as assistant secretary of defense and comptroller, and he brought in a system called Planning, Programming and Budgeting System or PPBS, known in government circles as "Hitchcraft." Every procurement and every defense decision was calculated according to its "real" cost—putting a dollar value on every possible aspect, from delays to extra training.

McNamara lost out in the government after opposing further bombing of Vietnam and disappeared to become president of the World Bank, later putting his imprimatur on a massively ambitious program of contraception—it's strange how the idea keeps coming up. The program went hand in hand, needless to say, with an enormous monitoring project to measure worldwide fertility rates, use of contraceptives, spending on family planning, financial sources and much else besides.

Despite McNamara's disappearance, Johnson was among those who was impressed, and he ordered Hitchcraft to be used in every government department from 1965 onwards. "I thought at the time that this was foolish, almost certain to lead to confusion and likely to end up discrediting the management techniques it was trying to promote," said Hitch later. It did. The problem was that actually this kind of approach suited the military better. The military was better at ignoring intangibles than other departments, and intangibles are at the heart of the counting crisis.

"Facts alone are wanted in life," said Dickens's character Thomas Gradgrind, and the early cost-benefit experts took the idea to heart. The

U. S. Army engineers used to congratulate themselves that they had completely ignored "intangibles"—like views or people's enjoyment— as they calculated which water management project to carry out next. The trouble was that, without the intangibles, their calculations weren't very accurate.

Cost-benefit faced its own counting crisis earlier than other aspects of calculation because of this very paradox. If you tried to find out what a major construction project *really* cost—including time saved, noise nuisance, and all the rest—you simply had to include intangibles. But if you included intangibles, it couldn't be very scientific. There was the dilemma: You had to have your answers either objective or accurate— you couldn't have both.

And it was this very paradox that was playing hell with the biggest and most ambitious attempt to measure a complex answer ever carried out. In 1968, the British government suddenly decided they would choose a site for the new Third London Airport north of the city by car-rying out a gigantic cost-benefit exercise that would measure absolutely everything.

For the next two and a half years, a commission chaired by a senior judge, Mr. Justice Roskill, combed the evidence. To make things doubly complicated, a third site had to be measured too. A campaigning think tank, the Town and Country Planning Association, put in its own plan-ning application to build an airport at Foulness—its preferred site—a stretch of marshland off the Essex coast much frequented by brent geese. The economists attached to the commission would put a value on the noise of aircraft, the disruption of building work, the delay of flights, the extra traffic, and so on, and then calculate the answer. For the Roskill Commission, there was going to be no value judgment at all. The figures would speak for themselves.

To avoid any chance of judgment and to keep the process completely "scientific," the measurements were put together in 25 separate calcu-lations. They were added up only right at the end of the process. And to the horror of some of the members of the commission, when the final addition was made, the answer was wrong. The site they felt was best— Foulness—was going to be £100 million more expensive in cost-benefit terms than the small village of Cublington.

After 246 witnesses, 3,850 documents, seven technical annexes, and 10 million spoken words, some of the planners on the commission felt cheated. In public, they stayed loyal to Roskill. The commission was excellent, said Britain's most famous planner, Colin Buchanan—a member of it—"it just got the small matter of the site wrong."

The team had managed to measure the exact cost of having too much aircraft noise by looking at the effect noise tended to have on house prices. But when it came to measuring the value of a Norman church at Stewkley, which would have to be demolished to make way for the runway, things got more confused. How could you possibly put a money price on that? One team member suggested they find out its fire insurance value. Everyone laughed, but the story got out and reached the press. Doing it like that would measure the value of the church at just £51,000.

A fierce political debate erupted. Commission members were accused of being "philistines." The geographer John Adams, from Jeremy Bentham's old college, drew up an alternative plan. Using similar cost-benefit methods, he showed that the cheapest option would actually be to build the airport in London's exclusive and royal Hyde Park—but that Westminster Abbey, where the medieval kings and queens of England are buried, would have to be demolished to make way.

The satire didn't work: The *Sunday Times* published a letter from a retired air vice marshal congratulating him for recommending Hyde Park for an airport, and pointing out that he had proposed exactly the same thing in 1946.

In the end, the government rejected the idea of building at Cublington or Foulness, and if you fly into the Third London Airport today you fly to Stansted instead. Meanwhile, one of the world's leading planning academics, Professor Peter Self, was organizing his revenge for the mauling he received at the hands of the commission's planning barristers. "It struck me at the time as strange," he wrote, "that so many intelligent people should apparently accept trial by quantification as the only sensible or possible way of reaching such a decision."

It infuriated him that the new "econocracy"—as he called it—were being so pompous about numbers that meant so little. Anyone like Buchanan who looked at the competing sites could see that building the airport off the coast was the best plan, he said. You couldn't calculate intuition and experience like that. Yet all the lawyers at the commission did was pick over the measurements: "The weight placed on cost-benefit analysis was then confirmed by the spectacle of the flower of the English planning bar gargling gingerly and reverently with the cost-benefit figures."

The whole thing was a "psychological absurdity and ethical monstrosity," said Self, noting that the experts had carefully calculated the cost of even a minute's flight delay—but completely ignored the cost of fuel, or pollution or the environmental effects or the effect on the geese. He advised economists to take Dr. Johnson's advice and kick a wall hard to convince themselves that the external world exists. His attack set back cost-benefit analysis for nearly a decade.

III

So here's the problem: Do you measure people—or churches for that matter—according to a number or according to a value? Put like that, the answer seems obvious. It's one man one vote, after all. In democracy, everybody counts the same. But it isn't as simple as that in the modern world. Or in a democracy, come to that, where a vote in Florida turns out to count considerably more than one in, say, Massachusetts.

The whole argument about measuring people and measuring money came to a head in the issue of global warming. How can we attach a value to carbon in the atmosphere or the trees in the rain forest? The United Nations Rio Earth Summit in 1992 agreed that some kind of action had to be taken. That meant some kind of economic framework. To produce one, they called in one of the best-known cost-benefit experts in the world.

David Pearce had been a consultant to the Thatcher government. He was—and is—a collector of porcelain, a cat lover, and a leading environmentalist. Pearce had devoted his career to finding a way of making the environment expensive. Because it's free to cut down the Amazon rain forest or pollute the atmosphere, everyone just goes ahead and does it. Yet there clearly were hidden costs when people did so—damage to the air we breathe causes health problems, for example. Damaged rain forest speeds up global warming, which means freak weather conditions and rising sea levels. There are real costs attached. The idea was to measure these costs and give threatened forests, views, and species a monetary value. If it could be measured—the value of elephants, the cash cost of aircraft noise, the value of the Grand Canyon—Pearce would measure it. And by measuring it, you could set a price to it and find a way of protecting it.

It was pragmatic in the extreme, but it was also hopeful. Yet within six years, Pearce was being condemned by the environmentalists of the world as a peddler of "racist economics," for assigning different market values to the lives of different nationalities. He had unleashed a torrent of international abuse on his head, and he was facing a vitriolic campaign against him—including a public letter signed by leading members of the chattering classes all over the world—culminating in the humiliating rejection of his framework by the United Nations itself.

The problem was the idea of Willingness to Pay or Willingness to Accept Compensation—known to the *cognoscenti* as WTP and WTA. This cost-benefit term means that you can measure the value of something—whether it's grizzly bears or bighorn sheep in America or Amazon rain forests—by asking people what they would be prepared to pay to rescue them.

Using WTP and other measuring techniques, Pearce came up with a figure of greenhouse damage of $20 per extra ton of carbon. Cutting down primary forest cost between $4,000 and $4,400 per hectare, said the environmental economists. People seemed to be prepared to pay between $40 and 48 per person to preserve the entire species of humpback whales—or $49 to 64 after seeing a video of them.

He and his colleagues were introducing a whole new jargon—bequest values, total user values, option values. Or existence values—what people are prepared to pay for the continued existence of things they may never see—like the Grand Canyon. Grizzly bears seemed to be worth $24 per person under this system. The Grand Canyon's existence he calculated at $4.43 a month.

There were many environmentalists who objected to the idea that you could put any money value on a species at all. Destroying the ozone layer, flattening the rain forest, killing whales was immoral and that was all there was to it. Their loss was of incalculable value, and anyone who said otherwise was immoral too. Pearce didn't agree. The point was to measure the world as it really was, to find a way of compensating people for changing their behavior. That meant assigning money values to things. So the confrontation over climate change was set.

When it came to their policy paper for the Intergovernmental Panel on Climate Change, Pearce and his team were commissioned to put a dollar value on every possible damage from the greenhouse effect. The trouble was that they valued a human life in the rich developed countries at 15 times the life of someone in a poor country—from $1.5 million for Americans down to $100,000 for the poorest peasants. And their ability to pay was similarly lower. A hectare of Chinese wetland was worth just 10 percent of a hectare of Western wetland. It wasn't what people wanted to hear.

The storm broke over Pearce's head, coordinated in an effective campaign around the world by professional viola player Aubrey Meyer. Meyer never looked like an international negotiator, with his trademark pigtail and white T-shirt, but his London-based organization, the Global Commons Institute, successfully drummed up signatures of protest from all over the world. "Why, if one spotted owl equals one spotted owl, doesn't one human equal one human?" he asked.

And Meyer won. When the representatives of world governments met in Berlin in April 1995, they carried with them a letter from Indian environment minister Kamal Nath rejecting the analysis as "absurd and discriminatory" and urging other governments to do likewise. When they reconvened in Geneva three months later, all the delegates were greeted with a copy of a newspaper clipping the previous weekend with the headline ONE WESTERN LIFE IS WORTH 15 IN THE THIRD WORLD, SAYS UN REPORT. In Montreal, three months after that, the two sides were yelling abuse at each other. This time, delegates threw out the analysis and figures altogether. Kamal Nath later resigned over bribery charges, which rather undermines his high moral tone, but it was no comfort.

"It is a result of poor communication by economists," says an unrepentant Pearce today. "Because we were used to using shorthand when we were talking about the value of an elephant, we knew what we meant by it—but it isn't the intrinsic value of an elephant. It's just what someone's willing to pay. We're just measuring people's preferences. But a lot of the opposition was based on sheer pig ignorance. People who couldn't be bothered to read anything or learn anything, thought that in five minutes they can pick up 200 years of economics. To an economist there's no surprise about what's being said. But if you want to discredit it, you don't have to be a master of the media to do that."

What Pearce and his team were trying to do was to measure the way of the world. It may have looked pragmatic—and that's exactly what it was—but it was designed to create an agreement based on real exchanges of resources. It was just what everyone does in their own homes: "The rights of individuals are not separate from costs," he says—and one glimpse around the world shows that, sadly, he's right. Nor has the world managed to knit together a climate change agreement without him.

Yet there is a big problem if you want to measure WTP with anything like accuracy. For one thing, many people can't afford to pay to protect bald eagles, even if they want to. And if they did, about a quarter of the people asked what they would be willing to pay to preserve bald eagles, woodpeckers, coyotes, salmon, or wild turkeys refuse to reply on the grounds that you can't put a price on such things. And of course you can't. One Frankfurt woman, Frau Kraus, discovered in 1989 that she had a veto over a proposed new skyscraper they wanted to build next door, and refused to play the game at all. She turned down a million deutschmarks, then she turned down 10 million. "Not even if they were to offer me 20 million would I change my mind," she told the papers. "It would block out my sunlight and spoil the place where I was born and bred."

Then there is the usual problem of measuring. Cost-benefits will always have a problem valuing the intangibles. This mixture of careful measuring of the things that can be measured and a vague rule of thumb for the rest led John Adams to call the process a "horse and rabbit stew." The rabbit is skinned and dressed with great care. The horse—size unknown—is just tossed into the pot with no preparation at all. "It is an ethic that debases that which is important and disregards entirely that which is supremely important," he says.

Valuing "horses" creates the most peculiar effects. One Washington economist valued the world's population of elephants at $1 million on the grounds that it was an easy figure to remember. The world's largest pharmaceutical company, Merck, actually bought the rights to Costa Rica's entire genetic diversity—plants, seeds, and soil—for $1 million plus royalties. It's strange how the figure of $1 million comes up when people don't actually know what something is worth.

Yet cost-benefit analysis is on the increase. Ronald Reagan's controversial executive order 12291, insisting on cost-benefit analysis for every new federal regulation, was announced within a week of his inauguration in 1980. All over the world, the technique is seen as a way of controlling politicians, or of politicians controlling bureaucrats—taking the politics or the uncertainty out of decisions. When the *Exxon Valdez* spilled its oil off Alaska in 1989, they had to work out the cost of the damage so that the tanker's owners could pay it, and they have been paying compensation practically ever since.

That's the heart of the counting crisis. Measuring is often impossible, but sometimes you have to try anyway. The question is: Can we find ways of counting people or work in such a way that it doesn't have ludicrous effects, or—worse—undermine everything we value in the world. That's where Edgar Cahn came in.

IV

Imagine you could somehow square the circle between counting up the value of everyone on the world markets and counting everyone equally and valuing equally what they can do—whatever it is. If cost-benefit is really an "ethic that debases what's important"—as John Adams says— imagine you could find a method of measurement that somehow gets it right.

That wasn't really the way Cahn was thinking in his hospital bed. He just wanted to invent a new kind of money that valued the old, the young, and the unemployed. But in practice, that's what time dollars became.

The first six time-dollar projects began in 1987 with a large grant from the Robert Wood Johnson Foundation. At its simplest, the idea uses a broker at the end of the phone and allows people to earn time dollars for each hour they help out in their local community—anything from peer tutoring by schoolchildren to telephone counseling by housebound older people. Cahn described the idea as working like a blood bank or baby-sitting club:

> *Help a neighbor and then, when you need it, a neighbor—most likely a different one—will help you. The system is based on equality: one hour of help means one time dollar, whether the task is grocery shopping or making out a tax return. . . . Credits are kept in individual accounts in a "bank" on a personal computer. Credits and debits are tallied regularly. Some banks provide monthly balance statements, recording the flow of good deeds.*

One of the original schemes, Member to Member in Brooklyn, has since become famous all over the world—and a major selling point for its sponsor, the Social HMO Elderplan. "Does Medicare send you a friend like George?" "Does Medicare lift your spirits?" asks Elderplan's advertising today. The health insurance company's managers know that a picture of George, an elderly volunteer doing minor home repairs, carries a kind of shock value at a time when the health-care industry is treated with some cynicism by the public.

On the face of it, the idea that people might volunteer for their insurance company—and with enthusiasm—is pretty peculiar. Yet in their first 12 years of existence, Member to Member volunteers have put in over 100,000 hours helping each other, teaching each other, and supporting each other to be independent. In turn, the time dollars they earn can be spent on help from other people in the same system—or on lower premiums, discounts on merchandise, or local services. Dollars needn't be part of the formula. The program was designed as a kind of bank, so that older volunteers could earn and pay time dollars for helping each other. It meant they could offer each other shopping, escorts, friendly visiting, bill paying, hospital visiting, home repairs, walking clubs, support groups, self-help courses, and others, all funded by time dollars earned through the scheme.

To the surprise of the organizers, the real effect wasn't so much helping seniors stay healthy and independent—it was that the older volunteers also stayed healthier too. They had a new purpose in life, in other words. They felt needed again. Better still, many of the services provided by Member to Member were beyond anything that can normally be offered by a health insurance company. Many are also services that money can't buy anyway. "Often you can't buy what you really need," says Mashi Blech, Member to Member's organizer throughout. "You can't hire a new best friend. You can't buy somebody you can talk to over the phone when you're worried about surgery."

A decade on, they also have an ambitious program of training courses and self-help courses, helping the recently bereaved, for example—hoping that they can train the graduates of those courses to teach in their turn. They also have telephone bingo, regular phone quizzes, walking clubs, and peer counseling along the lines of a successful program in California that pioneered the idea.

But because participants became healthier than average, Elderplan let them use their time dollars to pay a quarter of their health insurance costs. Now they're zero premium, and to replace this perk, Member to Member launched CreditShop in 1998, which allows participants to use their time dollars to buy goods and services outside the system. These include health-care products like blood pressure monitors—unexpectedly popular among the people of Brooklyn—plus movie and theater tickets, transport vouchers, and supermarket and luncheon vouchers. Organizers even negotiated fixed-price lunches in restaurants in Brooklyn.

Member to Member keeps people healthy by keeping them in touch with each other, in a corner of New York City where—until recently—you often had three generations living within walking distance. But the modern world, being what it is, has spread them to all four corners of the globe, and you need to find a way of linking people together again.

By measuring what people do for each other—but doing so in a new way, an hour for an hour—time dollars seem to be able to do this.

The idea spread agonizingly slowly. But by the end of the 1990s, there were 16-year-olds in Chicago earning time dollars for tutoring 14-year-olds, and spending them on recycled computers. There were young offenders in Washington, D.C., tried by juries of other teenagers who earned time dollars for doing so. There were tenants in Baltimore paying part of their rent in time dollars. There were seniors in Long Island earning time dollars for learning Internet skills.

Sometimes all the time-dollar volunteers are being "paid" to do is gather information—like those in St. Louis who go door-to-door visiting seniors making sure they are not showing early signs of depression. Or in Denver where they are phoning patients to check postoperative symptoms or to make sure they are sticking to a medical regimen. Often it's just checking up after somebody has been discharged from hospital that there's food in the house. There wasn't enough money to pay for these things in ordinary dollars—but they were critical nonetheless. People who had been designated "useless" were producing something absolutely vital.

What's more, the idea was spreading abroad. There are 500 or so time-dollar systems in Japan, called *hureai kippu* ("ticket for a caring relationship") and others using a small plastic currency called DanDan ("I thank you very deeply"). There are now time dollars springing up in England, France, Curaçao, and Slovakia—each one of them measuring people's effort, and yet not quite measuring either.

In that time, Cahn had faced as many setbacks as he had successes. His wife, Jean, died of cancer in 1992. The accountants got hold of many of the original time-dollar schemes and closed them down because they cost money to run. His attempt to bring time dollars into the National Legal Services Program—and by making it reciprocal, save it from the new Republican Congress—failed miserably. Time after time, the idea seemed to be rolling out with a new energy, only to find another major obstacle in the way.

But there were successes too. He persuaded the IRS to zero-rate time dollars for tax—people weren't, after all, volunteering for the taxman. He found himself invited into 10 Downing Street in London and to speak in front of the French prime minister. And in 2000, he married again—and with his new wife, Chris, set about organizing time dollars as a worldwide movement.

There are now somewhere between 700 and 1,000 time-dollar programs around the world, from Banco del Tempo in Italy to Time Banks in Britain. The result is a kind of parallel economy, using time as the medium of exchange, which can count people whatever they are able to do, even if they are bed-ridden or hopelessly depressed or so scared of the world that they daren't venture outside. But somehow, because time dollars measure the things that money ignores, they can build trust.

"Market economics values what is scarce—not the real work of society, which is caring, loving, being a citizen, a neighbor and a human being," said Cahn. "That work will, I hope, never be so scarce that the market value goes high, so we have to find a way of rewarding contributions to it."

Time dollars go to the heart of the counting crisis because they seem to be able to achieve some of those intangible things that proper measuring by professionals just can't. Doctors can cure disease, after all, but they can't cure loneliness, isolation, or unhappiness. If they think they can—or if their patients think they can—they will not just fail, they will find their time and money is increasingly eaten up hopelessly trying to force health on reluctant and passive people.

As the counting crisis mounts, even the most numerate researchers suddenly find themselves discovering intangibles at the root of what they are trying to measure. Take, for example, the massive recent study of crime in Chicago by the Harvard School of Public Health, which studied nearly 350 different neighborhoods and found that none of the usual measures—poverty, racial discrimination—had much to do with the crime rates. After 8,872 exhausting interviews, they announced the missing factor. They called it "collective efficacy"—and it meant the willingness of local people to intervene with children when they see them playing truant, painting graffiti, or hanging threateningly around in gangs on street corners. Absolutely real, but impossible to measure directly.

"Hard-headed, bottom-line policy makers want data, hard data—such as crime statistics or property values reflecting the prevalence of criminal activity," writes Cahn. "Now, suddenly, soft stuff takes on hard, statistical significance. Neighborhood interaction, networking, local custom and just being nice can no longer be dismissed as fuzzy, irrelevant concepts. In this context, time dollars earned in neighborhood roles can be used as a measure of collective efficacy and as a reward to stimulate such conduct."

Time dollars, in other words, would be a kind of magic potion tossed into the world to reveal everything that measuring with money had missed out—a kind of antidote to amnesia.

Before the late twentieth century, most societies knew without being told where the limits to measurable medicine were. They knew that if they needed people to visit seniors or give them lifts or just keep an eye on them, they would have to organize it themselves. One of the original meanings of "money" was memory, and time dollars seem to be unlocking this memory too. And when they do so, they find there are some things that are of much higher quality when they are provided by friends and neighbors than when they are provided by a reluctant and cash-strapped insurance company or by professional strangers.

"Time dollars are both a measuring tool and an unmeasuring tool," says Edgar Cahn. Sometimes unmeasuring can provide a side of life that measuring never can.

V

The problem, as the cost-benefit people found, is that economists measure and celebrate the wrong things—because money isn't a very good measuring rod. Somehow you have to use it as a guide, but if you take it too seriously, it can have a perverse effect on the world. It measures Wall Street pretty well, but it ignores some of those things that are most important—bringing up children, looking after seniors, creating a good and healthy environment—because they're not measurable with money. Then it forgets them altogether.

The futurist Alvin Toffler—author of *Future Shock*—used to supply executives with dramatic evidence of the importance of this hidden, unmeasured, unmeasurable economy. He used to enliven business conferences by asking them what it would cost them in real cash terms if none of their employees had ever been toilet trained. They didn't know. The point was to make them aware of the enormous subsidy and underpinning that the unmeasurable families and communities provide for business. We all know that community trust is vital: The government can't produce that by itself and the market doesn't want to—but without it, neither of them can work effectively.

"Measuring is a way of conveying information, but also a way of obscuring it," says Edgar Cahn now—but the counting crisis is worse than that. Because if money is the main measure and it ignores all of these things, that isn't the end of the matter. It remakes the world as if they weren't there. We spend a generation measuring community life entirely in money terms, and turn around and find—sure enough—that's all we've got. The drug dealers control the streets, the communities have disappeared behind bars and locked doors, and seniors die alone in municipal old folks homes.

These are what economists call "externalities"—the costs that the economy throws on the rest of us and never measures. It's the job of cost-benefit to try and measure them and give them a money value. That can have a dramatic propaganda effect, but it may also compound the problem—because, of course, they don't actually *have* a money value. So the damage goes on.

"We are strip-mining our communities," wrote Cahn in his latest book, *No More Throwaway People*. "We are depopulating our neighborhoods, we are atomizing families. The process keeps accelerating as every asset we can lay our hands on gets sent to the market for sale at the prevailing price. The market is governed by a pricing system that devalues precisely those activities most critically needed in communities."

That was what Cahn meant when he said his time-based money was both a measuring tool and an un-measuring tool. It measures in the sense that it tracks the efforts people put in. But it unmeasures in the sense that it throws the net far wider than money does. It means that everybody has something to offer, and for the so-called problem people—who may never have been asked to give anything in their lives before—that can be transformative.

The two institutions that Cahn became famous for provided a dramatic demonstration of this. In 1994, the incoming Republican leader Newt Gingrich targeted the National Legal Service Program, cutting its funding by a third and restricting the tactics it was allowed to use and the appeals it could make. Of the 100 million or so households helped over the previous 33 years, not one came forward for the hearings at Congress to defend it

Cahn believes that if they had abandoned the idea of just having professional lawyers helping people, and instead charged their time in time dollars—paid off by the recipients by helping out in their local community—it would all have been different. "I can help stop someone getting evicted, but I can't make their home somewhere they would like to be," he says. "For that I need their help too. And when professionals just give their time away without asking for any help back, they unwittingly provide the message to the recipient that 'you have got nothing that anybody could possible want.' And that's disempowering. You can change people's lives by asking for something in return."

That was the story with his other institution, the District of Columbia School of Law, the successor to his Antioch Law School, which is still teaching on the medical school model and sending students out to give legal support in the community. But at the DC School of Law, they don't give the support away for free; they charge in time dollars and expect that people will pay back in some way to the community. For a moment, as the deficit in Washington gaped larger, it looked as though the school would go the same way as the Legal Services Program. Even the *Washington Post* was calling for it to be closed.

But hearings organized by the DC Council didn't go the same way as the ones in Congress. Those who had been helped, and paid back, came out in droves to support it, and the school stayed funded. Somehow charging their services in this new kind of time-based money had made people equal. It wasn't charity anymore.

Cahn calls this "reciprocity," and it's part of a wider battle he has been fighting to measure people differently, not according to what they *can't* do—as problem people caught in the grasp of the professionals. Nor according to what they can earn but according to what they *can* do. It's another kind of unmeasuring because it doesn't categorize people—it starts from their uniqueness: Whatever they *can* do gets counted.

The point is that counting isn't actually neutral—however objective it might or might not be. You can see people's hidden beliefs shining out in what they choose to count. Those who just concentrate on money believe that's all that matters, but that hidden belief starts to remake society *as if* that was so—and we find we've got drug cartels and tax havens instead of trust. Those who try to value the hidden effects of the market—on whales or grizzly bears—realize there are other things in life. Those like Cahn who count something else are also "moral statisticians" trying to reveal to us all the hidden resources of people that money values don't see. "I count for a reason," says Cahn now. "The counting may be objective and precise, but it is really a form of advocacy. Only when I start counting can I begin to generate focus on the external costs of counting with money and a market driven by money."

But then, of course, time dollars are not just numbers. They can buy things too. Maybe that was what the old doyens of moral statistics missed. They should have given their numbers buying power.

VI

The trouble is that the world remains in the hands of the people who measure money, and will do so for the foreseeable future. So what can be done? The options seem to be either to give up measuring in money altogether—which seems unrealistic for the time being—or to broaden the bottom line by measuring with lots of different kinds of money. That's the choice: no currency or many currencies.

If one currency only measures some things—capital flows, income, and so on—maybe many currencies might act like lots of measuring rods.

The idea of other kinds of currency sounds a little far-fetched, but—largely thanks to the Internet—it's happening already. It isn't just Cahn's time dollars: Suddenly there are London businesses making donations to police charities in an international barter currency. There are a range of Internet currencies competing for space on the Web, and there are successful local currencies springing up from Aberdeen to Argentina.

What's going on? According to think tanks like the Cato Institute—not to mention the deputy governor of the Bank of England, Mervyn King—a new generation of private currencies exchanged on the Internet is emerging that might sideline central banks altogether. King had to go to Wyoming to say it, but he may be right. The point is that, thanks to the Internet, almost any asset is now transferable electronically. It can be precious metals, as anyone with an account on e-gold.com will know. It can be spare hotel rooms. And at a local level, it can also be people's time.

Loyalty points programs like the Internet currrency beenz and frequent-flyer miles are playing an increasing role in our lives. Credit cards issued from companies like L.L. Bean or Mobil give points for every dollar spent, exchangeable for gas or clothes. And in case you didn't think this is money: Until recently Northwest Airlines has paid its entire worldwide public relations account in frequent-flyer points.

International barter is also getting increasingly sophisticated; involving some of the biggest companies in the world and increasingly using electronic barter currencies like trade dollars. If your local exchange can't immediately find what you need, you can use an international currency called universal to barter it from elsewhere. If you have one of the Minneapolis dual-track HeroCards, you can buy products at the Mall of America—the biggest mall in the United States—partly in dollars and partly in a local time-based currency, earned by helping out in the local community.

The future looks likely to be dominated by a range of competing, interconnected virtual currencies, mixing the traditional aspects of money—as store of value and medium of exchange—in different ways, and which can be used for different aspects of life. There are time currencies, and there are all local currencies—about 2,000 of them in circulation around the world. They range from the Scottish currency, scotias, based in Perth to the highly successful printed currency Ithaca hours in upstate New York, backed by local banks and the chamber of commerce.

Currencies are money, but they are also measuring systems. Other kinds of currencies are able to recognize and measure the assets that the big currencies miss. Barter currencies like trade dollars are able to access the surplus stock, the apparently unsellable purple toothpaste, the wasted space, or the nearly outdated hotel rooms. Time dollars can access all the time, care, and effort put in by the young and old, not to mention those 15 million perfectly good computers thrown out by U.S. business every year, and give them a time value.

They can recognize all those unmeasured, wasted resources and direct them at the vast, unmeasurable, unmet human need—often loneliness, often the need for guidance—which we live next door to in the richest nations on earth. Currencies are measuring systems that can direct surplus toward need. Programs like Edgar Cahn's time dollars or Brooklyn's Member to Member and others are both a solution to the counting crisis and a symptom of it.

This is, I suppose, the main criticism of time dollars: However much it is an unmeasuring system, it is also a measuring one. It is also, in its way, a system of cost-benefit analysis, and as we know, measuring misses out what's most important. In theory, having rebuilt the sense of mutual trust in a neighborhood, the time-dollar system should be able to wither away.

That's why I was fascinated to hear about Miami's pioneering time-dollar system, organized by a former banker, Cuban-born Ana Miyares. She became so convinced that time banking was superior to money banking that she changed the rules as she went along. After a while, nobody had to sign to agree that they had done a time-dollar "job." They would just leave a message on the answering machine and she would take their word for it. She trusted them, and it seemed to work. She was wise enough to realize that, after a while, the measurements get in the way of the machinery. And that, in a way, is what this book is all about.

Because, in the end, although multiple currencies can measure better, rolling back the idea of measuring a little—if it works—is probably the most efficient way forward. "The non-monetary exchange of value is the most efficient system every devised," wrote Dee Hock, the founder of the Visa network, about communities and families. "Evolution and nature have perfected it for centuries. It requires no currency, contracts, government, laws, courts, police, lawyers, and accountants. It doesn't require anointed or certified experts at all. It requires only ordinary, caring people."

That's unmeasuring for you. Any measuring system we have simply must recognize that intangibles like love and trust underpin all our lives. The problem is how to sustain that idea in a world that recognizes only what it counts.

THE BOTTOM LINE

*"You are to be in all things regulated and governed" said the
gentleman, "by fact. We hope to have, before long, a board of fact,
composed of commissioners of fact, who will force the people
to be a people of fact, and of nothing but fact.
You must discard the word Fancy altogether."*

Charles Dickens, *Hard Times*

*Surely there is something unearthly and superhuman
in spite of Bentham.*

John Henry, Cardinal Newman

I

"IT WAS IN the beginning a modest initiative, almost confidential,"
wrote the prestigious French newspaper *Le Monde* in September 2000.
"It has now become a subject of an important debate which has created
a state of effervescence in the community of economists. Should not
the teaching of economics in universities be rethought?" What had
happened was that a small group of students had put a petition on the
Web protesting against the "uncontrolled use of mathematics" in economics. They claimed that the result was that mathematics had
"become an end in itself," turning economics into what they called an
"autistic science," dominated by abstractions that bore no relation to
the world as it really was.

Within two weeks, the petition calling for reconnection with the real world had 150 signatures, many from France's most important universities. Soon newspapers and TV stations all over France had picked up the story, and even senior professors were starting a similar petition of their own. By the fall, the campaign had led to a major debate at the Sorbonne, and the French education minister Jack Lang had promised to set up a commission to investigate the situation and come up with some proposals to change economics teaching.

It was a rare display of resistance against the overuse of numbers. Fear of too many statistics isn't a major issue in most parts of the globe. People who don't like to be measured do have a voice and some power—witness their recent campaign against Intel for its software tracking individual purchases over the Web. But people who worry about measurement in itself have not yet made an impact on the international consciousness.

Into the 21st century, companies like NCR have detailed figures about company targets and performance on the walls in every office, under every clock and every lunchroom—though so far they've drawn the line at toilets. Psychiatrists are increasingly relying on a fearsome numerical system of diagnosis called the *Diagnostic and Statistical Manual of Mental Disorder*. Doctors are being encouraged to diagnose according to programmable criteria, on the grounds that it would be more "open and scientific." Companies are developing the idea of microchip implants for their workforce to measure their timekeeping. One company in Virginia is even color-coding staff badges according to a numerical approximation of their personality type. Worse still, British Telecom's Soul Catcher project aims to find a way of digitizing every sense and experience in a lifetime so that it can all be held on computer.

Then there are the measuring machines. Panasonic has developed a "smart" fridge that measures what you eat and orders more milk when it thinks you want it. Matsushita has developed a "smart" toilet that measures your weight, fat ratio, temperature, protein, and glucose levels every time you give it something to work on. Their VitalSigns medical kit then sends this data automatically to your local clinic—probably the last thing they want.

It's hard to object to any of these measurements by themselves, but taken together they represent a massive loss of faith in our own judgment, intuition, and trust in other people.

Measurement as obsessively practiced by our society is about standardization and control. It is the byproduct of empire, but not the kind of empires we were used to historically. This is *our* empire. The measurements are a reflection of what we believe and what we fear the most. We collect them because we no longer trust politicians, professionals, or natural processes. We insist that their ways, methods, and progress are measured every step of the way.

"The more strictly we are watched, the better we behave," said Bentham. Although his Panopticon was never built—the prison where every cell can be watched by a single guard—his calculating has created a world like it, and we live in it.

Right back in the 1830s, philosopher Georg Friedrich Pohl used the metaphor of understanding a journey through beautiful landscape and fascinating people by using a train timetable. The figures were accurate enough, but they left out most of the experience. Now we are all a little like Jedediah Buxton, the 18th-century prodigy who tried to understand Shakespeare by counting his words. Buxton probably suffered from autism, and so in a sense do we—just as the Paris students in 2000 complained about "autistic" statistics. We don't suffer from it as individuals, but as a society. Like autistic children, we are slow to smile, unresponsive, passive, and we avoid eye contact. We find it hard to understand other people's emotional expressions.

It's not surprising that our institutions are being built in this image too. We will soon have a workforce recruited by categorizing aspects of personalities on a scale of 1 to 10. We will have our nannies graded for their caring abilities on the basis of some kind of checklist. We will have children who can pass exams but have no judgment. We will measure all our institutions by numerical "best practice" standards and wonder vaguely why nobody innovates anymore. And we will have doctors who translate our symptoms into numbers before feeding them into the computer. We will be turning ourselves ever so slowly into machines.

II

This practice of counting everything—which used to be known as pantometry—is changing human nature and making us mechanical, because our employers, political rulers and bureaucrats treat us like machines when they discount our humanness. We are—in Kurt Vonnegut's words in *Slaughterhouse Five*—Tralfamadorians. "Tralfamadorians, of course, say that every creature and plant in the universe is a machine," he wrote. "It amuses them that so many Earthlings are

offended by the idea of being machines." Number crunchers and technocrats are Tralfamadorians too, convinced that we are nothing more
than machines or computers—the sum of our parts.

"The human being is the only computer produced by amateurs,"
said a General Electric executive named Dr. G. L. Haller, a little omi-
nously, echoing the behaviorist B. F. Skinner. He even predicted we
might soon speak a "precise" machine language, shorn of all but one
meaning. In half a century he said—writing 30 years ago—"Juliet may
say of Romeo: 'Delta symbol not imply delta referent attribute end.' "

As far back as 1962, Motorola executive Daniel Noble wrote the following:

> At birth the infant will be clamped in front of the TV eye by means of
> a suitable supporting structure, and two sections of tubing will be
> connected to provide nourishment and to carry away the waste
> materials. From this time on, the subject will live an ideal vicarious
> life, scientifically selected for compatibility with the fixed influences
> of the inherited genes and chromosomes.

Noble was talking about what he called a recipe for "race suicide";
Haller and Skinner were quite keen on the idea. This was, after all, the
high point of brave new technological hope, and we have, in some
ways, spent the past 40 years shaking off these kind of predictions. I can
remember when space technologists were predicting that all food
would soon come in easy bite-size tablets and tubes—just like in the
Apollo capsules. But the futurists never predicted Martha Stewart or
the boom in authentic home cooking. There is a constant human longing for what is "real" that seems to go beyond the merely calculated.
Hence the unexpected survival of live performance, adventure holidays, and organic food. But there are also ways in which the depth of
our reliance on counting and measuring in every area of life demon-
strates that the pantometrists are still winning.

We may not be machines yet, but we think like them—and do so
increasingly as we forget there was any other way to think. Because, as
we've seen, relying on measurement doesn't just miss those other
human skills we have—it actually drives them out. Our big problem
then is what numbers *won't* tell us. They won't interpret. They won't
inspire and they won't tell us what causes what, yet overreliance on
them sweeps away our intuition along with everything else. It leaves
policymakers staring at screeds of figures, completely flummoxed by

them, unable to use their common sense to interpret the babble of competing causes and effects—unable to tell one from the other.

Number crunchers and pantometrists reduce complex connections to simple habitual links. They assume the world is a simple machine where one simple cause connects with a simple effect, when the truth is that the universe is a blooming, buzzing cacophony of competing causes and effects that no amount of measuring will interpret. Pantometry will throw up these unexpected connections, but it won't explain them: That requires human judgment, experience, common sense, and intuition—those very human attributes we have been losing faith in.

If men with long ring fingers are subject to depression—as they are for some reason—what does that mean? If there is really a connection between finger length and homosexuality, we are not being given a scientific law but a minute glimpse at the interacting soup of causes and effects. The same is true of other peculiar links: High stress makes you much more likely to catch colds and accident rates among children double when their mothers are miserable. These odd connections might surprise and inspire us to think about problems in new ways, but it still won't tell us what causes what. "Scientists try to avoid emotions and intuition," says the biologist Stephen Hardin, "but it is exactly those that give them ideas."

The current frontier is genetics. Perhaps no other recent advance in medical history has so much threatened to reduce us—on a personal and universal basis—to a number or code. Of course, there's nothing wrong with the study of genetics in itself, but it is constantly portrayed as a ceaseless counting of genes to find the one simple number that makes people happy, or allows animals to sense earthquakes, or gives us free will—as if any one gene could do anything of the kind. As if every human characteristic can be measured to a specific gene, each with a specific number, so that every human being could be completely reproducible. As if every human characteristic, good and bad, could be numbered according to genes and their combinations. As if human characteristics could be switched on and off, without reference to the complex interaction of different genes, different environments, and goodness knows what in-built spiritual destiny. The way some scientists and journalists describe it betrays the depths to which they have fallen victim to the measuring culture—driving out our sense that we are paradoxical beings, with at least some small measure of control over our lives.

That's not all. Pantometry tries to turn politics into a sports league table. We now share the central delusion of the number crunchers that we can get rid of politics altogether and measure ourselves an objective, unarguable, nonpolitical decision—that we can take all that human prejudice and error out of politics or management. It is a dream from the foundation of the London Statistical Society in 1830, whose first rule of conduct was "to exclude all opinions."

We can see where it goes wrong all around us. The more politicians urge us to look at the scientific evidence, the more their numbers seem to contradict each other. Red meat has a statistically proven link to bowel cancer in the United States but not in the UK. Tea is statistically proven to be good for you and bad for you—the same with margarine, wine, Q-tips, jogging, breast implants, and practically everything on the market. Our overmeasured world has become the victim of some social version of Heisenberg's Uncertainty Principle—that the observer in a scientific experiment affects the result.

By poring over the measurements, and little else, we have also convinced ourselves that we are living through accelerating change. We must be because the numbers change all the time. Yet if we step back from them a moment, we find that the really important things don't change. Death from disease or highway robbery may often be nightmares of the past, but ill health and crime—as far as we can tell—are with us still. We may be able to communicate by e-mail around the world, or leap on a transatlantic flight, but if we live in a big Western city like New York or London, our lives are remarkably similar to those in 1900. We live at the same addresses, work similar hours, and do similar things in bars on weekends. Even the bus routes in London have the same numbers.

Pantometry drives out our sense of paradox, which is a key tool we need in order to understand the way the world changes around us. We measure our way to success—money or whatever else we've decided we need to be happy—only to find that wasn't it at all. Even political success tends to work in the ways we least expect. Change doesn't happen like that: "Men fight and lose the battle," wrote William Morris in *A Dream of John Ball*, "and the thing that they fought for comes about in spite of their defeat, and when it comes it turns out not to be what they meant, and other men have to fight for what they meant under another name." You can't measure this kind of progress with figures.

Too much reliance on numbers drives out history—it gives us no sense of the different ways in which people measured in the past. It drives out creativity, locking away Keynes's dark woolly monster of ideas—even Henry Ford's intuitive "hunches." And it drives out moral-ity too—leaving our poor beleaguered ethics committees desperately trying to measure themselves a coherent attitude to the threat or prom-ise of genetically modified human beings.

The pantometrists will tell us that, without numbers, we risk falling into the clutches of those postmodern relativists who believe that noth-ing is firm and nothing is certain—but actually people who think every-thing is relative are as much an enemy of common sense as those who have to measure everything. To get through the next few perilous decades, to look after each other and solve the looming problems ahead, we're going to need as much of that—as well as all the judgment, intu-ition, history, creativity, and morality—as we can possibly muster.

III

Nobody is suggesting we should stop measuring altogether. Counting things is a vital human skill. Using numbers can help predict who gets cancer, reveal problems in social or engineering systems, and above all, sometimes still shock people into action. They can let us orient our-selves in our world and—to some extent—compare like with like. They allow us to take the world unawares, to prove theories wrong. All the figures that have appeared in this book without my being able to help it fall into that category. They may not be precisely right, but they let us see the world differently for a moment. They are a tool for visualizing problems.

But if we don't stop counting, what can we do about the counting cri-sis? We can hold to the belief that we are complex beings and more than the sum of our parts. And we can take heart from the fact that there is a crisis. The very fact that number crunchers are becoming aware that there are more complex, intangible truths beyond their measurements is mak-ing them push forward the boundaries of what can be measured.

The key question is what we should do about measuring, and here I think the clue is Edgar Cahn and his currencies. To tackle the narrow measure of money we could either stop trying to measure with money altogether or measure with a whole range of different kinds of money. It's the same with all measurements. To make sure our vital human qualities like love, creativity, intuition, and imagination survive, we could try measuring more, and we could try measuring less. Actually, of course, we can probably do both.

Take IQ tests, for example. The controversy over IQ has been raging for most of the past century, and in some ways it prefigured more recent versions of the same issue—that one number can't possibly measure the success of companies, nations, or cities in any meaningful way. But IQ has a darker side, catalogued in Stephen Jay Gould's book *The Mismeasure of Man*, because of the way the figures are used—as if they measured something fixed and unchangeable about people. As if IQ tests—which originally included questions about baseball players to people who spoke no English—could be used to rank classes or races. As if they could somehow measure "worth": "This will ultimately result in curtailing the reproduction of feeble-mindedness and in the elimination of an enormous amount of crime, pauperism and industrial inefficiency," wrote IQ pioneer Lewis Terman chillingly. Terman tested every U.S. Army recruit in the First World War and went on to try measuring the IQ of long-dead scientists and artists by analyzing the length of their entries in encyclopedias.

But there's no bottom line with intelligence either, for exactly the same reason. There is more than one kind—the great discovery of the visionary educationalist Howard Gardner, whose 1983 book *Frames of Mind* pointed out something that now seems obvious. Some psychologists are even now talking about "spiritual intelligence." Measuring people's intelligence by IQ alone means almost nothing unless you measure their other kinds of intelligence too—unless you find their individual brilliance and teach to that. That's the solution: measure multiple intelligence or stop trying to measure it altogether.

Multiple bottom lines, like multiple currencies, are about measuring more—and that's what many of the pioneers in this book have been doing. By measuring more, you base your conclusions on more variables, and that reveals greater complexity, not simple reduction. John Vasconcellos measures the success of schools and prisons by their ability to give people self-esteem. Simon Zadek and the social auditors measure corporate ethics. Measuring more destroys the tyranny of the bottom line. It undermines the great importance of the big number. It punctures the pomposity of the men in white coats or the men in gray suits.

This is how the management writer Charles Handy put it in an extraordinary lecture he gave to the Royal Society of Arts in London in 1996, describing the argument as the "fallacy of the single criterion":

Trying to find one number that is the sum of everything is misguided. There is never any one number that will actually explain success in life and we are foolish ever to think that it might be there. Money certainly isn't it. Businesses know very well that profit is not the only measure. Sensible organizations now have about 18 different numbers that they look at. Nevertheless, the myth pervades our society is that if you are profitable you are successful. Or if you're in the public sector, then efficiency is what matters. But efficiency is not quite the same as effectiveness. You can have a very efficient hospital if you don't take in very sick people or people who are not going to get better, like the old ones. So you push them outside. You're efficient but you're not terribly effective. Looking for the one number has corrupted our society.

We can do more than that too. We can recognize that single measures are about control. So instead we can encourage people to measure locally what they think is important, not what they're told to measure. If one neighborhood feels it wants to measure the number of people in the park as the key indicator of success, then it should do so—and those numbers should be considered alongside those of the distant bureaucrat who measures the mugging rate and nothing else.

We can also destandardize the counting process so that the subjects of measurement do their own measuring—the pupils, the patients, the poor. When ordinary people do the counting and measuring themselves, there's some chance that it might create change. Remember the story of the Latin American town that measures air pollution by whether or not its residents can see the Andes. That is a measure that can inspire and involve people, when measuring ozone parts per million has to be done silently in a laboratory by a technician.

Measuring more is the trendy radical solution, but my heart is probably in the opposite. We could also try measuring less. This is a trusting, conservative approach. Good professional doctors or development economists will tell you that they can know very quickly what is wrong with the patient or economy—but they then have to spend a great deal of public money collecting the figures in order to persuade anybody else. Measuring less saves money. It also requires considerable faith in other people, and that's in very short supply these days. It means giving more hands-on experience to schoolchildren, managers, civil servants, and police. It means lecturing less and listening more. It means decentralizing power. Most of all, it means practicing using our imagination and intuition.

Measuring less means trusting enough to lay aside occasionally some of those systems or policies that ensure we make appointments without discrimination, or decisions without ignoring the people who will be affected by them. Those are worthy reasons for counting, but we die a little if we do nothing but count. A world where we count more is stricter and sometimes fairer, but it has less life than the world where we count less. When we count less and get it wrong, we risk inefficiency, bigotry, ignorance, and disaster. But when we count less and get it right, we probably get closer to joy and humanity than we can any other way. Human beings can deal with a complex world better than any system or series of measurements.

Measuring less means telling stories more, and it means asking questions more. Telling stories, because they can often communicate complex, paradoxical truths better than figures. Asking questions, because they can devastate most political statistics. Yes, the carbon monoxide rate has been reduced, but is the air cleaner? Yes, our local university professors have produced a record number of learned published papers, but is their teaching any good? Yes, the exam passes top the league tables, but what about the education? Are the children happy? Can they deal with life? Numbers and measurements are as vulnerable as the Emperor's New Clothes to the incisive, intuitive human question.

The closer any of us get to measuring what's really important, the more it escapes us, yet we can recognize it sometimes in an instant. Relying on that instant a bit more, and our ability to recognize it, is probably the best hope for us all.

IV

Let me end with two stories from China, one using numbers in the modern measuring style and the other much, much older.

The first is the recent report from one Chinese city that alarmed their government by reporting an enormous rate of mental handicap among their children. It turned out that the local school system—thoroughly overmeasured—had discovered it could leave out any "special needs" children from their educational league tables altogether. So they had fallen into the habit of classifying anyone they thought might not pass their exams as disabled. Actually, of course, many of the kids moved to other school districts and did very well; others never shook off the classification. It is a classic story of the dangers of too much aggressive measuring, repeatable all over the modern world.

The second story is an ancient Chinese legend. "There were once eleven generals who had to decide whether to attack or retreat in a battle," wrote Carl Jung's interpreter Marie-Louise von Franz, introducing the story that changed her understanding of numbers. The generals got together and had a long debate, at the end of which they took a vote. Three wanted to attack and eight wanted to retreat—so they attacked. Why? Because three is the number of unanimity.

The story was so shocking, she said, that it woke her up. Suddenly she understood that the Eastern view of numbers was different from the Western one. For us modern Westerners, numbers can only count. Our numbers mount up to cumulative totals—things get bigger, we demand more. In the East, they have significance, meaning, and quality. Since Pythagoras's day, it's been hard to bridge the gap between the two, but—with Western figures driving out our sense of such things—we may be at a moment in history when we have to try.

When our decision makers seem to be able to do nothing but count, you can see in reaction a new longing for significance and complex truth, for poetry—despite Bentham's denial of its existence—and for the sacred. People want rhythms and music rather than bald statistics. They don't just want data, they want enlightenment. They don't want just numbers, they want meaning. And most of all, we all need to stop muddling them all up, to realize where the former stops being helpful in the endless search for the latter. We need to help people disentangle from numbers and connect with the kind of understanding that can help them change—because change, and whether it is possible politically or personally, is the key issue for our generation. Change without numbers may well be impossible; but change without anything else is impossible too, and we need some Universities of "Unlearning" to help us to find it. In short, we need a Campaign for Real Wisdom.

This is how Prince Charles made the point in his millennium broadcast on the BBC:

Two and a half thousand years ago, Plato was at pains to explain through the words of Timaeus that the great gift of human rationality should not be disparaged. Far from it, he said—it should be exercised to its utmost, but it must not make the mistake of believing it has no limits.

The same is true of counting. Western numbers that split things up, that see only the parts, that are blind to the most important things in life, can get us only so far.

But in case this doesn't convince you, I'll end with an old Scottish proverb that seems to put this point in just nine words, two verbs, and 13 vowels: "You don't make sheep any fatter by weighing them."

FURTHER READING

Adams, John. *Cost Benefit Analysis: Part of the Problem, Not the Solution*, Oxford: Green College Centre for Environmental Policy and Understanding, 1995.

Bell, Simon, and Morse, Stephen. *Sustainability Indicators: Measuring the Immeasurable*. London: Earthscan, 1999.

Cahn, Edgar S. *No More Throwaway People: The Co-Production Imperative*. Washington: Essential Books, 2000.

California Task Force to Promote Self-Esteem and Personal and Social Responsibility. *Towards a State of Esteem*. Sacramento: California State Board of Education, 1990.

Chambers, Robert. *Whose Reality Counts? Putting the First Last*. London: Intermediate Technology, 1997.

Cohen, Patricia Cline. *A Calculating People*. Chicago: University of Chicago Press, 1982.

Crosby, Alfred W. *The Measure of Reality: Quantification and Western Society 1250–1600*. Cambridge: Cambridge University Press, 1997.

Cullen, Michael J. *The Statistical Movement in Early Victorian Britain*. Hassocks: Harvester Press, 1975.

Daly, Herman E., and Cobb, John B. *For the Common Good*. Boston: Beacon Press, 1989.

Dantzig, T. *Number: The Language of Science*. New York: Free Press, 1967.

Dehaene, Stanislas. *The Number Sense: How the Mind Creates Mathematics*. London: Allen Lane, 1998.

Douthwaite, Richard. *The Growth Illusion*, revised ed. Totnes: Green Books, 1999.

Elkington, John. *Cannibals with Forks*. London: Capstone, 1999.

Epstein, Mark J., and Birchard, Bill. *Counting What Counts: Turning Corporate Accountability to Competitive Advantage*. New York, Perseus Books, 1999.

Fallowfield, Lesley. *The Quality of Life: The Missing Measurement in Healthcare*. London: Souvenir Press, 1990.

Flegg, Graham. *Numbers: Their History and Meaning*. London: A Deutsch 1983.

Gilbreth, Frank B., and Carey, Ernestine Gilbreth. *Cheaper by the Dozen*. London: Heinemann, 1949.

Gleik, James. *Chaos: Making a New Science*. London: William Heinemann, 1988.

Gonella, Claudia; Pilling, Alison; and Zadek, Simon. *Making Values Count*. London: Association of Chartered Certified Accountants, 1998.

Gould, Stephen Jay. *The Mismeasure of Man*, new ed. New York: W. W. Norton & Co, 1996.

Henderson, Hazel. *Paradigms in Progress: Life Beyond Economics*. San Francisco: Berrett-Koehler, 1995.

Himmelfarb, Gertrude. *Victorian Minds*. London: Weidenfeld & Nicolson, 1968.

Ifrah, Georg. *From One to Zero: A Universal History of Numbers*. New York: Viking Press, 1985.

Kakar, Sudhir. *Frederick Taylor: A Study in Personality and Innovation*. Cambridge: MIT Press, 1970.

MacGillivray, Alex; Weston, Candy; and Unsworth, Catherine. *Communities Count! A Step-by-Step Guide to Community Sustainability Indicators*. London: New Economics Foundation, 1998.

Mill, J. S. *Autobiography*, ed. John M. Robson. Harmondsworth: Penguin Books, 1989.

Pearce, David; Markandya, Anil; and Barbier, Edward B. *Blueprint for a Green Economy*. London: Earthscan, 1989.

Petersen, William. *Malthus*. London: Heinnemann, 1979.

Porter, Theodore M. *Trust in Numbers: The Pursuit of Objectivity in Science and Public Life*. Princeton: Princeton University Press, 1995.

Porter, Theodore M. *The Rise of Statistical Thinking 1820–1900*. Princeton: Princeton University Press, 1986.

Schumacher, E.F. *Small is Beautiful: A Study of Economics as if People Mattered*. London: Blond & Briggs, 1973.

Seed, Philip, and Lloyd, Greg. *Quality of Life*. London: Jessica Kingsley, 1997.

Self, Peter. *Econocrats and the Policy Process*. London: Macmillan, 1975.

Skidelsky, Robert. *John Maynard Keynes: The Economist as Saviour 1920–1937*. London, Macmillan, 1992.

Steinem, Gloria. *Revolution from Within: A Book of Self-Esteem*. London: Bloomsbury, 1992.

Steintrager, James. *Bentham*. London: Allen & Unwin, 1977.

Stewart, Thomas A. *Intellectual Capital: The New Wealth of Organisations*. Naperville: Nicholas Brealey, 1997.

Wrege, Charles D., and Greenwood, Ronald G. *Frederick W. Taylor: The Father of Scientific Management: Myth and Reality*. Homewood: Business One Irwin, 1991.

Zadek, Simon; Pruzan, Peter; and Evans, Richard. *Building Corporate Accountability*. London: Earthscan, 1997.

ACKNOWLEDGMENTS

"Why are boys obsessed with numbers?" girl asks boy in Bill Forsyth's film *Gregory's Girl* as they lie on their backs on the grass and gaze at the night sky—and I've got a feeling she was right to ask. Boys like numbers: There was a time in my life when I could list battleship statistics until far, far beyond the tolerance threshold of Admiral Halsey himself.

So this book is partly an act of contrition to anyone unfortunate enough to hear me do so, but also an attempt to redress the balance a bit. Because, just as many of us imagine we are building a more feminine and caring world, the new place also seems to be underpinned by hard, unemotional, and ultimately distorting statistics. I believe there's a contradiction here somewhere. I want to live where people can see beyond the figures to embrace complex truth.

This is intended as a polemic. I'm not against the idea of measuring, nor have I tried to write an academic critique of quantitative versus qualitative research—there's enough of them out there already, and I probably wouldn't be qualified to write one. Nor is it intended as a critique of scientific method: I concentrate on the dilemma at its sharpest—with the businesspeople, economists, and politicians who are busy shaping our world. In short, this isn't a book about statistics but a book about a pervasive blindness that I believe is creeping insidiously into the way we understand things.

I am enormously indebted to countless conversations about aspects of this labyrinthine subject with a range of friends and relatives on both sides of the Atlantic. I can't list them all, but they will recognize the discussions we had from these pages—and I hope it's a happy memory. I've certainly enjoyed it.

There are a number of others I'm ever so grateful to for specific nuggets of wisdom, help, and advice, including Alan AtKisson, Sarah Burns, Edgar Cahn, Clifford Cobb, Carol Cornish, Kate Cutler, Christine Gray, Lesley Harding, Sue Holliday, Amanda Horton-Mastin, Sanjiv Lingayah, Serena and Tony Ludford, Alex MacGillivray, Mark MacKintosh, Rachel Maybank, Sara Murphy, Gill Paul, Alison Pilling, Peter Raynard, Melita Rogelj, Jonathan Rowe, Catherine Rubbens, Andrew Simms, Marian Storkey, Karen Sullivan, Mathis Wackernagel, Perry

Walker, Gavin Yamey, Simon Zadek, and everyone at the New Economics Foundation and Time Dollar Institute for their patience, friendship, and shared excitement over the years. And Ed Mayo, who read many of the chapters in draft and made a series of incisive and sparkling suggestions that made the book much better than it otherwise would have been—and introduced me to e e cummings.

I am enormously grateful to Myles Thompson and Jena Pincott from TEXERE for all their wisdom and encouragement—and to my agent Julian Alexander and Lucinda Cooke at Lucas Alexander Whitley. Their advice and support has been one of the most luxurious aspects of writing this book—writing anything, in fact.

The mistakes are of course all mine, but I couldn't have done it without them all—and their contribution is another excellent example of the unmeasurable.